POWER AND GLORY

POWER AND GLORY

France's Secret Wars with
Britain and America, 1945–2016

R. T. HOWARD

Biteback Publishing

First published in Great Britain in 2016 by
Biteback Publishing Ltd
Westminster Tower
3 Albert Embankment
London SE1 7SP

Maps by FreeVectorMaps.com

ISBN 978-1-78590-116-4

10 9 8 7 6 5 4 3 2 1

A CIP catalogue record for this book is available from the British Library.

Set in Caslon by Adrian McLaughlin

Printed and bound in Great Britain by
CPI Group (UK) Ltd, Croydon CR0 4YY

'The conflict (in Indochina) may be popular,
as vindicating the power and glory of France'

—US CONSUL, SAIGON,
TO THE SECRETARY OF STATE, II JULY 1947[1]

CONTENTS

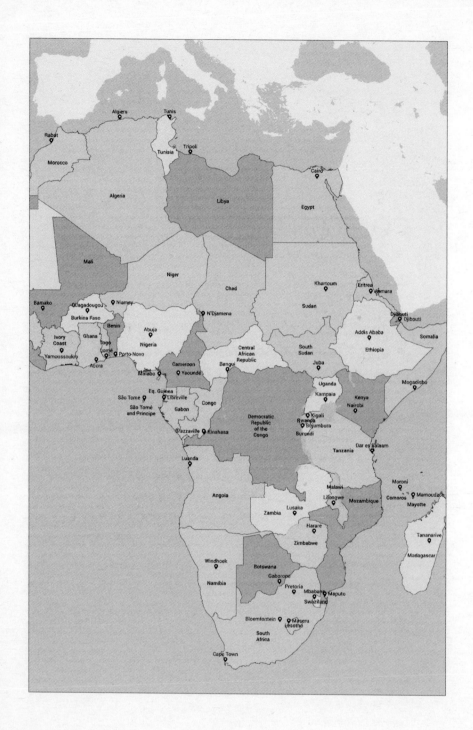

Africa

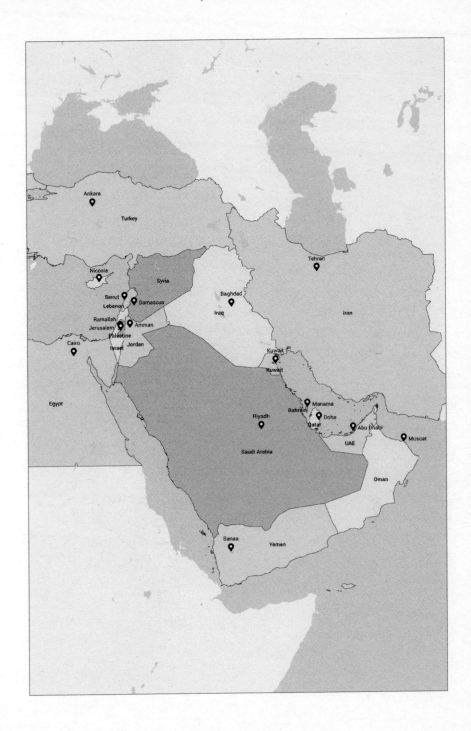

The Middle East

INTRODUCTION

One day in the summer of 1969, the Cabinet Office in London received an urgent and alarming report that was immediately brought to the attention of the Prime Minister, Harold Wilson. A British-owned oil installation at Kokori in Nigeria, ran the cable, had come under heavy and determined attack from a number of aircraft that had flown fast and very low – barely above the treetops – to slip through air defences. No lives had been lost during the bombing and strafing, which had lasted just a few minutes, but the attackers had inflicted considerable damage.[2]

The British government had always known that Royal Dutch Shell and British Petroleum could easily get caught in the crossfire of Nigeria's bitter civil war, which had erupted two years before. And they had always been well aware that any such damage would be very costly. Investors would panic and company profits would be hit, while the flow of oil to the British mainland would be disrupted. But there was also another reason, on that July day, why news of the attack caused such consternation in Whitehall.

Over the preceding weeks, spies working for British intelligence had discovered that the French government had been actively helping the rebels in Nigeria, who were fighting for the independence of the south-eastern region of Biafra, to acquire the resources and capabilities to carry out such an attack. In other words, the British government was now confronted, as a senior Whitehall official put it, by 'a situation in which French rockets fitted in France were used to attack British oil installations'. Of course Paris may not have ordered the attack on Kokori or have had any prior knowledge of it. But it would have been well aware that the Biafrans would want to strike the installations there, since their enemy – the Nigerian federal government – was dependent on the proceeds of oil exports to sustain its war.

There was also a wider dimension to the incident at Kokori because officials in London were convinced that French support for the Biafran cause was also motivated largely by anti-British feeling. There was no other plausible explanation or motive for the backing, which was covert and considerable, of French officials for the Biafran leader, Colonel Odumegwu Ojukwu, who they regarded as an ally against Anglophone influence in west Africa.

Not surprisingly, the media quickly picked up the story. Some months before, one British tabloid had already declared that the Biafran war had been transformed 'into a giant post-colonial battle between Britain and France for political and economic dividends in West Africa as a whole'. But this was not an empty media hyperbole, for the two countries were fighting a war by proxy. This was, quite plausibly, the last Anglo-French war.[3]

The incident at Kokori represents just one part of a much bigger 'Great Game' of competition and rivalry that France has been playing with Britain and America since the end of the Second World War. Its stakes have been high – to guard, and to raise, France's national prestige and standing in relation to the two English-speaking nations. And it is a game that has often been played out on a large and varied playing field. This has encompassed France's colonies and former colonies, and places where some French policy-makers have wanted to extend their influence, such as Israel in the mid-1950s. At other times, the French have tried to undermine the influence of their English-speaking rivals, as some officials in Paris appear to have done against the British in the Falklands in 1982, or indeed in Nigeria at the time of the Kokori attack.

Of course this is just one side of the story. It has long been said that there are two French nations and that there are constant, unavoidable tensions between them. And just as France has been deeply split over domestic issues, between the political left and right, between modernity and traditionalism, so in the same divisive spirit has it needed Britain and America at the same time as competing against them. For this reason, the French have typically played their 'Great Game' as cautiously and covertly as possible, allowing them to plausibly deny their actions and maintain their close relations with their two Anglophone allies. And it was in just such a spirit of covert hostility that the French fought British influence in Biafra, consistently denying the provision of any material support for Ojukwu other than humanitarian relief.

France has played this game of rivalry in all sorts of different ways, not just on the battlefield. On some occasions, for example, it has fought hard to carve out a diplomatic and political role that excludes Britain or America, as it did in the Middle East in the mid-1950s. And there have also been times when France has closely cooperated with its English-speaking allies but at the same time harboured a strong sense of rivalry. This was true, for instance, of Indochina in the early 1950s, when the French and Americans fought side by side in a secret war against a mutual enemy, even though their own relationship was also ridden with underlying tensions.

The players of this 'Great Game' have been equally multifarious. Some have been the policy-makers of the presidential palace, the

Élysée. Others were members of different ministries, including the ministries for foreign affairs (the Quai d'Orsay), defence and finance, overseas departments and territories and, since 1961, the Ministry of Cooperation. Other important and influential individuals have sometimes been more shadowy figures, perhaps affiliated to the mysterious networks (*réseaux*) and lobby groups that continue to shape developments in some of France's former colonial territories.

The picture that emerges is of course a highly diverse and complex one. Sometimes specific individuals within particular ministries in Paris have pursued their own private agenda, one that may be wholly at odds with the rival approach articulated or pursued by other power-brokers in the French capital. And some of these policies have been pitched against both the British and Americans, while at other times they have been directed only at one and perhaps ignored, or been allied with, the other.

The central theme of this book is that France's enmity and rivalry with Great Britain and America entered a new era from the end of the Second World War. This was most obviously because, from the moment of the defeat of Nazi Germany and the final liberation of their homeland in May 1945, France's leaders were in a position to pursue an independent foreign policy. And one pressing priority was to restore their country to the elevated status that it had enjoyed before the war, during the course of which it had been relegated to the position of a second-rate power, below and beneath its English-speaking rivals. In May 1945 Britain and America were the victors of war, having avoided the humiliation and shame of defeat and occupation. France, by contrast, was just a survivor. However, this book also argues that France's 'Great Game' against Britain and America is far from over. It is, on the contrary, a struggle for power and influence that is still being played out on the battlefields of Syria and it underwrote France's involvement in Libya in 2011.

Sometimes, France has vied with Britain and America only because those two countries happen to be, or be seen as, the most important or powerful threats to its own influence. But at other times this merges with a distinctly French perception of what they call the 'Anglo-Saxons'. This is not easy for anyone other than a Frenchman to understand but it has been described by Dr Gérard Prunier, an academic and a former adviser to the French government. 'Anybody who speaks English can be "Anglo-Saxon",' Prunier has revealed, and this includes British, American, Australian or English-speaking Canadian officials at the United Nations in New York, rap artists who sing vulgar lyrics or even people who 'plan hamburger invasions against French cuisine … ride skateboards and drink Coca-Cola'. Those who use the term, he adds, feel that 'the Anglo-Saxons want our death – that is our cultural death. They threaten our language and our way of life, and they plan our ultimate anglo-saxonisation'.[4]

There have been times when the 'Anglo-Saxons' have been viewed essentially as an economic and technological threat to French interests: in 1967, for example, the French writer Jean-Jacques Servan-Schreiber wrote a bestselling book, *The American Challenge*, in which he described this apparent menace in these terms. Two decades on, Britain and America also seemed to present a powerful cultural threat. President François Mitterrand's energetic minister for French culture, Jack Lang, made constant references against America's 'cultural hegemony' and made determined efforts to reinvigorate the French language: for example, during the protracted international negotiations to draw up a General Agreement on Tariffs and Trade (GATT) between 1986 and 1993, French representatives championed the creation of 'cultural exceptions' for French films. At other times, the two Anglophone nations have appeared to threaten the political independence of the French mainland, as they seemed to do in the closing stages of the Second World War, or pose a threat to the security of its colonies and former colonies. More generally, they have seemed to threaten France's national prestige.

Prunier points out how Great Britain has always been seen as standing right at the very centre of this political and cultural menace. He argues that:

> The arch-enemy of this cosy relationship (between France and its colonies or former colonies), the hissing snake in the Garden of Eden, is the 'Anglo-Saxon', the modern reincarnation of '*les Anglais*'. Everybody in France knows that '*les Anglais*' are amongst the worst enemies the French ever had: they burnt Joan of Arc alive, they stole Canada and India from us in 1763, they exiled Napoleon to a ridiculous little rock in the South Atlantic, and they sank our battle fleet at Mers-el-Kébir in 1940. And to top it all, their women are ugly and their food is terrible, traits which show a basic lack of civilisation. From all eternity, they have tried to spoil things for the French, and unfortunately they have usually succeeded. Nowadays they are greatly weakened and do not represent the threat they once did, but they have spawned an evil brood scattered over the four continents, the 'Anglo-Saxons'.

By 1945, rivalry and competition with Britain was too deeply entrenched in the French national psyche to just suddenly disappear. The entire French nation and its identity had been forged by a collective rivalry with the English: as a great French historian, Jules Michelet, argued, 'the struggle against England has done France a very great service by confirming and clarifying her sense of nationhood'. Over the course of whole centuries, and even when they had shared France's Catholic faith, the English had consistently been France's chief rival and enemy. Since the Middle Ages, the two countries have played out their rivalries on a succession of battlefields, both on land

– Agincourt in 1415 during the Hundred Years War, and Waterloo in 1815 are of course the best known – and, at places like Trafalgar in 1805 and Cartagena in 1758, on the high seas. Whole generations of schoolchildren were nurtured on the heroes and heroisms of such battles and conflicts, and of the sacrifices their ancestors had made to keep at bay 'Perfidious Albion', a term for England that was said to have been coined by the great seventeenth-century bishop Bossuet, as he watched Protestantism take root across the Channel. And in the middle of the twentieth century, French animosity towards Britain was not just a fading legacy of earlier ages. On the contrary, one episode that had caused the French particular bitterness was still well within living memory.[5]

This was an incident at an obscure, dusty town, set in a 'landscape of desiccation and rubble populated by scorpions', called Fashoda, situated on the White Nile in east Africa. The French had long had designs on British-controlled Egypt, and London feared that they would try to dam the Nile at Fashoda to disrupt the flow of water northwards. In practice there was never any chance this would happen, because throughout the wider region there was a total dearth of stones and other building materials that the French would have needed to carry out such an ambitious project, but in British eyes it seemed to be a place worth making a stand for.

In the autumn of 1898, military contingents from both countries had met there and confronted each other, each standing their ground and waiting for the other to stand aside and allow it to pass to win control of the town and then the surrounding area. But while the British were reinforced by gunboats and bayonets, the French were much more vulnerable: General Jean-Baptiste Marchand's tiny force of just 150 men, who had marched hundreds of miles, only had some light arms, a bicycle and a French flag, which snapped in half when he tried to raise it outside Fashoda Fort.

For several long and extremely tense weeks, the governments in Paris and London exchanged a fierce barrage of threats and constant salvos of deep insults, both refusing to order their forces to move and instead mobilising their entire fleets amidst talk and speculation of outright war. But the French blinked first and ordered Marchand's men to stand aside and let the British advance, allowing them to secure control of the Sudan. 'And so we moved on,' one Frenchman recorded in his diary as his fellow countrymen raised their hats to the passing British gunboats, 'sad but proud, eyes wet but heads held high, knowing that we had done nothing to deserve the humiliation inflicted on us.' Another wrote, more simply, that 'we are fleeing'.

News of the outcome caused deep consternation in France. Hundreds of ordinary Frenchmen headed for South Africa to join the Boers in their armed struggle against the British, while in Paris the President, Félix Faure, even told a Russian diplomat that Britain, not Germany, was now France's main enemy. A whole generation of Frenchmen, including its future President, Charles de Gaulle, grew up in the dark shadow of what was regarded as a moment of terrible national humiliation. When, in his memoirs, de Gaulle made a list of the national calamities that he thought his country had endured during his lifetime, and which had prompted him to devote his career to the restoration of its greatness, he put the Fashoda incident in first place. In his eyes, it ranked alongside the humiliation of 1870–71, when Bismarck's Prussian Army had invaded France and inflicted an overwhelming defeat, and the shocking losses of the First World War. But it was not just de Gaulle, or indeed his generation, that was afflicted. The 'Fashoda complex' was to prove both deep and enduring.[6]

Such traditional, deeply entrenched French fears were discernible even at France's most desperate hour during the Second World War. This was in the summer of 1940, when Hitler's legions scythed through the French Army in a matter of just weeks and a First World

War hero, Marshal Philippe Pétain, signed an armistice with Germany and set up a new authoritarian French state in the town of Vichy in central France. But even at this dark moment, many Frenchmen still harboured strong suspicions about Britain and its motives. Pétain's plan was to keep France's empire safe from acquisitive British hands as well as from the Germans, and Admiral François Darlan, who had had an ancestor killed at Trafalgar, was heard to mutter how he 'hated Perfidious Albion'. 'Anglophobia seems to be almost universal in the French army,' the writer Claude Jamet noted in his diary, as French soldiers and civilians accused the British of barely bothering to help save their homeland from the German onslaught.[7]

As the Second World War raged, the 'Anglo-Saxon threat' acquired a completely different dimension. From 1942 onwards, the French were suddenly confronted not just by Great Britain but also by another 'Anglo-Saxon' power, emergent and rapidly expanding, which seemed to pose a clear threat to the sanctity of their empire. Not only did the United States have vast resources that would allow it to win possession of France's colonial territories, but some Americans also spoke openly about their own imperial 'mission', closely echoing the view that many French people had of their own country and of its role in the world. Both countries shared the same sense of being 'exceptional' and of diffusing their values throughout the wider world. Presidents Thomas Woodrow Wilson, Franklin D. Roosevelt and George W. Bush have actively championed highly idealistic plans to promote democracy in different parts of the world, just as French imperialists of the nineteenth century proclaimed an ambition to enlighten and civilise the outside world, pursuing what they called *la mission civilisatrice*.[8]

French fear and resentment of American imperial ambitions was nothing new. On the contrary, such feelings had been clear enough eighty years before, in 1862, when Emperor Napoleon III had acted alongside Britain to deal with a truculent Mexican government that was refusing to repay its debts. Both countries assembled and dispatched a joint force to Mexico to seize and occupy the port of Veracruz, allowing them to recoup their money from customs duties. But they also had another motive. As the British Prime Minister Lord Palmerston expounded, they wanted 'to stop the North Americans … in their projected absorption of Mexico'. At the same time, the French leader disliked the American attitude to established traditions and instead wanted to restore the Mexican monarchy. 'It was his custom,' remarked Benjamin Disraeli, 'to say that there were two powers who hated old Europe: Russia and the United States of America.'[9]

In the years that followed, French fears of America, and feelings of hostility, continued to grow. After America's defeat of the Spanish in Cuba in 1898, derogatory references to *les anglo-saxons* became ever more prevalent. And America seemed to be an ever greater menace during and after the First World War, when much of the French economy came under the indirect control firstly of the British and then, from 1917, of the Americans, who directed a number of inter-allied commissions that were responsible for the production of food, coal and shipping.

A generation on, there was a resurgence of such sentiments. The central reason was that America's imperial star was rising in a dramatic and unmistakable manner, at the same time that France's own, and its national standing in general, was already waning. France's economic and political muscle was badly diminished by the experience of defeat in 1940 and by its subsequent occupation by German troops. As one American diplomat later wrote, France's collective mindset had been abnormal since 1940, while the loss of its global status remained a trauma 'the explosive character of which was not fully understood in the US or elsewhere'. But by 1945 France was also confronted by other challenges. Nationalist sentiment was already growing in its colonies. This was partly because thousands of colonial soldiers had joined the war effort against Nazi Germany and demanded something in return for their support. But at the same time America's own power, even before it had developed the atomic bomb, which added so much to its political as well as military weight, was also increasing sharply. This was true not just of its economic power but also, more importantly, of its global reach as it entered the Second World War in December 1941.[10]

The French were particularly sensitive about their national standing and had been ever since the French Revolution, when 'the nation', rather than 'the monarchy', became a unifying force that the French people rallied around. At the same time, the universal values of the Enlightenment took hold in France, and many French men and women regarded their country as the embodiment of its high ideals, such as 'liberty' and 'justice'. Such faith inspired Montesquieu, the eminent eighteenth-century lawyer and thinker, to note 'the general passion [that] the French nation has for glory'. Decades later, the aristocrat and political philosopher Alexis de Tocqueville described how 'national pride is our greatest remaining sentiment', a description that was echoed over a century later by Charles de Gaulle, who emphasised how 'France is not really itself except in the front rank … and cannot be France without greatness'.[11]

The British and the Americans seemed to pose a particular threat to French prestige because France's sense of national self-worth was very closely linked to its territorial possessions. The French had staked out much of their empire in the later nineteenth century in order to compensate for humiliating defeats and their loss of status in continental Europe during and after the war of 1870–71 against Prussia. As their troops seized Tunisia, Madagascar and the north of Indochina, many French citizens came to regard their country as great once again, years after the spectacular triumphs of Napoleon

Bonaparte. The nation could now fulfil its mission to spread civilisation and universal values across the world. 'France is becoming a great power again,' proclaimed a triumphant Léon Gambetta in 1881. At the same time, the colonies offered raw materials and markets that could help guarantee the health and prosperity of the French mainland. At its zenith in 1939, the French Empire covered four and a half million square miles and had around 65 million subjects.[12]

In 1945, this empire was still the second largest in the world, and after the defeats and humiliation of the wartime years it was one of the very few things – another was the allocation of a permanent seat on the United Nations Security Council – that allowed many French men and women to convince themselves that their country had retained something of its grandeur. As a result, any threat to the empire's integrity, which the Americans and the British seemed to pose, was all the more untenable. If France lost its empire, then it had no hope of ever becoming *la plus grande France* ('Greater France') of days gone by.

The geographical and cyclical overlap between the two powers, France and America, was to have politically explosive consequences in the post-war years, and the result was a mutual rivalry and jealousy that merged with France's traditional competition with Britain. In the course of the 'Great Game' that was subsequently played out, the French have fought wars by proxy with one or other of the two Anglophone countries. At other times, intense mistrust, fear and suspicion of Britain and the United States have driven French policy-makers to instigate coups, carry out assassinations and order invasions of places where they fear London or Washington might otherwise step in at their own expense.

There is, of course, a wider dimension to this 'Great Game'. Were French fears of British and American motives towards their colonies or former colonies justified? Or was France afflicted by any degree of paranoia at this time?

There is no instance, in the course of this book, of Britain ever harbouring any such acquisitive motives towards France, its territorial possessions or its *pré carré* ('fiefdom'). In the post-war years, Britain was too overstretched by its existing commitments to entertain such hugely ambitious goals. Financially ruined by the cost of fighting the Second World War, it was heavily dependent on American aid in the years that followed, and then too badly afflicted by a succession of monetary crises to have ever even searched for any further imperial commitments. These constraints became clear in the course of the Suez crisis in 1956, which was aborted by investor flight, and again in 1966, when the British government announced that Britain would no longer have any significant military presence 'East of Suez'. Britain's retreat from its own empire, as it forfeited its control over territories such as Palestine and India in the mid to late 1940s, was also so bloody and difficult that it scarcely had the opportunity to wrest any additional territories from any other power, let alone any interest in doing so.

French fears of American acquisitiveness were not, however, wholly unjustified. There are instances in this book of American policymakers, not always acting with congressional approval, working to undermine France's grip over its territories. This was true of Indochina in 1954, and of Africa during the presidency of John F. Kennedy. It was true, too, of Central Africa in the mid-1990s, when American soldiers covertly supported Washington's allies in Zaire. In these cases, the United States was continuing to play the imperial role it had taken ever since the days of the early settlers of the seventeenth and subsequent centuries. They seized land from the native Americans and then looked further afield, wresting Puerto Rico, the Philippines and parts of Cuba from the Spanish while also prising other territories from the Mexicans during the war of 1846–48. And when, in 1942, American soldiers invaded French territory in north Africa, it was not altogether surprising if some French men and women had wondered if the United States was continuing to play the same imperial role, at their own expense.

The 'Anglo-Saxon' threat that many French officials thought they saw at the end of the Second World War, in other words, was not always an imaginary one.

CHAPTER I

MASSACRE IN DAMASCUS

In the early evening of 29 May 1945, French troops had put on a show of force outside the parliament building in the Syrian capital of Damascus. Scuffles broke out and, as tension suddenly mounted, the officer in charge, a general called Fernand Oliva-Roget, barked out an order to open fire. His soldiers now unleashed a deafening and devastating barrage of artillery and mortar fire on their targets, and shortly afterwards French warplanes appeared overhead, flying low to drop their deadly cargos with maximum devastation and accuracy. The city, in the words of one eyewitness, had 'suddenly exploded into utter chaos' as heavy fire 'rained almost unceasingly from the French forces'.[13]

In their official residence, British diplomats had to dive for cover as bullets raced around them. Shocked by what they had witnessed, they cabled back to London to describe the French 'reign of terror' that they could see with their own eyes. 'I have never been in such difficulty,' wrote one terrified official. 'Apart from indiscriminate shelling, their troops are behaving like madmen, spraying the streets with machine-gun fire from vehicles and buildings … they are clearly out to win a merciless war on the Syrians.'[14]

Oliva-Roget had judged that his hard-hitting measures were the most appropriate response to the outbreaks of rioting that had swept through the country over the preceding ten days. In that time, large numbers of demonstrators had swarmed into the streets of the major cities of Aleppo, Homs and Hama as well as Damascus, to demand the departure of the French 'oppressors' and the declaration of national independence.

But ever since the end of the First World War, the French had regarded Syria and the neighbouring territory of Lebanon as their own *domaine réservé* ('zone of exclusive influence'). Their troops had occupied Syrian and Lebanese lands in 1919 and three years later the League of Nations formally approved a French mandate there. Now, whole decades on, Paris would only bow to growing nationalist sentiment if it was granted a privileged relationship, one that guaranteed economic, cultural and strategic privileges, with a new, independent Syrian state. 'France is prepared to crown her recognition of the independence of Syria and Lebanon with the withdrawal of her garrison troops, but first wishes to settle a number of outstanding questions,' as the French Foreign Minister, Georges Bidault, reportedly told his fellow members of the Cabinet. Paris had already agreed in principle to Syrian and Lebanese independence but in practice soon started to work against it, quietly transporting extra contingents of soldiers into a region that it was supposed to be evacuating. In effect, the French government was trying to intimidate and threaten the Syrian and Lebanese leaders to get the concessions it wanted.

Almost as soon as the fighting in Damascus broke out, the Syrian Prime Minister, Fares al-Khoury, appealed to the British to broker an armistice, and to ensure that France would not bully an independent Syria into its political orbit. The British, like the Americans, had not only recognised Syria's independence but had a large military presence there: the British Ninth Army had exerted ultimate responsibility for law and order ever since the Levant states – Syria and Lebanon – had fallen under the remit of Britain's Middle East Command during the Second World War.

The British Cabinet now met in an emergency session, while the Foreign Secretary, Anthony Eden, informed the House of Commons of 'a serious loss of life and destruction of property' and a situation that had 'greatly deteriorated' in the region. Meanwhile, the Prime Minister, Winston Churchill, urgently contacted Washington, asking President Truman to give his full support to British intervention and to make an official protest to the French government. The following day, on 31 May, Truman held a press conference in Washington in which he openly supported Churchill's position on Syria.[15]

Now that he had the green light from the White House, Churchill dispatched an urgent telegram to Paris, ordering an immediate cease-fire. The senior British commander in the region, General Sir Bernard Paget, imposed martial law in Syria, confining French troops to their barracks. 'No French soldier will go out into the streets without my permission!' thundered the general, adding that he would order his own men to bomb French positions if necessary. At Paget's insistence, General Oliva-Roget was also relieved of his command.

The hush of peace fell over Syria but hundreds of civilians lay dead or injured: an estimate by the American government put the death toll at 641, although the real figure may have been much higher because the French buried many of the dead in mass graves. More may have died from starvation, aggravated in Hama by the actions of French troops, who reportedly burnt large amounts of wheat and other cereals.

French officials had long harboured deep suspicions about British motives towards Syria and Lebanon. There were bitter recriminations over an agreement about Syria's future that had been struck in July 1941, when the British official Sir Oliver Lyttelton had effectively subordinated French jurisdiction over its internal politics to Britain's strategic priorities. For a brief, tense moment, de Gaulle had even threatened to unleash his own 'Free French' troops against British soldiers to claim back the regions that he thought rightfully belonged to France. Four years on, the French were convinced that the British had been stirring up the unrest that their troops had tried, with such ferocity, to suppress. This was not just because British officials were busily helping the Syrians to take over the reins of power. It was also because some of the Arabs, who were involved in an initial outbreak of rioting earlier in the month, had served with the British Army elsewhere in the Middle East, notably the mandated territory of Palestine. Entire Syrian communities had also turned to the British for protection against alleged French brutality, while French officers complained that the British Army had failed to intervene and stop their own soldiers from being attacked. Soon, French officials were openly accusing their British counterparts of secretly supplying Syrian insurgents with arms.[16]

Now, on 31 May, news of Britain's actions in Syria seemed to justify all their suspicions. The British were forcing the French to retreat. At the very least, it was a major humiliation for France, all the more so when, the following day, Paget arrived in Beirut and was escorted by a large contingent of British troops who were ordered to take up firing positions, poised ready for an imminent clash of arms, as they drove past French soldiers on the roadside and at checkpoints. The French soldiers were ordered to stay confined in their barracks while the British took over responsibility for public order, preparing the way for Syrian and Lebanese independence.

In Paris, the acting President of the post-war government, Charles de Gaulle, held a press conference in front of hundreds of journalists from the world over. Known for his volcanic temper as well as his intense patriotism, he struggled to keep his cool, and his voice cracked several times as powerful emotions overwhelmed him. After outlining a long, discursive history of the region, he described recent 'British intrigues' that were being orchestrated by 'a considerable number of agents on the spot' against French interests in Syria. A disturbance had broken out, he continued, 'in which bands armed with British weapons attacked isolated French posts, and compelled our forces to retaliate and re-establish order'. He had, however, agreed to a ceasefire on 30 May in order to avoid the 'monstrous absurdity' of an Anglo-French clash. The following day, de Gaulle also summoned the British ambassador in Paris, Duff Cooper, to the Élysée and vented the full force of his intense anger. 'I recognise that we are not in a position to fight a war against you,' he fumed, 'but you have outraged France and betrayed the West. That cannot be forgotten.'[17]

The Anglo-French confrontation in the Levant in the weeks that followed the end of the Second World War was an unmistakable reminder of the febrile tensions that lay between two Western powers. Rivalry between the two countries was of course centuries old and had surfaced even at moments of great national crisis, when both had been confronted by the same, overwhelming threat. French suspicions of Britain had emerged almost as soon as the Second World War started, and even at France's most dangerous hour. In mid-June 1940, as the German Army overran France, the British government had proposed setting up a Franco-British Union that would have allowed the French to keep fighting the Nazis. But although the idea won the support of the French Prime Minister Paul Reynaud, it was viewed with strong suspicion by his Cabinet ministers, who saw it as a British conspiracy to seize control of the French Empire.

Other incidents, after the rapid defeats of 1940, had aggravated French anger towards the British. On 3 July, Churchill had ordered the Royal Navy to attack and sink the French fleet at Mers-el-Kébir, off the Algerian coast, to prevent it falling into Nazi hands. British fire killed around 1,300 French sailors and sank six warships, and news of the tragedy shook France, playing into the hands of Vichy and Nazi propagandists, fuelling a rabid Anglophobia and testing the loyalties of those who opposed the Vichy regime. Why, asked many French men and women, was such an act of violence necessary when Vichy commanders had given an assurance that their fleet would not fall into Nazi hands and had taken safeguards to prevent such a worst-case scenario? Shocked and outraged, the Vichy leaders retaliated by bombing Gibraltar and breaking off diplomatic relations with London. For a brief while, it even seemed possible that Vichy would strike up an anti-British alliance with Germany against Britain, and the political echo of the gunfire continued to reverberate years later, when the incident was still deemed to be a 'major stumbling block in Anglo-French relations'. In May 1945, such tensions remained as real as ever, with France struggling to retain and regain as much of its national glory as it could against another imperial power that seemed to harbour sinister designs over it.[18]

But this ancient rivalry now had a new and much wider dimension. This was the involvement of the United States in world affairs. A few weeks after the bombing of Damascus, Foreign Minister Bidault had accused London of colluding with Washington to evict France from the Middle East, and resentment in Paris grew as American representatives joined their British counterparts in condemning French policy in the region. The 'Anglo-Saxons', as the French called them, seemed to be working secretly together to rob France of its colonial territories and demote it, or to keep it demoted, to the status of a second-rate power. In fact, these fears were hardly without foundation: the Foreign Office and the State Department both wanted a French withdrawal from the Middle East, and diplomats like Shone and his American counterpart, George Wadsworth, openly condemned the French presence there.[19]

Shattered and demoralised after *les années noires* – the long years of war and occupation – France was nonetheless still an imperial power. It had numerous colonial possessions that it was most anxious to safeguard, including large parts of west Africa (Guinea, Ivory Coast, Niger, Mauritania, Senegal and French Sudan) and equatorial Africa, which covered Cameroon, Congo-Brazzaville, Chad and Gabon. Further to the east, French explorers had also won areas of Somaliland and the islands of Madagascar and Réunion, while in the Far East its major possession was Indochina, which was a federation of Vietnam, Cambodia and Laos. In north Africa, Tunisia and Morocco were both part of France's empire, while Algeria had constitutionally been part of the French mainland since 1848.

But, in French eyes, the 'Anglo-Saxons' had posed a direct threat to their empire ever since 1942, when American, as well as British, forces had started to make their presence felt against both Germany and Japan. American and New Zealander soldiers had also arrived en masse in parts of the French Empire, notably New Caledonia in the Pacific, where over 100,000 GIs had been stationed in the summer of 1942. And on 8 November both Britain and the United States had undertaken Operation Torch, a hugely ambitious operation, one that involved 700 ships that moved 100,000 men over long distances and often through supremely dangerous stretches of water, to invade and capture French north Africa, prising it out of the hands of those who de Gaulle called Nazi 'collaborators'.

From the moment of the Torch landings on that November day, it was not just Great Britain that posed the 'Anglo-Saxon' threat to French interests. British power and influence had now merged with that of the United States. As Roosevelt wrote to Churchill, 'in the last analysis, north Africa is under British-American rule'. Under a deal struck between the Americans and the governor, Admiral François Darlan, the Allies had a degree of authority that was 'analogous to an occupying power' and had control over north African naval bases. The overall commander of the Torch operation was an American, Dwight D. Eisenhower, to whom the British reluctantly admitted their subservience. 'We acted the part, as it were, of lieutenants of the Americans,' sighed senior Foreign Office officials, 'and if this relationship continued, we should find ourselves in the position of having our relations with the whole of the French Empire governed by the United States.' From this moment on, de Gaulle and many Frenchmen regarded Britain, with much justification, as the *demandeur* (junior partner) of the United States and a 'Trojan Horse' that bore Washington's hidden influence.[20]

This was a clear, unmistakable sign that France's role, and its national fortunes, were in a state of sharp decline. France had not only suffered the humiliation of wartime defeat and occupation but was now forced to watch two Anglophone countries act as its effective overlord. Until the mid-1930s, France had boasted the most powerful army in Europe as well as a large and highly successful economy. It also had colonial holdings in Asia, Africa, South America and the Middle East, while its language was the lingua franca of international diplomacy and had been so for centuries. And little more than a decade before, the United States had been an insular and introspective nation, ravaged by economic depression and barely in a position to assert itself on the international stage even if its leaders and electorate had had the will to do so.

But now the supremacy of the French-speaking world, *la francophonie*, seemed to be under real threat for the first time since the Berlin Conference of 1884, when France had formally established its colonial presence in Africa. Such a drastic and profound loss of status would not be easy to come to terms with. When he arrived in Algiers on 30 May 1943, an unsettled Charles de Gaulle, who was at this stage the leader of the 'Free French' exiles, who were sworn to liberate their homeland from the rule and influence of Hitler's Germany, even told his wartime colleague, Jean Monnet, about the 'mounting threat' of 'Anglo-Saxon' domination in the world. He argued that, if such a threat persisted, a post-war France would have no choice but to lean towards Germany and Russia. And in a letter written shortly before to his senior commander, General Georges Catroux, he made derogatory remarks about the United States, stating that France would soon have to 'unite against the power of America'.[21]

For some historically minded French men and women, the American advance was perhaps all the more difficult to accept because of the historic ties between the two nations. This emerged a few months earlier in a telegram that Admiral Darlan had written to an American wartime ambassador, in which he made a reference to the Marquis de Lafayette, the French aristocrat who fought for American independence against the British in 1780–81: 'I realize that my defeated country is placed in a painful situation,' wrote the admiral, 'but I did not believe that the Government of a nation [America] that owes its independence in great part to it would take advantage of this fact to treat it with scorn.'[22]

Doubtlessly it was such historic ties that had helped to shape de Gaulle's initial sympathy with the United States in the weeks and months that preceded Washington's entry into the Second World War. In August 1941, four months before America's declaration of war, he had even offered America the use of its naval bases in Cameroon, at Port-Gentil in Gabon and at Pointe Noire in French equatorial Africa. 'Should Vichy retake Free French territory in Africa,' he was quoted in the press as stating, 'American defences would be pushed to the Caribbean.'[23]

It is likely that at this early stage in the Second World War de Gaulle viewed America as a counterweight to Great Britain, his historic enemy 'the Perfidious Albion'. For at the same time as Whitehall officials were still complaining openly about his visceral anti-British sentiments, de Gaulle allegedly commented that 'the Americans would shortly come into the war and it is principally to them that the Fighting French must look for Salvation'. He had added that 'I always had faith that the United States would keep her word, and I know that America does not covet territorial aggrandizement in Africa especially as I am sure that France's African possessions would be in safe hands if strategic points were occupied by the American navy.'[24]

But in the months that followed America's entry into the Second World War in December 1941, his attitude changed drastically. In overheard conversations that he had with American officials in north Africa, *le Général*, as de Gaulle was sometimes called, had clearly reversed his views and 'launched a long critique of American policy since before the collapse of France for which he thought the US was at least partly to blame'. And as a British telegram of 'particular secrecy' pointed out in June 1942, de Gaulle felt that:

> [America] had entered an era of imperialism and colonial expansion. The British Empire was strong enough to stand up for itself, but the French Empire, under the control of Vichy, was like a ripe cheese, a constant temptation for a hungry appetite. For that empire, said the general, he was a trustee to the French people, and he would betray them if he continued to collaborate with any nation which endeavoured to seize French territory for its own purposes.

At almost the same time, he had sent a cable to General Catroux in which he expressed his fears that the Allies had ulterior designs on the French Empire, notably Senegal.

De Gaulle said that he had really very little suspicion of us but deep
suspicions of the Americans. There had been much talk in Washington about an operation against Dakar and he seemed to fear
that something was being planned there without our knowledge ...
their policy was to disintegrate and neutralize the French Empire.[25]

Recognising the danger, Washington did its best to alleviate such
fears. The Allies, President Roosevelt had publicly declared in a radio
broadcast just after the invasion began, 'seek no territory and have no
intention of interfering with friendly French authorities in Africa.
We come among you to repulse the cruel invaders who would remove
forever your rights of self-government, your rights to religious freedom and your rights to live your own lives in peace and security.' But
privately he had been furious at de Gaulle's attitude, all the more so
when, on Christmas Day 1941, the Free French seized two islands
off Nova Scotia, located just 500 miles from the American coast
and lying well within a region that Washington regarded as its own
exclusive zone of influence.[26]

Tension mounted again when the general had sent a cable to the
Empire Defence Council, a body of Free French leaders who were
responsible for organising the war effort, in which he expressed fears
that both countries, Britain and America, were planning attacks on
Senegal and Niger. If this happened, he reiterated darkly, he would
sever his links with the two Allies and simply send his troops to fight
alongside Russian troops instead. At the same time, the British and
Americans seemed to be reaching out, quite unnecessarily, to Pierre
Boisson, the Governor General of large areas of Vichy France's African territories.[27]

But it soon became apparent that de Gaulle's fears were not
unfounded. For, in January 1943, the American President issued a
public statement about Dakar, the capital of Senegal, which American

defence chiefs regarded as a perfect submarine base. 'The coasts of West Africa and Dakar,' he asserted, '[must] never again under any circumstances be allowed to become a blockade or an invasion threat against the two Americas.' He seemed to imply that the American government was prepared to get involved in French territory. Roosevelt had also repeatedly asserted that New Caledonia should not remain a French colony after the war but instead be mandated by the United Nations.[28]

In the months that followed the invasion of north Africa, such political pressures were adding to the difficult relationship between Roosevelt and de Gaulle. These had become obvious at the time of the Casablanca Conference in January 1943, when Churchill and Roosevelt had met to discuss strategy. De Gaulle was invited but refused to take part, knowing that he would play only a peripheral role in a meeting held by two 'Anglo-Saxon' powers that directly concerned the future of France, and which was being held on French soil. He eventually relented but then refused to dine until American soldiers, whose presence on French territory infuriated him, were replaced by French personnel. Even then, he exploded with anger, exclaiming that it was 'odious that they should finally get together behind barbed wire manned by foreigners'. Privately, he was determined to 'bring back to France independence, the Empire and the sword'.[29]

Others noted the rising tension. 'Anti-American feeling is growing,' wrote a British official from Cameroon in April 1943. And there was a risk, noted Anthony Eden in the same year, that the British and Americans 'would find ourselves accused … of interfering improperly in French internal affairs with a view to treating France as an Anglo-American protectorate'. If this happened then 'our relations with France would be … dangerously affected'. He knew that 'the French suspect us of intending to keep the territories we occupy for ourselves'.[30]

There were other disagreements. In July 1943, Churchill and Roosevelt once again decided to sideline the French from their invasion of Sicily, and de Gaulle was not informed of the attack in advance. And when de Gaulle refused to work with the governor of Dakar, Roosevelt threatened to send American troops and ships to west Africa to keep the Free French out. Several weeks later, the American President once again infuriated *le Général* by suggesting that a post-war France could be administered by an Anglo-American occupation force until elections were held. De Gaulle's anger grew even more as the Allied invasion of occupied France drew closer but the Free French were excluded from the planning and given no indication of when 'D-Day' would take place or where it would happen. And when Churchill made a trip to Corsica without even informing the French in advance, an infuriated de Gaulle told the governor to simply ignore the British leader.[31]

But *le Général*'s suspicions that America was 'already trying to rule the world' and had ambitions to subjugate post-war France, had started to grow much earlier in the war, some time before the invasion of north Africa. Perhaps the most decisive single event took place in August 1941, before Washington's entry into the Second World War, when Franklin Roosevelt and Winston Churchill had signed an 'Atlantic Charter'. This was intended to raise morale and give hope to their own people, as well as those who were ruled by the Nazis and other tyrannical regimes, and to explain exactly why any sacrifices they made would be worthwhile.

On paper at least, the charter's 'common principles' were admirable enough. While neither the United States nor Great Britain would seek 'territorial aggrandizement', the document solemnly declared, they were committed to liberalising trade and universal standards of welfare. But some colonialists were alarmed by its declaration that 'all peoples [would] have a right to choose the form of government under which they will live'. The signatories had also added that 'they wish to see sovereign rights and self-government returned to those who have been forcibly deprived of them'. These principles were soon to become embodied in the United Nations Charter, which in 1945 specified the principle of 'equal rights and self-determination of peoples'.

Of course this applied to the British Empire and perhaps even to the American nation, which was created by the expansionary and forceful drive of the early settlers. But for French imperialists, it seemed to be a justification for meddling and interference. The Americans, it appeared, would want to drive France out of its colonies so that they could move in.

The American President appeared to be particularly inimical towards France's colonial territory in south-east Asia. Soon after America's entry into the war, it became clear that Roosevelt had acquisitive designs on Indochina, the federation that France had created in the late nineteenth century out of the three regions of Vietnam, Cambodia and Laos.

At a meeting held in Washington in October 1943, a representative of the French Committee on National Liberation had listened with horror to the views put forward by some State Department officials about what the post-war world would resemble. In particular, an Assistant Secretary of State, Adolf A. Berle, had raised the question 'of whether, in the Far East, we are re-establishing the western colonial empire or whether we are letting the East liberate itself if we can do it'. He added that the Chinese should be given a free hand to move into Indochina to help drive the Japanese out.[32]

In fact, Roosevelt had been interested since at least the beginning of the year in promoting Indochinese independence. He had watched the French nation collapse in the summer of 1940 and had lost faith in its powers, thinking that France no longer deserved its pre-war status as a major imperial nation. Just weeks after the German Army had stormed through France, the Vichy government had once again given up ground, allowing the Japanese armed forces to build airbases in Indochina. Roosevelt regarded this as shameful behaviour, and decided that a vastly preferable outcome would be for the United States or one of its allies, such as the Chinese nationalist leader Chiang Kai-shek, to push the French out altogether and step into their shoes instead. Aggravating his hostility towards France was his genuine conviction that 'after 100 years of French rule in Indochina', the people 'were worse off than they had been before'. Instead he was interested in establishing 'a trusteeship [under] a Frenchman, one or two Indo-Chinese, and a Chinese and a Russian ... to educate them for self-government'.[33]

Lying at the heart of Roosevelt's remarks was a vision of the world, and of America's role in it, that clashed directly with France's view of its own self. But, curiously, each vision also closely mirrored the other. Both countries cherished high ideals, and had done so at almost the same time. In 1776, American revolutionaries had proclaimed a Declaration of Independence that championed the 'self-evident truths' of life, liberty and the pursuit of happiness. A unified, homogenous American identity had not at this stage been formed, but these ideals were rallying points around which it was now to evolve. In Paris, as the tumultuous events of the French Revolution unfolded thirteen years later, the National Constituent Assembly issued the Declaration of the Rights of Man, which heralded the free and equal rights of every individual in comparably idealistic language. There was a close connection between these events: French soldiers, under the Marquis de Lafayette, had fought alongside the Americans and, after the victory of 1776, had then returned to their homeland echoing the language of liberty.

Such high idealism went hand in hand with a sense of being

unique, or 'exceptional'. At some point in the eighteenth century, many French people had come to regard their nation as morally superior to others and felt that it that had both a right and a duty, a *mission civilisatrice* born of French *exceptionalisme*, to disseminate its values and language throughout the world. The French language, which became the standard idiom of diplomacy from the nineteenth century until the 1990s, was viewed as the expression and means of conveying these values. But such sentiments were also harboured on the other side of the Atlantic. The early Americans believed that they, like the French, were God's chosen people and that their emergent country was blessed by Providence to play a unique role in the world.

Such declarations as the Atlantic Charter also fostered the nationalist sentiments that were already growing in parts of France's empire and elsewhere. After the war, a top secret American document admitted the charter's impact on north Africa:

> US wartime propaganda was in part responsible for the recent spur to North African nationalism and for the present unrest in the area. Descriptions of the Charter and of the Four Freedoms were extensively spread among the native inhabitants at the time of the Allied landings in order to create a favourable atmosphere for our forces.

Tellingly, the document then adds: 'There is strong evidence that President Roosevelt, during the Casablanca conference of 1943, personally encouraged the Sultan to hope for American support ... in preparing Morocco, possibly under a joint US–British and French protectorate, for independence some years hence.'[34]

As the Second World War continued to rage, it became increasingly difficult for de Gaulle to turn a deaf ear to the voices of nationalism that cried out from within France's own empire. In December 1944, for example, mutiny broke out amongst demobilised African infantry in a camp near Dakar, provoking a savage French reaction. And in Senegal, a highly revered prophet of nationalism, Léopold Senghor, began to speak out with increasing audacity against colonial rule.

Nationalist sentiment had grown partly because a defeated France, far from looking invincible as it had done before 1940, had so suddenly and dramatically been rendered vulnerable by the experience of defeat in both Europe and Indochina. But it was also because the colonies, particularly those in west Africa, were providing increasing numbers of soldiers to de Gaulle's Free French, and were also acting as bases and staging posts for vital supplies. This colonial support endowed the Free French with an independent base that bestowed upon them a much higher standing in the eyes of the British and Americans, who were sceptical of just how much following de Gaulle and his movement really had inside France. De Gaulle owed them a huge token of gratitude.

In January 1944, de Gaulle held a conference in Brazzaville to discuss the future of the French colonies before announcing some token concessions to nationalist sentiments. But at the same time he issued a warning to Roosevelt to keep out of France's own business: 'It belongs to the French nation, and only her,' he continued, 'to proceed when the time is opportune to make reforms in the imperial structure which she [France] will decide upon in the context of her sovereignty.'[35]

But by the end of the war there was another global force, besides the influences of nationalism and *les anglo-saxons*, that the French would have to contend with if they were to keep a grip on their empire. That force was Communism. At almost exactly the same time that the Anglo-American invasion fleet was landing on the north African coast, the Red Army was inflicting a decisive defeat upon the German Army at Stalingrad. At this stage, de Gaulle had close and cordial relations with Stalin's regime, but he would still have wondered what would happen – to western Europe, France and its colonies – when Nazi Germany was defeated. He knew that Communism often went hand in hand with nationalism, and that many of the emergent nationalist leaders in the French Empire, and the British, had associations with the Communist Party. It seemed only a matter of time, in other words, before France's imperial possessions came under pressure from Communism too. If or when that happened, he would need the support of Britain and America to keep it at bay.

In the meantime, *le Général*'s mistrust of the United States was growing. At the Bretton Woods summit in July 1944, as representatives from the world over met to formulate a new global economic order, French delegates were enraged to find their country apparently relegated to a status well below Britain and even China, prompting one of them to start shouting in protest at his American counterparts. And as Allied forces pressed ahead in western Europe after the D-Day landings, President Roosevelt invited de Gaulle to Washington to discuss the future of France, and of Europe in general, after the defeat of Nazism. It was now, at a meeting in the President's study at the White House, that de Gaulle's worst fears were borne out.[36]

Roosevelt outlined a grandiose vision of the new starring role that the United States would play on the stage of the post-war world. Great Britain and the Soviet Union were the other two powers in the post-war 'directorate' he imagined, but ultimately America was the only Western power that really mattered. He added that Washington would recognise and support self-determination everywhere in the world, and emphasised that the United States would need bases in French territory, mentioning Dakar as an example. De Gaulle responded that he had no intention at all of surrendering any part of the French Empire, and added that he was troubled by the President's vision of American hegemony.

De Gaulle also felt sure that Washington was deliberately keeping

France's role in the advance towards Berlin to a bare minimum. The likely reason, he surmised, was to sideline France from post-war negotiations about the future of Germany and other key matters. He told a press conference in Paris that his forces hadn't received any heavy weapons or armour to equip even a single division, pointing out how deeply unfair this was when Germany had invaded his country three times over the preceding seventy years.[37]

He was not imagining things. In November 1944 the British Foreign Secretary Anthony Eden noted how the American leader was 'snarky to the French', had 'refused to agree that the French should attend at the next three-power meeting to discuss Germany' and 'was not forthcoming about equipment for the new French army'. Eden also added that there were grounds for believing that:

> Some of the governing authorities in Washington have little belief
> in France's future and indeed do not wish to see France restored as
> a great imperial power ... to my mind the danger was that Amer-
> ican policies towards France might jeopardize their relations and
> ours with that country for years to come.

Then, in early February, Roosevelt, Churchill and Stalin met at Yalta to discuss the shape of post-war Europe. To his fury, de Gaulle was excluded and the French went unrepresented, deemed by Roosevelt to be 'a complicating and undesirable factor'. By this time, many French men and women also wondered if Washington intended to set up a military administration in their country rather than allow them to choose their own government.[38]

Matters did not improve when unarmed French soldiers in Indochina were massacred by Japanese soldiers but Roosevelt refused outright to provide any air support that might perhaps have saved them. De Gaulle wanted American arms for an expeditionary force, which Churchill would have allowed him to station in Burma, but the President turned the request down. And when General Gabriel Sabattier, fighting his way to the Chinese border with the remnants of his force, contacted the American command centre at Lai Chao in China, and pleaded for urgent support, his appeal was rejected. The French, de Gaulle told American representatives, 'have the impression that you no longer consider the greatness of France as necessary to the world or yourselves'.[39]

But de Gaulle was determined not to surrender easily to American and British pressure, or indeed to the pressure of Communism and nationalism. This was not just because of the material benefits that empire bestowed on the French government, which was able to buy and import raw materials at well below the open market premium. It was essentially because, in his own eyes, France's empire was an integral part of its national identity and importance. The empire bestowed upon France grandeur, and this qualified it to stand tall, *au premier rang*, on the international stage. 'France is really itself when it is at the forefront of the leading nations,' he once said. 'France cannot be itself without her greatness.' It was the empire, he added, that had allowed France to carry on fighting when the Nazis had invaded and overrun the mainland.[40]

By the war's end in August 1945, de Gaulle appeared to have gained some ground. Opinion polls showed that most ordinary French men and women thought that their country had regained something of its lost stature and had now once again become a great power. France had by this time won a permanent seat on the United Nations' Security Council and become an occupying power, alongside Britain, America and Russia, of post-war Germany. Yet, less impressively, France had been given both roles only by virtue of those three other countries, and had been excluded from the two international conferences, at Yalta and Potsdam, where such decisions had been taken.[41]

But those French men and women who associated their country's grandeur with its empire were confronted with a clear dilemma. On the one hand they wanted to continue to exert their national grip over the territories that the United States, Britain and Russia seemed to be prising away from them. But on the other hand, they needed the support of those two 'Anglo-Saxon' countries against a mutual enemy, Communism. A great many nationalists also had strong connections with Soviet or Chinese Communism, and this meant that London and Washington would sometimes have strong sympathy with France's position.

The result would be that France would play a 'Great Game' for national influence against both English-speaking countries, competing with them but at the same time doing so covertly because it was also heavily dependent on their support.

It was just such undercover tactics that the French used in Lebanon in 1943. Lebanon, like Syria, had been a French protectorate since the end of the First World War but, under pressure from growing nationalist sentiment and from the British and the Americans, Charles de Gaulle agreed to hold national elections and recognise Lebanese independence if a majority demanded it. But the 'Fighting French'– as the 'Free French' now called themselves – were in fact desperate to maintain their grip over Lebanon, and the election campaign was rife with dirty tricks, bribery and intimidation. The British representative, General Edward Spears, accused the French of distributing paper, a highly valuable item at a time of wartime rationing, only to newspapers that towed their line, and even of murdering one voter in a polling booth. Infuriated by the electoral outcome, General Jean Helleu then placed the entire Cabinet under arrest, dissolved the chamber, suspended the constitution and appointed the defeated candidate, Émile Eddé, as the new head of state. But within days the French had to back down as they came under massive pressure from both the Lebanese masses and the British government to respect the true wishes of the Lebanese people.

Then, just as the Second World War drew to a close, the French Army fought a similarly secretive operation in the Algerian market town of Sétif, around 200 miles east of the capital, Algiers.

On the morning of 'Victory in Europe', 8 May 1945, thousands of people had come out into the streets of Sétif to celebrate the defeat of Nazi Germany. But it was not long before violence, stirred by nationalist agitators, flared up. Shots were fired and the situation quickly escalated as bands of young Muslim men went on the rampage. Heavily outnumbering and overwhelming the meagre number of policemen, they looted shops and went in search of European settlers who they could rape or kill. Over the next few days, around one hundred Europeans were slaughtered, their bodies typically mutilated and hacked apart.

The Governor General, Yves Chataigneau, now ordered his troops to launch a savage counter-reaction to ensure that the rioting was crushed before it started to spread. Suspects were rounded up and shot without trial, or even without proof. Planes and warships, anchored some distance offshore, bombarded villages and districts where they suspected nationalist rebels were hiding. How many died in these long weeks of repression is unclear, but even the most conservative estimate, ventured by a government report, puts the figure at between 1,000 and 1,300. As Alistair Horne, the distinguished historian of the Algerian War, wrote, this 'still represents a ten-to-one "overkill" in relation to the numbers of Europeans massacred; especially when, as was later estimated, no more than five percent of the population had been tainted anyway'. This bloody affair went completely unreported in the French press, and the foreign media was kept well away from the disturbances. De Gaulle only made one brief reference to the troubles, a single sentence which appeared in his war memoirs.[42]

The French authorities felt sure that, unless they crushed the Algerian protests, then the subversive influence of the 'Anglo-Saxons' and of international Communism would merge with nationalism. In 1943, the Algerian nationalist leader Ferhat Abbas had produced his own political manifesto, the *Manifeste du Peuple Algérien*, which was explicitly modelled on the Atlantic Charter, and he had also held a number of meetings with Roosevelt's representative, Robert Murphy. Unless any violence was quashed immediately, then Paris was afraid that the Americans would have an excuse to intervene in such strategically valuable territories and prise them away.

Hundreds of miles away, in Damascus and other Syrian cities, French officials also thought they saw a secret 'Anglo-Saxon' hand at work, stirring up violence and protest. The British–American response fulfilled their worst fears and suspicions towards the two 'Anglo-Saxon' powers. In north Africa, French administrators such as Jacques Soustelle, the minister of the colonies, accused the British and American soldiers of encouraging Arab nationalism. And in the Levant, as Syria and Lebanon prepared for the moment of independence, French spies kept close watch on British administrators and tried to find clues to London's long-term plans for the region.[43]

Over the months that followed, the French became increasingly convinced that 'Anglo-Saxon' influences were also prising their grip off one of their most strategically important colonies. This was Madagascar, 'the Red Island', off the south-east coast of Africa.

CHAPTER 2

ENGLISH SPIES ON THE RED ISLAND

In early January 1947, French intelligence officers were alarmed by a series of reports about the activities of a nationalist movement, the *Mouvement Démocratique de la Rénovation Malgache* (MDRM), in the colonial territory of Madagascar.

Over the preceding few months, rumours and indications of an armed rebellion by the MDRM had been steadily growing. Documents found on the body of a dead Madagascan man revealed that 'members of this group are each sworn to kill Europeans when the rebellion breaks out', warned Captain Chesneau of the Deuxième Bureau, one of France's foreign intelligence agencies. The French spies knew that the nationalists were numerically much stronger than ever before. With just 300 or so active members in 1945, the MDRM was now thought to have a following of around 14,000 men and women. Its agents were also travelling throughout rural areas to recruit, and bribe, new members. The intelligence officers pointed out that its numbers and its fighting capabilities had been bolstered by the sudden influx of Madagascan nationals who had served in the

French Army during the Second World War before returning home. There had been previous occasions when the Deuxième Bureau had felt sure that the activists were ready to launch a coup attempt: it had expected such an eventuality between Christmas and New Year's Day 1945. Now, a year on, the rebels were stronger than ever and ready to flex their muscle.[44]

But it was not just the MDRM's growing band of followers that deeply alarmed the French spies. For according to 'a well informed source of information', warned one Bureau officer, the MDRM had just received a large and highly secretive cash transfer of 400,000 francs. One of the donors was the Chinese government, which had used its embassy in the capital, Tananarive, to spirit the funds into the party's hands: this was alarming because the Chinese leader, Chiang Kai-shek, was a strong American ally. But another party had also been involved. The culprit, continued the report, was another 'foreign consulate, the identity of which remains unclear'.[45]

Days later, another memorandum gave further details:

> A sum of 400,000 francs received by the MDRM's Central Committee has been handed over by the Chinese and American consulates. A second sum of 300,000 francs would have been paid by the consulates of Great Britain and America by an intermediary, who is an English missionary (his identity is not known), and by another religious preacher.[46]

Then, in March, more reports emerged that seemed to confirm the Deuxième Bureau's worst fears. The nationalist party was not only stepping up its activities and its state of readiness for some big operation but it was reaching out to foreign powers for supplies of arms. Some of its agents were attempting to buy weapons from Syrian mercenaries and traffickers, or from cargo ships docked at the ports of Tamatave and Majunga. And on 11 March, at a major meeting at the MDRM's headquarters, a party leader called Rahenja Ralison had addressed the delegates in these terms: 'According to our intelligence operatives, the French government has started to become concerned about Madagascar and has started to monitor our activities ... we are subject to very intense surveillance, and the arrest of several influential members is proof of that. We must avenge those who have been arrested.'

And then, as he called for financial support for the purchase of a radio transmitter and demanded the release of several followers who the French authorities had just arrested, he proclaimed that: 'The purchase of arms for our future state is going well. Let us thank the English!'

The French spies also knew that the MDRM deputy leader, Joseph Raseta, had visited London over the preceding months. They wanted to know exactly who he had been meeting. 'It would be of the greatest interest to question Raseta about his links with the British and perhaps with the Americans,' ran one report. The previous year, the visit to London by another nationalist leader, an individual known only as Ravoahangy, had deeply alarmed senior ministers in Paris, who had asked the French ambassador to London to find out, as a matter of urgency, as much as possible about the 'meetings with British personalities'.[47]

The spies had other indications of foreign involvement, noting that 'every one of the leading members of the MDRM who we have arrested has declared that the deputy leader Raseta promised time and time again that a [nationalist] revolt would have the support of other countries'. The report continued by adding that 'in any future Madagascan government, we expect that Raseta would be Foreign Minister. So it seems that if there have been dealings with any foreign powers, the leader who has been responsible for it is Raseta.'[48]

The French authorities thought they knew the identity of one of the troublemakers who was stirring up nationalist sentiment. He was a former British national, who lived and worked in Madagascar, called 'Major' John Morris.

A 46-year-old former soldier, Morris had first arrived on the island in 1942, immediately after the British Army had invaded and seized it from Vichy forces. His role was to act as a liaison officer between French officials and the British Army, but although he was well qualified for this role, since he was born and raised in Belgium and spoke perfect French, he soon started to clash with the French administrators. They quickly suspected Morris and his chiefs at the British consulate, two colonels by the name of Watson and Holt, of economic and political espionage. In particular, they resented British efforts to survey the land and its resources, and to strike up trade deals with local people.[49]

Morris had left the army in 1945 but stayed on in Madagascar to work for a British–American company called Socimex. He continued to raise strong French suspicions. Not only did this 'talkative and somewhat boastful' individual like to drop hints that he had links with British intelligence, a French spy reported, but he seemed to act in an almost official capacity when a British diplomat, Sir Philip Mitchell, visited Madagascar. French officials in both Tananarive and Paris were particularly alarmed by the connections that Morris appeared to have forged with Madagascan nationalists. Until September 1946, Morris had been in touch with Joseph Raseta through an intermediary by the name of Rakotomalala, who worked as an official in a British company, based in Madagascar, called Caltek. Subsequently, another nationalist figure called Dr Raherivelo had taken on the same role. And when Raherivelo visited the English Consulate in the capital Tananarive in January 1947, French intelligence officers felt certain that British officials

would have assured him that the rebel cause would get assistance from Great Britain. British aid, channelled via Morris, would have consisted of advice and promises – advice on establishing links between the MDRM's reps and foreign countries, and on military preparations for the revolt. And there would have been promises of funding ... arms and naval reconnaissance during the campaign.[50]

By March 1947, the French intelligence service was keeping a close and careful watch over Morris and another official, Major Nicholson, who worked at the British consulate in Tananarive.[51]

These alleged links, real or imaginary, between the nationalist rebels and the 'Anglo-Saxons' play an important part in explaining the course of events in Madagascar over the months ahead. Fearful that the British or Americans might start to support the rebels, and undermine Paris's grip over its colonial territory, the French governors were prepared to deploy, or at least turn a blind eye to, a degree of brutality and heavy-handedness against the nationalists that was completely disproportionate to the actual threat they posed. Like General Oliva-Roget in Damascus, the colonial administrators in Madagascar seemed to see foreign spies all around them.

This presented a curious irony. Madagascar was, as it remains, one of the most isolated and unspoiled environments in the world. It had changed little in the half-century that had passed since a 3,500-strong French force had landed on its north-west coast and hoisted the tricolour, dashing the hopes of American rivals who wanted to get there first. After the conquest of 1894–95, a succession of French colonial explorers, agriculturalists and businessmen had arrived, cultivating coffee and rice, examining the island's geology, particularly its distinctively dark red soil, and studying its plants and wild animals. These colonialists did succeed in building a number of main roads and several rail links, mainly in and around Tananarive, and constructed some impressive buildings in the main cities, which firmly stamped France's imperial authority on the island.

Otherwise the traditional landscape of 'The Red Island' had remained largely unchanged.

Curiously, however, the political events of the late 1940s were shaped, to an important degree, by some very contemporary influences.

With whatever foreign support they had, the rebels braced themselves to attack. On 28 March an urgent French intelligence report warned that an armed rebel assault was 'very probably' going to take place the following night in the town of Moramanga. Commanders were put on a state of alert.[52]

But although they were issued in time, the warnings were not acted upon. Late in the night of Saturday 29 March 1947, two groups, totalling around 2,000 indigenous militiamen, launched simultaneous attacks on the military camp at Moramanga. Moving with stealth in the early hours, the attackers reached the camp perimeter completely undetected and then hurled a succession of incendiary bombs at the outposts before storming through barbed wire and gates. By the time the remnants of the attacking force withdrew the following morning, they had killed twenty-two people and wounded twelve. The town, in the words of one witness, was 'devastated'. All outside communications had been cut and the streets were 'littered with bodies'.[53]

The attackers seemed to have had some inside knowledge of the camp and some assistance from within. A subsequent investigation also pinned the blame on serious administrative failings in the wider area. Local government representatives, ran the report, were hardly ever seen by the local population, allowing MDRM propagandists to plausibly claim that the French were no longer even the rulers of the island. 'There has been a total abandonment of all authority and of every activity on the part of the administration,' it continued. The MDRM's activists had been openly campaigning and operating over the year that preceded the outbreak of the revolt, yet had still succeeded in taking the defenders by surprise.[54]

The Madagascan Revolt had begun.

Over the next year or so, before the last pockets of resistance were driven back into the remote forests and mountains and finally suppressed, the French armed forces fought a brutal and bloody war against lightly armed insurgents who launched sporadic attacks, mainly on towns and railways, that were designed to intimidate the French colonial rulers into surrendering the island to local rule.

Exactly how many Madagascans died during the conflict remains deeply uncertain. In 1948, the commander of French forces on the island stated that the toll surpassed 89,000, while the following year the high commissioner estimated that the number exceeded 100,000. Two years later, an official figure came up with a drastically revised figure of just 11,200 deaths. But independent observers estimated that the death toll considerably exceeded this figure within just weeks of the revolt breaking out: as a result of Colonial Minister Marius Moutet's 'pacification programme', wrote an American official, Robert Fernald, who was in Tananarive, '25,000 innocent (more or less) bystanders were killed by the French' in the first six weeks of the revolt alone. On 3 June he pointed out that 'probably thousands of rebels have been killed in fighting (or) during the reprisals and destruction of villages', adding that there were reports of 'police tortures and ... acts of barbarity'. Even after the revolt ended, the following year, he still noted how 'bodies are now found in the streets and roads or drowned in the rice and lotus swamps around the city'. As a Catholic priest called Father Jacques Tronchon, who was undertaking missionary work on the island for the Franciscan Order at the time of the rebellion, concluded in his own study, 'it was a real bludgeoning'. Paraphrasing the Roman historian Tacitus, he added that 'they called it pacification once they'd flattened everything'.[55]

Others bore witness to French reprisals. In the spring of 1947, as he travelled through the colony, a French colonial administrator witnessed some sights that shocked and horrified him. Although he was a former soldier who had been awarded the Military Medal in the First World War, he was not afraid to admit that he was sickened by what he saw.

One incident he witnessed took place after a rebel attack on a village, in which several European settlers had been killed and their bodies mutilated. In the hours that followed, the French Army had rounded up several hundred suspects, herding them into a heavily guarded building. 'Around 500–600 prisoners,' he wrote, 'were crammed together like animals and forced to stay lying on their stomachs.' He continued:

> Then, as soon as one man made a move, bursts of automatic fire raked through groups of ten, twenty or thirty of the prisoners, hitting them in the back. Around 150 people were killed like this. Stories and memories of this carnage will live in the minds of the local people for centuries.

Afterwards, he was asked to witness the interrogation of three suspects. But he didn't last long. 'I couldn't stay more than 5 minutes in each interrogation,' he wrote, describing how:

> The prisoners were stripped to the waist while two European men struck them hard and constantly with a bullwhip until they confessed. But all this ended at night when the two Europeans shot them dead and dumped their bodies in the common grave a short distance away – having said that their lives would be spared if they confessed. I would never have guessed that the French would carry out acts that are worthy of the Gestapo, and in the presence of an interpreter-writer and of a number of local people who were in nearby offices and who couldn't help witnessing what happened.[56]

Father Tronchon also discovered that much of the brutality unleashed on the Madagascan population was the result not of nervous or heavy-handed commanders but of deliberate government policy. Some of these atrocities could only have been carried out with the approval of commanders at a high level: for example, there were numerous reports of French military transport planes being filled to capacity with prisoners who were then flown over rebel-controlled territory and thrown out of the planes to their deaths. But to deploy military aircraft, and then load them with prisoners at an airfield, clearly requires some planning and organisation. The same could be said of the mass executions that took place in French-run prisons where suspects were held, often for no good reason, and of the numerous villages in rebel-held territory that were set alight and reduced to ashes.

Years after Tronchon published his findings, declassified documents confirmed the raw brutality with which the French armed forces had conducted their campaign. Some of them refer openly to prisoners being immediately shot on capture. Others refer to acts of random and unprovoked atrocities, particularly by Senegalese tirailleurs (infantry). Two years before, many of these Senegalese troops had served in Damascus and at Sétif in Algeria, winning a reputation for brutality on both fronts.

To quash the rebellion, the French high commander diverted a whole detachment of them to Madagascar, and they soon lived up to their reputation. 'It is likely that the Senegalese and mercenary troops stopped at nothing ... and they seemed to have lost control of themselves,' admitted one commander after the initial attack on 29 March. 'They caused considerable damage. We should condemn their excessive reprisals which undoubtedly affected innocent people ... they weren't able to contain themselves and overstepped the mark in the enthusiasm of their first repressive action.'[57]

A French colonial administrator also added that:

As for the Senegalese and mercenaries, although they currently
make up the most trustworthy and brave soldiers, their lust for pil-
lage and their bloodthirstiness is only curbed by the authority of
the leaders who, in the confusion of recent events, have not been
able to keep them in constant check.

He also noted that: 'some troops carried out initiatives less praise-
worthy than others [in places where] the distinction between loyal
citizens and the rest was not clear, and where soldiers, acting without
any officers, took reprisals that undoubtedly spilled innocent blood'.[58]

Other documents spell out *certaines brutalités* of Senegalese soldiers towards civilians, such as random assaults, rapes and thefts. The
situation was so serious, one French official acknowledged, that, in
some places, shopkeepers and merchants would almost certainly shut
up shop and move elsewhere to avoid the Senegalese men. Others
note the prevalence of venereal disease amongst the French colonial
soldiers, and pointed to the 'disastrous' effect of stationing them so
close to villages. Military camps should be ringed off with barbed
wire, urged one commander, to keep contact to a bare minimum.
Such atrocities were not new – in 1945, an American officer had
been shocked to witness similar behaviour by Senegalese troops in
Madagascar and complained to his seniors in America – but they
became far more prevalent now. Many of these tirailleurs were known
for abducting young women from villages, or for cutting off the heads
and ears of their victims and parading them as trophies. In another
report, an administrator urges commanders and political chiefs to act
to prevent soldiers, Senegalese and Syrians but also some Westerners,
from carrying out 'looting and bad behaviour to avoid provoking the
wrath of the local people'. Other letters or memoranda refer openly
to the summary execution of prisoners.[59]

These reports suggest that the French were deliberately perpetrating a policy of 'collective punishment'. To crush a rural insurgency, the thinking seemed to run, it was necessary to destroy the insurgents' local support base and networks. That meant killing or, at the very least, intimidating innocent people in rebel-held areas with murder, torture and mass rape.

Judging by the savagery of such tactics, the French government was prepared to stop at nothing to win this particular war. Equally, in the National Assembly, politicians from across the political spectrum urged the government to quell the uprising as quickly as possible. 'It is necessary for us restore law and order with the utmost urgency,' argued one representative during the parliamentary debate on the crisis, on 8 May 1947. It was the same savagery that the French authorities had deployed in Damascus less than two years before.[60]

In both Madagascar and Damascus, there was a clear mismatch between the actual threat the rebels posed and the armed response of the French. The Madagascan insurgents were, on the whole, poorly armed and, despite the alarmism of some French intelligence reports, had very little if any logistical support from abroad. Most of them relied upon spears and machetes, although some had very simple and antiquated pistols. They never controlled more than about one-sixth of the island, since they were concentrated mainly in the forests that surround the eastern coast, in areas where the local people had a good number of grievances about how land and its produce was shared. Only a relatively small number of Westerners, around a few hundred expatriates who lived and worked in remote parts of the island, and three hundred soldiers, were killed in the eighteen-month conflict. And the local people had long had a reputation for being docile and peace-loving, having never previously posed any serious threat to French rule there.

There were certainly occasions when the rebels seemed to pose a very real challenge. 'The Westerners are feeling threatened and feeling extremely nervous,' reported the High Commissioner Alexandre Conty in Tananarive on 19 April 1947, as a result of 'the suddenness of these events, the revelation that numerous Westerners had sometimes been massacred with a certain type of cruelty, the knowledge that everyone was confronted by a similar fate, and the huge disparity of forces.' For several weeks, Moramanga, for example, was confronted by nightly attacks. But such incidents were generally rare after the first few weeks of the outbreak of violence.[61]

Otherwise, French administrators and soldiers give the rebels little weight. The rebels used mainly knives and had only a very limited number of firearms, admitted one senior officer, who pointed out that, instead of being trained soldiers, they mainly belonged to 'very primitive tribes ... that have taken heavy losses during their engagements with our soldiers'. This lack of training became clear from the rebels' occasionally suicidal behaviour: 'a tide of insurgents tried to overrun our position and threw themselves straight into machine gun fire', as one officer wrote. 'Rarely has any rebel group displayed such a crazy zeal when making its attack.' And when, on 16 April, his men were ambushed, a French commander pointed out that '*for the first time* since 29 March one of our reconnaissance patrols came face to face with an enemy force that was well armed, well led and possessed a considerable fighting spirit. Fortunately such attacks are rare enough' (italics supplied). Other documents refer to the 'ease' with which the rebels were beaten back, or their 'fatigue'. 'At the moment the rebels are a bit disorientated,' wrote one official in April 1947, 'and I don't think they are being given any more orders for the moment.'[62]

Confronted by such an enemy, the French were very quickly able to keep the security situation in check and contain the rebel advance around the coast, in the forests and on the island's central plateau. Whole areas, such as the North Sector that lay south of Diego-Suarez, 'had been barely troubled in the days following the attack, [and are] no longer a source of concern', as one commander wrote. On 18 May, an official admitted that 'the rebellion is plainly not regressing [and] no let-up in the number of attacks against Mahanoro, Nosy-Varika, Mananjary and Manakara', but added that the rebels 'haven't won any successes … in spite of their losses'. Their attacks on the railways, for example, had been unsuccessful, either because they 'lacked explosives or expertise'. By early September, after reinforcements had arrived, the rebels were being pushed right back into the most remote forest areas.[63]

Prime Minister Paul Ramadier's government was not under any public pressure to strike at the rebels; on the contrary, the situation and campaign in Madagascar was little-noticed on the French mainland. The general public and the political elite were more preoccupied by economic troubles and political deadlock at home, and conflicts elsewhere in the colonies, notably Indochina, than by events in a remote island off the east African coast.

Not surprisingly, the French authorities were anxious to keep the truth about their campaign as quiet as possible and there were few media reports about events on the ground. But Ramadier's government did not have to work hard to suppress the truth about what was happening in Madagascar. This was not just because of the island's geographical distance from the French mainland or its insularity, but was, instead, essentially because France's media was generally subservient to the government of the day, which it depended upon for subsidies.[64]

Why, then, was France waging this secret war with such a savage and hugely disproportionate use of force?

Perhaps the French are temperamentally inclined to overreact when things go wrong, lashing out with an excessive, emotional use of force in the way they had done in Damascus and Sétif. Perhaps, too, the Madagascan campaign was also a reaction against the humiliating defeats of 1940, while some specific incidents were also provoked by the insurgents' classic hit-and-run. Because the rebels frequently melted away into the hills and forests after ambushing or attacking French or governmental targets, the soldiers became frustrated by their inability to see, let alone strike, their enemy. As a government report stated:

> In a guerrilla war like this one, we can only tire ourselves out with-
> out ever reaching our destination. Our enemy slips away whenever
> it is confronted by a superior force and then reappears where we
> least expect it and where we are unprepared, and then it disappears
> again before we can engage.

It is also possible that some of the senior French officers had been too optimistic about how quickly the revolt could be completely sup-pressed and were prepared to do anything rather than lose face. As he stepped on board a plane at Orly airfield to fly to the Red Island, the head of French forces, General Marcel Pellet, proclaimed that he was 'heading off with every confidence and certainty about a military mission that I hope will be as short as possible'.[65]

More importantly, French politicians and officials were afraid that the revolt might prove contagious. If France lost its grip over Madagascar then other colonies would be inspired to drift away. Parliamentarian René Malbrant said: 'The events in Madagascar have repercussions for our other overseas territories. What has hap-pened in Indochina and is happening in Madagascar will soon happen in north Africa, in Black Africa and beyond if we don't con-tain it. On the outcome rests the future of the entire French Union.'[66]

What Malbrant was saying was that the French Empire was under pressure. What he did not spell out, however, was that this had something to do with France's relations with two distinct ene-mies – Communists and the 'Anglo-Saxons'.

CHAPTER 3

MADAGASCAR, COMMUNISM AND THE 'ANGLO-SAXONS'

The revolt in Madagascar badly unsettled French administrators, partly because it coincided with growing tension between the French government and Communist organisations, both at home and within the French Empire. For several long months, it seemed that the Malagasy uprising was just one ripple in a vast wave of popular support for Communism that could engulf the French mainland as well as its colonies. In the general elections of 1947, the French Communist Party claimed a quarter of the popular vote and its representatives sat as ministers in the Cabinet led by the Prime Minister, Paul Ramadier. There was a real chance, American officials warned their French counterparts in February 1946, of a Communist uprising in France. Rumours of an impending coup, supported and supplied by secret air drops from East Germany, Yugoslavia and other Communist-controlled countries of eastern Europe, were rife in the early months of 1947. Predicting that the rebellion would start with industrial unrest and then spiral out of control, the French intelligence services bugged Communist headquarters and paid party insiders for information, waiting anxiously for any sign of trouble.[67]

The Reds, it seemed, were everywhere. When, in May 1947, Ramadier dismissed the Communist ministers from his Cabinet, he discovered that his former chief of reconstruction, Charles Tillon, had placed more than 1,500 Communist militants on his ministry's payroll. And when industrial tension grew markedly over the summer, the threat of Communist revolution appeared to be a very real one. Millions took to the streets of Paris to protest about their pay, workers in key industries went on strike, riots broke out and large caches of weapons were discovered. Armed soldiers were ordered to surround and guard the National Assembly building, and the government prepared to call up nearly 100,000 reservists.

Unrest was also growing fast in the colonies, where the leaders and members of some pro-independence movements often had close links to either the Soviet Union, China or both. As a result, French officials feared that a nationalist revolt in Madagascar could easily prove infectious and trigger nationalist revolts elsewhere in the empire.

At almost exactly the same time that the rebellion broke out, for example, French officials in west Africa were struck by 'increasingly frequent and systematic anti-French propaganda', which African nationalists such as George Padmore, 'a British subject of West Indian origin', were publishing from their offices in Nigeria and in Manchester. In particular, the Madagascan revolt had broken out just weeks after an uprising elsewhere in the French Union – Indochina. On 19 December, soldiers of the Viet Minh Communist militiamen had massacred forty Frenchmen in Hanoi, sparking off a wider uprising against French rule that their leader, Ho Chi Minh, had long been planning. But to make matters even worse, the Prime Minister was then forced to divert thousands of troops to Madagascar as they sailed to Indochina. 'We can't deceive ourselves', one parliamentarian warned, 'that the future of the French

Union depends on how we deal with the crisis in Madagascar.' This was all the more important when Communism had made its presence felt on the island: the sizeable Indian population, noted the French, was 'somewhat susceptible to Communist propaganda', essentially because 'only the USSR had helped them to shake off British rule'.[68]

This also had a party political dimension too. Prime Minister Ramadier was at this time doing his best to hold together a fragile centre-left coalition and knew that he was vulnerable to attacks from his chief rival, Charles de Gaulle. France and its empire were at risk, argued de Gaulle with increasing fervour. He, de Gaulle, had personally saved France from Nazi tyranny in the Second World War but now, just a few years later, his country was once again confronted by real danger that the Prime Minister was incapable of confronting. France had already lost its protectorates over Syria and Lebanon, continued *le Général*, and nationalist sentiment in north Africa seemed to be on the rise. Decisive action was needed to maintain control. But de Gaulle also argued that the United States and Great Britain, as well as the Soviet Union, posed a threat to the French colonies.

It was this fear of American and British, as well as Communist, influence that helps to explain the sheer savagery of the French reaction to the revolt. The 'Anglo-Saxons' were stirring up the revolt, it appeared, and if the French lost their grip over the island then it seemed likely that the Anglophone enemy would quickly step in. As René Malbrant had argued in the National Assembly, any rebel victory against the French would be 'temporary' because: 'In the eventuality that we pulled out, there would be others who would immediately be interested in Madagascar. There is uranium down there. And the strategic importance of the island isn't lost on the world's leading nations.'

It was in this context that Major Morris and other 'Anglo-Saxon' spies seemed so important. Before and during the revolt, the French felt sure that British agents were searching for Madagascan resources, particularly uranium and precious metals, but also wanted to know more about possible links between nationalists and Communists. And in one particularly revealing confidential document, the French intelligence services wondered if the purpose of British espionage was 'to prove that France is incapable of guaranteeing, on its own, the defence of strategically valuable territory'.[69]

As a result of his 'activities contrary to our interests in our colony' and 'his contacts with insurgents', French officials expelled Morris from the island. In particular, they strongly suspected that he had lent or given money to the rebels, and thought he had used a British missionary, Pastor Hutchins of the London Missionary Society, as an intermediary.[70]

The French were also suspicious of other 'Anglo-Saxon' influences, notably the South African consulate, which they regarded as 'a centre of anti-French sentiment ... that welcomed nationalist leaders who came and went'. The consul, Jan Klerck van Petersen, was strongly suspected of making contact with 'certain British nationals who have long been known for their animosity towards France', and his diplomatic dispatches, which French agents intercepted and read before they left the island, were 'deliberately biased' and often 'very hostile towards France'. His likely tactic, they mused, was to win the sympathies of the white expatriate community, amongst which were individuals who were interested in forming a union between South Africa and Madagascar, and then use these links 'as a form of blackmail against France, which was regarded as distant and indifferent to their material welfare'.[71]

It was not coincidental that the Madagascan revolt broke out just as there was a change of American policy towards France, and to other countries in western Europe. This meant that, indirectly at least, Washington had some influence on even the early stage of the revolt.

Nearly all of the rebels were inhabitants of the most remote settlements that were relatively untouched by civilisation: a number of fanatical sorcerers had allegedly convinced some of the local populations that their ancestors had blessed an attack on French rule, and had also given them amulets that were supposed to turn bullets into harmless drops of water. This may have been why the rebellion began during a Malagasy pagan festival, *fandroana* (the festival of bathing), when ordinary Madagascans commemorated their homeland and the spirits of earlier generations. Paradoxically, however, the rebellion was in another respect very much in tune with the spirit of the age. The previous October, Joseph Ravoahangy had made a series of rousing speeches to his followers in which he pointed to the Atlantic Charter that Roosevelt and Churchill had promulgated five years before. 'A new world order' was emerging, he told his audiences in Tananarive, 'in which the people will be sovereign'. Within weeks he had founded a nationalist movement, the MDRM, whose constitution seemed to closely resemble the 'Four Freedoms' that President Roosevelt had championed.

Then, on 12 March, less than three weeks before the Madagascan revolt got under way, President Harry S. Truman had addressed Congress to make an important declaration. 'I believe it *must* be the policy of the United States', he decreed, 'to support free peoples who are resisting attempted subjugation by armed minorities or by outside pressures.' In Madagascar, rumours immediately swirled of American support for independence.

The French were well aware of this, and noted with alarm that the MDRM was turning to Washington and inspired by Truman's message. French officers heard the rebels shouting out that 'The Americans are coming to help us!', and 'Long Live the MDRM, Long Live America!' The rebels used another slogan, 'Ethiopians, led by the Americans, will come to help us', which referred to the links that Washington had been building over the preceding few months with the Ethiopian leader, Haile Selassie. One French soldier recorded how: 'Around Manakara all the rebels are convinced that the Americans have arrived on the island to come to help them, and have even approached our own men, who they have mistaken for Americans, allowing us to take quite a few prisoners.'

French spies were also aware that the MDRM was actively pleading with the American embassy in Tananarive for Washington's support: in June 1947, the organisation's leaders wrote a letter to the Consul General pleading for intervention by the United States, 'the mother of liberty', against 'the French Gestapo'. Gradually, French diplomats noticed, 'the idea is spreading throughout the world that America will emancipate people who live under colonial rule'. This, they added, was 'completely exaggerated and distorted' but nonetheless had 'grave repercussions'.[72]

But although it must have seemed otherwise to some of the nationalists of Madagascar and elsewhere, the Truman Doctrine was really directed not at imperialist powers like Great Britain and France but at Soviet Communism. In Paris and other capitals, this was obvious from the proper context, the context of that particular speech and of wider American foreign policy, of presidential remarks about 'free people'. But to the people of Madagascar, less able to see the wider challenges that confronted the United States at the time, the true meaning of Truman's words was not so clear. Given a choice between supporting a French Empire that was anti-Communist on the one hand and, on the other, a nationalist movement with even vaguely Communist sympathies, the US administration would, in the tense and difficult post-war climate, have unhesitatingly sided with the former.

By this time, the 'Cold War' between the Communist Soviet Union on the one hand, and the United States and its west European allies on the other, had already broken out. Before the end of the Second World War, Winston Churchill had already referred to the threat of an 'Iron Curtain' dividing Soviet-controlled eastern Europe from the West, and now it seemed that his predictions were being borne out. Instead of retreating from the territories that he had 'liberated' from Nazi rule, Stalin had tightened his grip on them. The governments of eastern Europe had become Soviet puppets, and in Greece, Communist organisations had tried to seize power. In the Far East, the Red Army had occupied both Manchuria and North Korea, where it had set up Communist regimes. Containing the Soviets and Communism was now becoming the major preoccupation of the American government.

Over the preceding months, the leaders and representatives of the MDRM had been in close and regular contact with American officials in both Paris and Tananarive, doing their best convince them that their movement had no links with, and was even hostile to, international Communism. One leader, Joseph Raseta, even showed a lot of interest in 'American capital to develop the resources of the island'. But American diplomats were unsure about where the MDRM's sympathies really lay, and a year before, in March 1946, Robert Fernald had warned his compatriots in the State Department that 'whatever political developments take place here [in Madagascar], a finger in the pie will be placed by the Communists in France and the few local Communists'. Later in the year he added that the MDRM was 'already largely influenced by Communists in France through Deputies Ravoahangy and Raseta'. Then, just shortly before the Malagasy uprising began, the ambassador reported that the rebels, for whom 'everything else is apparently secondary to the aim of independence', were openly looking to French and Indochinese Communists for support. Another American intelligence report pointed out that Joseph Raseta was not only a former member of the Communist Party but was also personally acquainted with Ho Chi Minh.[73]

Such fears were not entirely unfounded but nor were they absolutely fair. The MDRM had almost certainly been infiltrated by extremists but, if it had a 'foreign policy' at all, it entertained only a loose sympathy for other colonial people and proposed organising a regional community based on cooperation with its Indian Ocean 'neighbours', India and Australia. The local police also captured a number of the organisation's documents that singled out Madagascar's leading Communist, Pierre Boiteau, for assassination. But if State Department officials were aware of them, such truths did nothing to alleviate their suspicions.

Then, only a few weeks after the outbreak of the rebellion and the declaration of the Truman Doctrine, came another hugely important development in Franco-American relations.

On 5 June, the American Secretary of State, General George C. Marshall, had chosen a very unremarkable venue, a lecture hall at Harvard University, to make a very special announcement. He was in a position to launch a new 'European Recovery Programme', he proclaimed, which was designed to help America's Western allies recover from the devastating cost of the Second World War. Better known as 'the Marshall Plan', the programme offered Britain, France and West Germany, as well as other countries, huge sums of cash. The idea was that such massive financial injections would not only lift up their economies but also give them a degree of domestic stability, thereby reducing the appeal of Communism and other extremist parties. 'In the final analysis,' wrote the American ambassador in Paris, Jefferson Caffery, in a dispatch back to Washington, 'it is obvious that social and political stabilization in France and western Europe depends largely upon economic stabilization.' Washington had already been heavily supporting France and other Western economies – in December 1945 Paris had taken a $1 million American loan – but Marshall's announcement now promised even more.[74]

American assistance kept France financially afloat but did have strings attached. In return for granting so much financial support, Washington wanted some economic reforms. It also wanted political guarantees. 'The primary aim of the Marshall Plan', wrote a Parisian politician called Gilbert de Chambrun, 'is to serve American strategy. The economic order was a secondary factor.' Marshall even hinted that French foreign policy might need to alter course. In January, a few months before he announced the aid package, Marshall had written to the American embassy in Paris, expressing his 'increasing concerns over the situation as it is developing in Indochina'. He added that 'we [are] not interested in seeing colonial empire administrations supplanted by a philosophy emanating from and controlled by the Kremlin'.[75]

But if Washington was willing and able to impose any conditions on Paris, conditions about its domestic and foreign policies, then there was no reason why it couldn't also interfere in the French Empire, including Madagascar. If the Truman administration felt, with or without justification, that the French authorities were not doing enough to prevent Madagascar falling into Communist hands, then it seemed quite possible that they could make Marshall Aid dependent upon a very awkward condition: that they, the Americans, should assume responsibility for the island. Washington could perhaps have insisted on setting up bases on Madagascar, in the same way that it had on Greenland and Cuba. It might have wanted, at the very least, to be entrusted with the island's security and foreign relations, while the French remained responsible for its domestic affairs.

In other words, the French would have been very keen to stamp out a rebellion that might have appeared, in Washington, to be inspired by or linked to Communism. Otherwise the Americans would have had a reason to involve themselves in France's empire. Perhaps the Americans would use Communism as an excuse to get involved.

There were certainly occasions when it seemed that the Americans were overtly interfering in Madagascan affairs. At the port of Tamatave in August 1947, French security officials detected a secret delivery of arms by an American-owned civilian cargo ship. Whatever lay behind this arms-smuggling, which may or may not have had any official sanction from anyone in the American government, the revelation prompted a flurry of diplomatic activity in Washington, as French officials lobbied the State Department to publicly disassociate the United States from the rebel cause. While French diplomats did not dispute the good intentions of the State Department – 'we don't think that the US has officially backed the revolt,' mused one official – this left open the possibility that the arms delivery was the work of individual officers, within specific departments in Washington, who had their own anti-French agenda and the freedom to pursue them.[76]

On another occasion, an alarmed French administrator recorded how 'a member of the US consulate in Mauritius has publicly criticised the attitude of the French administration in the light of events [the rebellion in Madagascar] and has spoken of making an appeal to the British forces in Mauritius'. The same document also makes an intriguing reference to the presence of an American admiral during French operations against the rebels. It is likely that he was an attaché or formed part of a high-level delegation, perhaps to assess the strength of Communist activity, but, whatever his mission, such a visitor is likely to have exacerbated their insecurity about their colonial grip on the island.[77]

The French were also concerned about possible British intervention, or at least interest. 'Most of the rebels have said that they have been given orders to save British civilians,' ran one French intelligence report. 'In some areas, the rebels are led by Madagascan religious men belonging to the Protestant missions of the English.'[78]

In fact, Paris had good reason to fear foreign interest in Madagascar, which had considerable strategic importance. This was partly because of its natural resources. Before the war, it had been the world's largest exporter firstly of graphite, which was quarried by a British company, Morgan Crucible, and subsequently of phlogopite mica, which was mined in remote locations of the far south. Both materials were hugely valuable in wartime, since graphite acts as an industrial lubricant for engines while phlogopite mica provides a protective coat to metal. The island's other great asset was rubber, which also aroused strong interest in times of war: a single aircraft could use as much as 2,000 pounds of this commodity.

But it was not so much its natural resources that made the island such a valuable asset. What really mattered was its vital location. Whoever held possession of Madagascar had a superb, natural base from which to control the western stretches of the Indian Ocean. Long-range patrol aircraft could use it as a base from which to search for and destroy shipping or submarines that were moving hundreds of miles away, while the island's harbours made a superb staging post to control the surrounding seas. In particular, the deep water port at Diego-Suarez, on the island's northern tip, raised the eyebrows of foreign strategists. It boasted ten miles of quays and docks and was deep enough to accommodate an enormous fleet and sheltered by a huge jetty. And if the Suez Canal was ever closed and shipping would have to make its way round the Cape of Good Hope, then Madagascar would make a superb base to harbour en route, or from which to disrupt enemy movements. During the 1905 war between Russia and Japan, for example, the Tsar's Baltic Fleet had made an epic nine-month journey to engage the Emperor's warships, and stopped off in Madagascar for several days before continuing the last stage of its odyssey. In the same way, the island could have potentially acted as a base from which an enemy force could harass French lines of communication between the mainland and its empire in the Far East.

Not surprisingly, the island quickly became a prized asset in the Second World War, and the first British plans to seize it were floated in December 1940. If the Japanese captured Madagascar, asserted Winston Churchill, then they would use it as an aircraft and submarine base from which they could 'paralyse' Britain's communications with India and its eastern empire. Burma had just fallen to the Japanese and there was a real risk that India could follow next. India would also be much more vulnerable if the Japanese seized Diego-Suarez. 'The Japanese might well turn up [at Madagascar] one of these fine days,' cabled Churchill to Roosevelt in 1942, 'and Vichy will offer no more resistance there than in French Indochina', where they had allowed the Japanese to build air bases without even putting up a fight. During the war, the island had also had strategic significance because so many vital resources, such as Middle Eastern oil, provisions to Russia from the Persian Gulf, supplies for the defence of Egypt, aid to Australia and New Zealand, all moved across the Indian Ocean and would have been vulnerable if the Imperial Army seized the Red Island.[79]

French officials had been well aware that the British and Americans, as well as the Japanese, had good reason to want to occupy their territory. 'There has been a fear [in Vichy] for some time that the Allies might anticipate Japanese action by occupying Madagascar, Mauritius and Réunion,' wrote the American ambassador, Admiral William D. Leahy, in a letter to President Roosevelt in February 1942. 'It is difficult to understand,' he added, 'why these islands, flanking as they do the supply route from anywhere to the Red Sea and now from Good Hope to the Dutch East Indies, have not long ago been occupied by the Allies.' In May 1942, determined to deny the Japanese a base in the western sphere of the India Ocean, Churchill had then ordered the seizure of Diego-Suarez, and Operation Ironclad got under way.[80]

Ironclad not only fuelled mistrust between the British and the Free French but also aggravated a sense of vulnerability about the motives of foreign powers towards the French Empire in general and Madagascar in particular. But over the preceding few years, something else had happened that had added to France's sense of vulnerability about the island.

In the summer of 1937, a delegation of Polish officials, led by Mieczysław B. Lepecki, had set sail from Marseilles and headed for Diego-Suarez. They were doing so with the full knowledge and approval of French authorities in Paris and Tananarive.

The Poles wanted to assess the viability of a proposal, first put forward in the 1880s, to ethnically cleanse the Jews from Europe and resettle them on Madagascar. At a time of growing anti-Semitism in Poland, such an idea seemed to them to be at least worth exploring. But after spending several weeks on the island, Lepecki was pessimistic. Not more than 7,000 families would be able to subsist there, he argued, and Poland would have to find somewhere else to relocate the Jews. But after the outbreak of war in September 1939, the Nazi government revived the idea. In June 1940, a German official by the name of Franz Rademacher put forward a detailed plan to seize Madagascar from a defeated France and ship Europe's entire Jewish population there. Rademacher sketched out some of the details of his idea and continued to press the Nazi leadership to adopt his proposal. Nazi officials were still considering the 'Madagascar Plan' until November 1942, when the British invasion of the island ruled out the proposal.[81]

The French were well aware of how much international interest lay in the 'Madagascar Plan' after 1938, and such interest could only add to their sense that foreign powers might have their own designs on parts of the French Empire. This may also help explain why the Free French and elements within the Vichy regime secretly supported the cause of Jewish terrorism in Palestine: if the Jews found a homeland in the Middle East, the thinking may have run, then there would be no need for a Jewish colony on Madagascar.[82]

By the time the rebellion broke out in March 1947, there was certainly no prospect of any British intervention on the island nor any suggestion of creating a Jewish state there. The British did not have the will or the means to establish a base on the Red Island, all the more so when they were fighting for their lives in Palestine, and when India was about to win its independence. Great Britain was also in a state of financial crisis and dependent on American aid. Other than the Soviet Union, the only country that might have wanted to establish a presence there, and had the resources to do so, was the United States. And any French suspicions of American motives were not altogether unfounded.

In the spring of 1943, as the Germans started to lose ground on their eastern front, defence officials in Washington had started to consider and plan for America's post-war security. They knew that, after the defeat of Nazi Germany, they would be confronted by a supremely powerful Soviet Union that had a vast and seemingly invincible army capable of absorbing enormous losses. Numerous proposals to deal with this emerging threat were drawn up and nearly all of these had a consistent theme: that the United States needed a chain of bases that would guarantee its control over both the Atlantic and Pacific Oceans. These were necessary, ran the strategic thinking in Washington, to stop any future aggressor, in Europe or the Far East, from depriving the United States of its vital sources of supply. The bases could guard vital sea lanes and act as air and sea stations to attack a national enemy in the event of a future war.[83]

Within the vast French Empire, there were naturally a good many places that were of huge interest to American defence chiefs. In 1944, not long after he had dispatched Admiral Richard E. Byrd as an envoy to travel through sections of the Pacific region to assess whether, and where, America would need post-war bases, Roosevelt ordered the occupation of Clipperton Island, a French-owned Pacific atoll that he deemed to be 'of real importance in connection with certain air routes' and as a listening-post in the Pacific Ocean. His decision infuriated Georges Bidault, the French Foreign Minister in the provisional French government that Charles de Gaulle set up after the liberation of Paris in August 1944, who accused Washington of an arrogant high-handedness that was humiliating France. Bidault did not know that the Joint Chiefs of Staff had told a State Department official, John D. Hickerson, that American forces should occupy French islands in the Pacific because by doing so they would have a stronger claim to have post-war bases there.[84]

Then, as the war ended in May 1945, the US Secretary of War, Robert P. Patterson, instructed one of his generals, Henry S. Aurand, to 'make preparations for permanent rights at seven airfields in North Africa and Saudi Arabia', including Algiers and Casablanca (Port Lyautey). Soon afterwards, an American government document, marked 'top secret', pointed out that 'French North Africa is important to the security of the United States primarily because of its strategic geographical position flanking US routes to the Mediterranean and the Middle East as well as Great Britain's lifeline'. French defence chiefs, meanwhile, soon became aware of America's strategy.[85]

Washington officials now continued to look elsewhere, and were interested in building a base at the sea port of Cayenne in French Guiana and at Nouméa on the French-owned island of New Caledonia in the Pacific Ocean. In the course of 1947, Washington drew up proposals to establish 'joint' or 'participating' rights with the French in Algiers and Casablanca and also negotiated a secret agreement to use Port Lyautey in Morocco: although it remained under the command of the French navy, the Paris government allowed the Americans to station technical staff there to service their aircraft that were now authorised to use the base.

The outbreak of rebellion in Madagascar coincided exactly with the American drive to acquire bases and landing rights in parts of the world that Washington deemed to be of strategic interest. In French eyes, the British were just as untrustworthy: de Gaulle noted that when London and Paris withdrew their troops from Syria in 1945 and 1946, the British remained in much closer proximity than the French, pulling their troops back to Baghdad, Amman and Jerusalem rather than Algiers, Tunisia and Marseilles. This was quite consistent, felt de Gaulle, with a British plan to remain the dominant power in the region. Equally, the British could not be trusted in Madagascar.[86]

Not unreasonably, Paris would have been afraid of two things. It would have feared that the Americans might want an excuse to intervene in Madagascar and wrench it from French control. They could have made Marshall Aid conditional upon this, just as in 1944 some Washington officials had wanted to make the provision of aid and supplies to its allies, under a scheme known as 'Lend-Lease', conditional upon American occupation of Clipperton. Or else Washington might have regarded a Communist-inspired revolt on the island as a genuine threat to its own national security and insisted that its own troops invade and quell the uprising before the rebels won ground and invited the Soviets in.[87]

Desperate to maintain the independence of its empire, the French government was determined to quash the revolt as quickly as possible and was prepared to use ruthless and brutal methods to do this. For Ramadier personally, any failure to keep the revolt under control and the Americans out would also have played into de Gaulle's hands: *le Général* was out of office but he was always quick to argue that his political enemies and France's new constitution, the Fourth Republic founded in 1946, could not be trusted to safeguard France and its empire.

French fears were not entirely unfounded. Contemporary American documents do not reveal any fundamental hostility towards French rule, either in Madagascar or elsewhere. On the contrary, they show a 'desire to have France continue to bear the responsibility for the maintenance of peace and security' because 'we are not attempting to disrupt French rule'. But at the same time, some American officials also revealed an interest in having military 'facilities available to us *by right*' (italics supplied) and of ensuring that other foreign powers keep out of the region. However, they do not say what action the United States would have undertaken if the French had to any degree failed to impose law and order in their colonies, creating a void into which the Soviet Union or its allies could have crept. Nor, for that matter, can French intelligence reports about American support for the MDRM rebels be easily dismissed.[88]

Determined to keep the Americans at bay, the Ramadier government not only rushed to quell the Malagasy uprising as quickly as possible but also played the anti-Communist card in Paris. On 7 May, in a gesture to the Americans, Ramadier expelled five Communist ministers from his coalition government. There seemed to be, argued the American magazine *Newsweek*, a 'change of attitude towards the Soviet Union from within the French foreign ministry'. The measure drew the response he wanted, for within just hours Washington announced the release of a huge shipment of emergency food aid to France, and two days later the World Bank authorised a vast loan to the French government.[89]

The resistance in Madagascar had been completely stamped out by the end of 1948, abating both American fears of Communism and French concern about American intervention. But in the months and years that followed, French administrators closely monitored nationalist activity for any signs of American or British involvement. In June 1950, for example, Paris was alarmed to discover renewed contacts between American diplomats in Tananarive and a nationalist leader called Gabriel Razafintsalama, who claimed that Washington was prepared to back Madagascan claims for independence and to put pressure on Paris to support independence because of the 'geographical location of the island and its wealth of natural resources'. French officials were concerned that Razafintsalama was trying to portray himself and his followers as an anti-Communist force on the island. 'We can be certain,' noted one French administrator in Tananarive, 'that he has come across some sympathetic assurances' in Washington, where his warnings about 'the eventual expansion of communism' would have been 'well-received'. It is clear, he continued, that if the nationalist cause 'presents itself as a bulwark against communism, it will be capable of attracting foreign support'.[90]

Weeks later, the French ambassador in Washington was informed of 'contacts' between Madagascan nationalists and American diplomats, whose 'attitude risks conveying approval' for the nationalist cause. The American representative, continued the case officer, needed to show 'extreme care and reserve' to stop giving the nationalists a real propaganda triumph.[91]

Other incidents added to a climate of suspicion: when, in October 1951, the American representative in Tananarive offered to distribute radio sets to local people, French officials wondered if it was part of an elaborate 'propaganda effort' by the State Department. And French officials cancelled a visit that two left-wing British parliamentarians, Fenner Brockway and Raymond Blackburn, planned to make to the island. Both men proclaimed their interest in 'liberating oppressed colonial peoples' and working 'on behalf of the liberty of colonial peoples'. Alarmed that their visit would stir up nationalist sentiment, both men were refused visas.[92]

But by this time French eyes were more focused on another part of the world – the colonial territory of Indochina, where nationalist guerrillas were fighting a ferocious war to win independence from French rule.

CHAPTER 4

TENSION AND RIVALRY IN INDOCHINA

On the afternoon of 17 September 1951, an immaculate and revered French general, Jean de Lattre de Tassigny, stepped off a passenger ship, the *Île de France*, and onto the quayside at New York.

The 61-year-old 'King Jean' had arrived to win round American opinion and rally it behind the French cause in Indochina. He wanted the leaders and people of the United States to give it their whole-hearted support and to view the conflict there as indistinguishable from the war in Korea, where American forces, under the command of General Douglas MacArthur, were locked in a bloody and protracted combat with Chinese troops.

Indochina was a cause that he was utterly committed to. 'If we lose our grip on Indochina then Madagascar, Dakar, Tunisia or Rabat will also go their own way,' the general argued. 'As long as we keep control of the region, we will stay a great power. If we win our struggle, we will truly be one of the "great" powers. But if we lose it, we will become the "sick man" of the second half of the 20th century.'

France's struggle for Indochina, in his eyes, was a test case of French and Western willingness to confront Communism. But he knew that without strong American support the struggle would be lost.[93]

There was no better start to his mission than striking the right image. He posed for press pictures, standing alongside Lauren Bacall and Humphrey Bogart, who were on their way home after filming *The African Queen*. He also insisted on his picture being taken just as the passenger ship sailed past the Statue of Liberty, knowing that this setting presented a superb photo opportunity.

De Lattre, who nine months before had been appointed as France's high commissioner for Indochina as well as the commander-in-chief of its forces there, struck an impressive figure that was calculated, and virtually guaranteed, to command press attention and public respect in the United States. The general certainly had the credentials to seize the popular imagination. He had taken part in the last cavalry charge in the history of the French Army, and his chest was embroidered with numerous medals that he had won in the First World War, during which he had been quite badly wounded. He was France's youngest general at the time of the German onslaught in the summer of 1940 and had fought bravely before being taken prisoner. Desperate to continue the fight for his country, he had then managed to escape from a Vichy prison before making his way across France to join Charles de Gaulle's Free French forces.

The press was well aware that, long before he took up his new position in Indochina in December 1950, he had acquired something of a legendary reputation. After his appointment, morale amongst the French soldiers and *colons* (colonials and expatriates) in Indochina surged. Perhaps the war was winnable after all. One American reporter wrote how 'informed persons realize that the situation basically remains critical [but] both French and Vietnamese, nevertheless, have been infused with a new spirit and energy'. This was because their new leader had banished 'defeatism' and 'stirred widespread enthusiasm by a rare combination of showmanship, charm, energy and forcefulness'. He had shown enormous energy in travelling constantly throughout the region, delivering rousing speeches to his men in a 'husky voice that ranges from a whisper to a fortissimo' and making 'heart-stirring points' to his audiences. Another American observer noted that he was 'the chief military personality in France today … and his appeal for the average French soldier or civilian is comparable to the appeal which Eisenhower and Patton have for the average American'. As a result, he was said to have engineered a 'miracle' in French fortunes.[94]

The French had needed such moral support ever since Indochina had erupted into open revolt in December 1946. After the defeated Japanese Army had surrendered and retreated the previous year, the French had proclaimed that they, once again, were the overlords. But nationalist sentiment had been growing fast during the war years. Paris granted limited independence to Laos in 1950 and promised to give Cambodia its own freedom three years later. France also offered the Vietnamese a deal. They could govern their own affairs, the French proposed, provided they remained within the French Union and Paris retained responsibility for their defence and foreign affairs. But the Viet Minh rejected the offer and demanded outright independence. The fighting intensified.

Although de Lattre was now courting American support, he had always held strong suspicions of the United States. He had angered Washington by expelling from Indochina an American air force liaison officer, Edward G. Lansdale, who he suspected of harbouring an anti-French agenda. And in 1951 he had banned French newspapers from even mentioning American economic aid to the war effort, regarding this as an insult that made France look 'like a poor cousin in Viet eyes'.

There had been tensions between the two countries over Indochina even in the course of the Second World War, when both confronted the same enemy. In November 1944, a young American airman had been shot down as he flew over Cao-Bằng, in the Gulf of Tonkin in North Vietnam, and been forced to bale out. Almost as soon as he landed, Lieutenant Rudolph Shaw was surrounded by Viet Minh militia who escorted him to their base camp some miles further north, very close to the border with China. It was here that he met their leader, a diminutive, bearded and waspish man with a sharp smile and a gleam in his eye. Ho Chi Minh recognised an opportunity: if he could look after the airman and ensure his safe return, he reasoned, then he had a chance of winning American diplomatic support for his cause of Vietnamese independence.[95]

Ho's clever move worked brilliantly, and within weeks he had not only established links with the OSS, the forerunner of the CIA, but also set up a network of rescue teams composed of his own men, who were given responsibility for finding any downed American airmen and ensuring their safety. In return, the OSS parachuted supplies and a number of agents into Viet Minh hands.[96]

Ho went one stage further in his bid to win American support, using his contacts in the OSS to transmit messages directly to desk officers in the State Department. For a time it seemed that his tactics might be working, for on 4 February President Roosevelt issued a directive, specifying that any military operations in Indochina should only be undertaken against the Japanese Army and not to support the French, who were anxious to win back their Indochinese empire from the Japanese. Instead of allowing the French to rule over the region, Roosevelt wanted to establish a 'trusteeship' that would pave the way for outright independence. His enthusiasm waned prior to his death in April 1945, and his successor, President Harry S. Truman, took a more neutral line, cautiously accepting a restoration of French authority. It was vital, his officials warned him, 'to treat France in all respects on the basis of its potential power and influence rather than on the basis of its present temporarily depleted strength', adding that the French people were 'exceptionally sensitive to questions involving their national prestige'.[97]

Others in Washington harboured a much greater hostility towards the French. In August 1945, a young veteran of the Resistance, Jean Sainteny, had flown to Hanoi to establish a spy network on behalf of Charles de Gaulle. But at his side was an American intelligence officer, Major Archimedes Patti, whose purpose in Hanoi was to make contact with, nurture and support local nationalist forces. Just two weeks later, Patti attended a Viet Minh ceremony that proclaimed 'the Democratic Republic of Vietnam' and produced a revolutionary document with a preamble that seemed to closely echo the American Declaration of Independence.[98]

Abbot Low Moffat, the head of the State Department's Division of Philippine and Southeast Asian Affairs, also made a visit to French Indochina at the end of 1946 and urged his counterparts in Washington to distance themselves from France or even to actively work against it. If the war continued, he argued, then the French could end up turning the Vietnamese people 'against all whites' and destroy any chance of preserving Western political and economic influence in the area. The United States had to show 'moral leadership', he continued, and put pressure on Paris to end the war. Other American officials concurred. Going along with French policy 'would be catastrophic [for] American prestige, would turn Vietnamese who distrust and hate [the] French into [a] violent anti-white bloc', warned the American vice consul in Hanoi. His counterpart in Saigon concurred, adding that it would 'ensure irretrievable orientation [of] intellectuals and people towards communism and Moscow and against West ... and destroy confidence that natives still have in [the] US'.[99]

Meanwhile, in Paris, many French policymakers were deeply hostile towards the prospect of American interference in their colonial affairs. In a secret cable sent in September 1946, the Acting Secretary of State in Washington noted 'the French colonial tendency (to) picture the US as aggressive and imperialistic. This brings certain French colonials, unwittingly for the most part, very close to [the] Communist party line'. He also castigated a colleague who 'should know better than encourage anti-American suspicions'. The following year the American representative in Saigon reported back that 'many French, in Indochina at least, are suspicious of American motives'. He also referred to a number of articles in the French media 'charging American interference in affairs in this area for the purpose of securing a position of economic domination', and he added that

> the French have always believed that the Americans favoured the native cause and this belief has coloured their actions and reactions to Americans and to American organizations and institutions ... some opposition to the Americans arises from the fact that the Americans did not back the French for the recapture of Indochina, that the Americans wanted to be fair towards native aspirations, and because many French here fear that the United States, by opening up this country, will reap a part of the rich profits that formerly flowed into French coffers.

Unsurprisingly, when in late 1946 Washington officials offered to mediate and bring an end to the war, the French government refused the offer: the French embassy in Washington told State Department officials that France would handle the Indochina matter 'single-handedly' and would negotiate directly with the Viet Minh when it had gained the upper hand. The Americans were well aware that any interference in the region would inflict a 'loss of prestige' upon the French, and felt that in general the French public supported the conflict because it was 'vindicating the power and glory of France'. They did not have to search hard to find evidence of the resentment they were causing: in Indochina, for example, an undercover intelligence agent called Albert Meyer organised the arson of an array of vehicles and flats that belonged to an American contingent.[100]

But in the months that followed, there was a sharp shift of sentiment in both Paris and Washington. As the threat from Communist insurgents increased, French rivalry with the 'Anglo-Saxons' was pushed into the background. The unity was only superficial, however, and underneath there were real tensions between them that consistently surfaced.

In Indochina, French colonials and soldiers had quickly started to struggle to contain the insurgency. In September 1945, General Philippe Leclerc had led 80,000 troops to Indochina to reimpose French rule after the Japanese defeat, but even this considerable force soon proved to be insufficient. Five months later, recognising the strength of the Viet Minh's support in the northern areas of Vietnam, Leclerc urged Paris to offer Ho Chi Minh limited independence, while remaining under the ultimate sovereignty of Paris, as soon as possible.

At the same time, French and American leaders were becoming increasingly concerned about the new 'Cold War' against the Soviet Union. In April 1948, Washington organised a major airlift to reinforce West Berlin and prevent it from being starved into surrender by the Soviet Army, which had blockaded the city's road and rail links to West Germany. Communist movements seemed to be on the march everywhere – in France and the rest of western Europe, but above all in China. On 1 October 1949, Mao Zedong's Communist movement won a long and bitter civil war with Chiang Kai-shek's nationalist government and proclaimed the formation of the People's Republic of China. In Paris and Washington, and in other Western capitals, the threat of Communist encroachment into, or even engulfment of, the free world was becoming increasingly real.

Both the French and the Americans had to balance competing interests. Paris needed American support to keep a ferocious and tenacious Viet Minh enemy at bay, but at the same time regarded Indochina as its own territory in which the Americans had no right to interfere. Equally, Washington was increasingly concerned about Communist infiltration into the region, while at the same time wanting to disassociate itself from French imperialism, fearing that it would give America a bad name.

The turning-point came in the spring of 1949, when the French government had recognised that 'the attitude of Great Britain and the USA make it inconceivable to follow a policy of re-establishing our sovereignty on the old terms' and offered the Vietnamese a higher degree of autonomy than it had originally wanted. On 9 March, French officials then signed the 'Élysée Accords' with the Emperor Bảo Đại, granting Vietnamese 'independence' within the French Union, while allowing Paris to retain control over Vietnam's defence, foreign relations and finances. By doing so, the French had helped their supporters in Washington to gain the upper hand over their critics, who had argued that French obstinacy was simply stirring up more nationalism and playing into the hands of Communism.

President Truman now authorised limited support for the French war effort. Soon afterwards, on 21 June, Washington effectively ended its neutral position on the conflict and sided openly with France, proclaiming the formation of the Bảo Đại government and heralding French promises of a new Vietnamese constitution as 'welcome developments' that would allow Vietnam to assume its 'rightful place in the family of nations'. The March agreement, continued the presidential statement, would 'form the basis for the progressive realization of the legitimate aspirations of the Vietnamese people'.[101]

In November 1949, Chinese soldiers reached the border with Indochina and Ho Chi Minh was invited to Peking for talks with Communist leaders. The fate of Indochina, as a French government memorandum argued, was 'no longer a matter of concern for the French Union but had assumed an international character'. It was 'at the frontline of the anti-Communist struggle' in the wider region because of growing Sino-Viet Minh collusion and the distinct possibility of direct intervention by Chinese troops alongside Ho Chi Minh's men. When, two months later, Ho visited Moscow and pleaded for Soviet support in his anti-French struggle, America's worst fears seemed to be realised. President Truman told Congress that 'a large part of our military aid will go to Indochina, where French troops are valiantly fighting Communist forces', while Dean Acheson visited Paris and pledged more aid.[102]

Within weeks, Washington officials nodded their assent to requests from the French Navy to use American ports as transit bases en route to Indochina. The Pentagon also sold or leased a number of ships to the French, who picked them up from West Coast bases. The following May, Secretary of State Dean Acheson decreed that he had authorised the provision of 'economic aid and military equipment' to the French war effort in Indochina, and in August set up a US Military Assistance Advisory Group (MAAG) in Saigon. In the summer of 1950, Eisenhower allocated a $100 million package to support the French war effort, and a year later that amount increased again, reaching around $170 million. At the same time, the French spy chief in Washington, Philippe Thyraud de Vosjoli, struck a deal with the CIA, which agreed to provide French forces with intelligence and radio sets, and hold twice-weekly meetings to exchange information. The French Army established a special English-speaking unit in Saigon to liaise with their American counterparts and arrange delivery.[103]

Paris also urged Britain to play its part. When, on 7 April 1950, the Viet Minh unleashed a new offensive, the French made urgent calls to Britain as well as to America for assistance, pleading for hundreds of Bren guns and radio sets and an undisclosed quantity of Australian automatic weapons that the British had in their possession. In both Singapore and Saigon, high-ranking British officials declared their support for the French cause and proclaimed Tonkin to be the 'key' to the security of south-east Asia. In early July and mid-August 1950, British commanders met in secret in Singapore and Saigon with their French counterparts, who tried to link the fate of British Malaya with French Indochina. The British did propose establishing a radio link between Singapore and Saigon, but despite the 'very friendly' meetings, refused to commit themselves to helping the French and did not think that the fate of Indochina necessarily posed any threat to Malaya. More meetings with British and American officials were held in Singapore in mid-May, where representatives of the two 'Anglo-Saxon' countries agreed to exchange intelligence and to coordinate their naval movements, notably to curtail gun-running in the area, more closely. However, the French still wanted more and hoped that a visit to Saigon in January 1951 by the diplomat Sir Esler Dening amounted to 'a display of solidarity [that] will entail a change in British opinion'.[104]

Meanwhile, American aid was not arriving at the rapid rate that the French needed. Under ferocious pressure on the ground, French commanders bitterly complained that the flow of US material support, made up of jeeps, trucks, lorries and radios, had been tailing off noticeably. There was a 'chronic shortage' of vehicles, in particular a 'serious' and 'critical' shortage of lorries, noted officials, and a 'crisis' due to the shortage of barbed wire, which was vital for the protection of bases and fortifications. And while there were good reasons to be optimistic about the outcome of the war, concluded a French military report, a great deal depended on whether military aid from 'generous' America would continue to grow.[105]

French officials became even more frustrated when reports reached them from their counterparts in Washington. Closely monitoring the production and development of American arms, they sent dispatches back to Paris in which they noted, in detail, the proliferation of napalm, atomic-powered submarines and supersonic aircraft. France needed these materials so badly for its war in Asia but was not getting any of them.[106]

To win more support, de Lattre had sailed to America in September 1951. He returned to Europe with good reason to feel pleased. He had made a strong impression on the Americans and been 'a real success', noted the French ambassador in Washington, in the course of a trip that promised to yield 'highly fruitful' results. True, President Truman had not authorised the all-out use of force to support French forces, or the establishment of a joint Franco-American command. And there were certainly not going to be any American boots on the ground. But far more American resources were on their way.[107]

On his way back home, the general also visited London where he met with the Prime Minister, Clement Attlee, the foreign and defence ministers, senior Foreign Office officials and Winston Churchill. De Lattre and other French strategists thought that Great Britain could use its bases in Burma and Malaya to contribute to Indochinese security. British sea power, in particular, could disrupt enemy supply lines.[108]

Meanwhile, his counterparts were stepping up their efforts to sign up Britain and America to what they called a 'common strategy' for the defence of south-east Asia. On 11 January 1952, representatives of the three countries – General Omar Bradley, Viscount John Slim and General Alphonse Juin – met in Washington to discuss ways of building this front. They agreed upon the importance of establishing military bases around Tonkin and coordinating action against the 'prospect, perhaps an imminent one, of Chinese intervention', and advised their respective governments to warn China of the dire consequences of any aggression it showed towards Indochina.

The three men now set up an 'ad hoc' committee composed of French, American and British officials but also with representatives from Australia and New Zealand. At their meetings in Washington, they drew up plans to fight back against a possible Chinese invasion. In this worst-case scenario, the British promised to support Indochina with naval and air support, while the Americans refused to commit ground troops, although they hinted that this might change in the event of a Chinese attack. The French, however, privately expected the British to provide a brigade from Malaya and a division from Korea to beat off a Chinese attack. As the committee continued to draw up plans and proposals, in the spring of 1952, French officials felt confident that 'we are on track to establish a British–American security guarantee for Tonkin'. They were, however, disappointed because in the end no formal deal was ever signed.[109]

By this time, the Americans were subsidising nearly half the cost of France's Indochina war. American bombers and transport aircraft had started to arrive, as well as arms and logistical supplies. The Americans provided the French with some of their best rifles and arms such as 'Variable Time Fuses'; these bombs exploded in the air and then rained shrapnel onto the ground, decimating any enemy soldiers who were trying to take cover. By the following October, the Americans were sending twelve shiploads of supplies to Indochina every month. Supporting the war in Indochina, ran the thinking in Washington, would not only keep Communism in check in Asia but also allow the French government to 'make their full contribution to the security of Europe'.[110]

But despite so much cooperation, there was also tension between the two countries. One French general complained of the 'invading nature' of the Americans and their drive 'to control ... everything of importance'. American liaison officers on the ground in Indochina were also accused of trying to 'interfere', and the French refused to let any of the Americans train either their own soldiers or the indigenous Indochinese. The French also disliked the Americans' cultural interference. A French diplomatic counsellor in Saigon complained that the United States seemed to think that Indochina had been 'discovered in 1950 and that [the] history of civilization … began with the arrival of US aid'. The Frenchman continued by arguing that 'if a water pump or tractor is delivered to Indochina, it becomes, in [American] publicity, the first water pump and the first tractor that Indochina has ever had. If a medical first aid station opened, then it is the inauguration of public health in Indochina'. But the French, he continued, had been doing 'twenty-five times the volume and with 1/25 the publicity'.[111]

The Americans were also providing free English language classes, which was viewed as a grave insult to France and its *mission civilisatrice*, and which seemed to reveal ambitions to turn the region into 'a zone of US influence'. The efforts of the American cultural mission to promote English reminded French officials of how the Russians wanted 'to open Russian courses in the blind belief that all that is good is in Russia'. They added that 'the time and effort' of the local population 'might be better spent in acquiring really useful knowledge of French which will be much more important to them'. It would not be so sensible, cautioned one Frenchman, if 'America expects Vietnam not to remain in the French Union'.[112]

Other American officials quickly noticed the same hostility. 'The French have been viewing United States economic aid activities … with suspicion and some disapproval,' reported one diplomat. '[They] appear to want United States aid, but without the Americans, the American label or any augmentation of American influence here'. General de Lattre also made stinging criticisms of American citizens who were in Indochina. 'Yours is a rich country,' he told one

American representative, 'so why don't you build houses? Or get rid of some your ECA [Economic Cooperation Administration] men and your American missionaries, then we could house MAAG?' The depth of de Lattre's anger prompted his interlocutor to write a long telegram back to Washington, pointing out that there were serious tensions between the two countries.

One American who quickly noticed French hostility was a junior State Department diplomat called George Lambrakis. During his stay in Saigon in 1954, the American cultural centre and US Information Service offices were firebombed by a culprit who threw a hand grenade through its glass exterior, while one of his colleagues also found a suspicious-looking package, which turned out to be a small bomb, on one of the landings. Lambrakis himself was the victim of several sexual blackmail attempts, all of which were unsuccessful. On another occasion, in Laos, he was astonished to see a truck that 'pulled up outside my house and dumped a load of sweet-smelling manure all over the front lawn'. The American never found out who was behind this, but could guess: this incident, and the others, was 'the work of bitter but not terribly bright minds' in the French military.[113]

The American presence may also help explain why the French were lashing out at their enemy with the same brutal force that they used in Madagascar and in Damascus. In a dark reference that mirrored these other episodes and presaged events in Algeria, one American visitor noted that, after an enemy attack, 'the French military summarily punish all the natives in the neighbourhood, a practice which has not endeared them to the population'. French soldiers and intelligence officers routinely tortured suspects to gain information, regularly using 'waterboarding' techniques or the equally horrific death of 'the thousand cuts' in a bid to get their prisoners to talk. As in Madagascar, the French seemed to be overreacting to their defeat in 1940: feelings of guilt after the humiliation at the hands of the Germany Army, as one observer wrote, had 'taken on the aspect of a psychosis. Every little victory against the Viet Minh is an answer to the world.' But more generally, they felt under greater pressure than ever before to keep a grip on their colonies before any other powers, the United States chief amongst them, stepped into their shoes.[114]

French officials knew that, if they were to retain their colonial grip, they had little option other than to accept American military aid, not least because they were coming under greater public pressure at home to resolve the Indochinese crisis. French public opinion had shifted overwhelmingly against the war and in favour of a negotiated settlement followed by a phased withdrawal. Just a relative few wanted to send more troops to restore order. In April 1953, Georges Bidault had warned the American Secretary of State, John F. Dulles, that 'the [French] government is caught in a crossfire between some on the left who are opposed to the war and some on the right who wish to make economies'. The war in south-east Asia was consuming around one third of France's defence budget, and without massive American support there was no chance of placating public opinion. But at the same time many French men and women felt a strong sense of nostalgia for Indochina and worried that its decolonisation might prove infectious, stirring nationalist sentiment throughout the empire. Bidault, for example, fervently believed in the 'French Union' that had been established by the Fourth Republic in 1946, creating an alliance with colonies, including Indochina, that would remain closely tied to France. Pierre Mendès France, who became Prime Minister in 1954, was more lukewarm about colonialism but still wanted France to retain some of its ties.[115]

The French needed outright victory quickly, before the general public completely ran out of patience. At the end of 1953, Paris asked Washington to send American personnel to maintain a large consignment of planes that the Americans had already dispatched.

Eisenhower and the National Security Council concurred. They knew that without strong American support the French might suddenly cut their losses and run, creating a huge void into which Communism would immediately step. In January, the French premier decided that he wanted to negotiate a settlement, and placed the future of Indochina on the agenda of an international summit that was due to be held in Geneva at the end of April.

But by now a large, stranded French garrison was coming under intense pressure in a vast valley, close to the hamlet of Dien Bien Phu, in the far north-west of Indochina. Recognising just how dire this situation was, American officials stepped up their dialogue with their French counterparts into a higher gear. The President's judgment was now emphatic. 'We cannot become engaged in war,' he told his Secretary of State. The remnants of the French force at Dien Bien Phu now surrendered, having held out heroically for fifty-five consecutive days against a vastly superior, militarily ruthless and supremely efficient enemy. In this battle alone, the French Army had lost 7,700 men, although its total losses during the eight-year war were closer to 92,000. The Viet Minh had succeeded not just in inflicting a heavy and humiliating defeat upon France but also in holding the upper hand in international peace talks at Geneva. French negotiators were now entering the conference from a position of weakness.[116]

On 12 June, Prime Minister Mendès France promised to bring peace to Indochina by 20 July. If he failed to do so, he vowed, then he would resign. He managed to beat his deadline by taking a few liberties – the clocks at the Palais des Nations in Geneva were stopped for a few hours so that he could keep his promise and stay in office – and France now agreed to withdraw its troops from Indochina in return for an immediate ceasefire. Vietnam would be divided into two 'regroupment zones' followed by national elections. Within two years, North and South Vietnam, as well as Laos and Cambodia, had completely rejected any association with France and instead become independent states. Each of them, with the exception of North Vietnam, turned to the United States for protection.

Now that Dien Bien Phu, and North Vietnam, had been lost, the underlying rivalry between France and America surfaced in dramatic style as both vied for influence in the south. The French retained 80,000 men in South Vietnam while the American presence grew sharply. Both also carved out their own political factions in Saigon, each of which came to blows in the spring of 1955: the CIA's representative, Colonel Edward Lansdale, even accused French 'soreheads' of instigating attacks on American citizens in the capital, prompting him to retaliate against French colonists. One 'Top Secret' French government memorandum, written on 13 November 1954 and addressed to Mendès France, noted that:

> The primary movers in US policy in Vietnam are ... determinedly hostile to French influence [and] may have persuaded Washington that it would be sufficient for the nationalists to take over power and for the French to withdraw. Moreover in Bangkok ... a member of the US secret service may be supporting Prince Petsarah against the present king of Laos and Prince Savang, in spite of the denials made to us. It would not be too far-fetched to think that he was the real instigator of the recent assassination of the Laotian Minister of War.

Mendès France also accused the United States of 'replacing' France in South Vietnam and 'refusing to consider alternatives' to the leader, Ngo Dinh Diem. Such bitter disagreements continued until the following May, when Prime Minister Edgar Faure decided to withdraw the French Army from Indochina altogether and allow the Americans to take over.[117]

Faure knew that France's grip over other colonial territories, much more highly prized than Indochina, was becoming much more tenuous. Within the French Union, nationalists had taken heart from the Viet Minh victory, recognising not only the vulnerability of the French Army but also questioning if Great Britain and the United States would in future render Paris their wholehearted support.

In the protectorates of Tunisia and Morocco, nationalist parties were now making a determined effort to win control over local governing bodies and use their influence to demand independence. Soon after the signing of a peace deal in Geneva, violence suddenly flared up in both countries. In the first two weeks of August, Fez and Port Lyautey were rocked by violent and protracted riots, prompting the police to open fire and kill twenty-five people. Algeria was also simmering with increasingly virulent nationalist sentiment. In 1947, the French authorities had blatantly rigged elections to both local and national bodies, cheating nationalist candidates of any representation. Unable to find any voice in representative bodies, Algeria's nationalists became more restless than ever, looking beyond the moderate leader, Ferhat Abbas, and turning instead to more militant firebrands who scorned dialogue, cooperation and persuasion and instead preached a much more radical message of violence.

After the loss of Dien Bien Phu, even Charles de Gaulle, so deeply devoted to French rule in north Africa and elsewhere, had bemoaned that 'Algeria is lost. Algeria will be independent.' His warning proved prescient, for a wave of popular protests, an 'Arab Autumn', was now sweeping through the region. In the early hours of 1 November 1954, within just months of the ceasefire in Indochina, Algeria was rocked by a succession of bombs, and amidst the smoke, bloodshed, panic and mayhem that followed, the Algerian civil war had begun.[118]

In Paris, there was a cross-party consensus that *l'Algérie française* had to be saved. '*L'Algérie, c'est la France,*' exhorted Mendès France to the Chamber of Deputies, just days after the revolt broke out. 'And who among you … would hesitate to use every means to preserve France?' The mere possibility of failure was all the more painful to the tens of thousands of officers and soldiers who were returning to their homeland from Indochina, badly wanting to avenge their defeat at Dien Bien Phu and harbouring deep mistrust of civilian politicians.[119]

In the years ahead, France's chief enemy in Algeria was the National Liberation Front (FLN), but the war to save Algeria was fought on several different fronts. Amongst them was a conflict at Suez against President Nasser of Egypt. To fight this war, the French sought to strike up an alliance with Israel, prising it away from the United States in order to establish their own influence in the post-war Middle East. And they also sought to drive a wedge between the two 'Anglo-Saxon' countries by covertly enlisting Britain to their cause. A close relationship with Israel would also enable France to act quite independently of the British if it needed to. Israel, in other words, was viewed in Paris not just as an ally against the Algerian nationalists but as a pawn in the Great Game against Britain and America.

CHAPTER 5

A PAWN IN THE GREAT GAME

One foggy morning in September 1956, a transport plane came in to land at an aerodrome outside Paris. The flight control crew, who had only just been informed of its arrival, were told only that some 'Tunisian visitors' were on board. They were surprised to see that, despite its size, the plane was carrying just four of these 'visitors', three men and a woman, all of whom were wearing hats, pulled right down, and dark glasses. Then, almost as soon as they had stepped off the plane, all of them were quickly ushered by a team of plain-clothed officials into a car that sped off, closely followed by another black, unmarked vehicle.

The 'visitors' were not in fact Tunisian but an Israeli delegation composed of the Foreign Minister, Golda Meir, the Chief of the General Staff Moshe Dayan, the Defence Minister Shimon Peres, and a French-speaking former general called Moshe Carmel. Their mission to France was a closely guarded secret, and so too was the war that they had come to plan – a joint war between France and Israel to strike at the Egyptian leader, Gamal Nasser, and execute regime change in

Cairo. The architects of war in Paris did not want Washington to know of their plans to wage aggressive war in the Middle East, a war that the United States had the economic and political might to prevent or to cut short. This closeted elite had resolved to approach Tel Aviv 'secretly but officially', and now only a handful of select and highly trusted officials knew of this very high-level visitation to Paris. No one, even in the Quai d'Orsay, the French Foreign Ministry, was familiar with its very conception, let alone the details. All correspondence between the two sides had been compartmentalised and branded as top secret.

Israel, for its part, did not want to be seen by the outside world as the partner of a colonial power that was prepared to use brute force to suppress nationalist movements. Equally, the French did not want to be seen to be allies of a Jewish state whose very existence, not just its actions, deeply rankled the Arab world: they needed the support of oil-producing Arab nations, whose governments had declared their loathing for Israel ever since its formation in 1948.

As they stepped off the plane, the Israeli visitors had paused for breath, relieved that their ten-hour journey was over. They had left Tel Aviv the previous evening, completing the first leg of their journey, to Tunisia, on board a French bomber that was very cramped and uncomfortable. Golda Meir had been given the relative luxury of flying in the cockpit but the other three had volunteered to squeeze into the tiny compartment that was habitually used by the flight crew. By the time he arrived in Paris, however, Carmel was in real pain and needed to see a doctor immediately. The reason was that, as he had made his way to the lavatory during the flight, he had lost his footing and fallen into the bomb bay, cracking several ribs and clinging to the deck for dear life until a flight attendant scrambled to rescue him. Fortunately the next stage of the journey had been much easier, since they had stopped off in Tunisia and boarded a larger and relatively luxurious French transport plane.

The visitors spent the night of 29 September at an address at St Germain, outside Paris, before they were taken to an impressive private residence belonging to Colonel Louis Mangin, at nearby Montparnasse. A former Resistance leader, who had entered politics after the war, Mangin was now a senior adviser to Maurice Bourgès-Maunoury, the Minister of Defence. Underneath an impressive portrait of Mangin's father, a highly decorated general who had been revered for his role during the epic Battle of Verdun in 1916, these two men now sat alongside the Foreign Minister, Christian Pineau, and the deputy chief of staff, Maurice Challe, to form the French delegation at these highly secretive negotiations. On this occasion the Prime Minister, Guy Mollet, was absent, although he had arranged to meet the visitors the next day. But no representatives of the Quai d'Orsay were present. They had been deliberately sidelined because many of its staff officers were deemed to be too critical of Israel.

The French negotiators knew exactly what they wanted. Their priority was to plan a war that was ultimately not about Egypt and Nasser but about Algeria. Civil unrest in Algeria was escalating almost by the day, and they felt sure that the Egyptian leader was largely to blame. Every day and night, a radio station in Cairo, the *Voice of the Arabs*, broadcast Nasser's inflammatory speeches about 'the Arab nation' and 'freedom'. The Egyptian leader also hosted a nationalist leader, Ahmed Ben Bella, in Cairo and allowed him to broadcast radio messages to his followers in Algeria. French officials also claimed to have 'intelligence reports' about the FLN's 'training camps' on Egyptian soil, and to possess 'secret information' about the flow of arms into Algeria. Aggressive pan-Islamism, argued Mollet, was the message of Nasser's work *The Philosophy of the Revolution*. 'All this [is] in the works of Nasser, just as Hitler's policy [was] written down in *Mein Kampf*,' he asserted. 'Nasser has ambition to recreate the conquests of Islam.'[120]

Many of Mollet's contemporaries echoed his thoughts. Robert Lacoste, the Governor General in Algeria, argued that 'one French division in Egypt is worth four divisions in North Africa', while Foreign Minister Pineau felt that 'defeating Nasser is more important than winning ten battles in Algeria'. And Jean Chauvel, the French ambassador in London, was also sure that 'if Egypt's act went without a response then it would be impossible for France to pursue the struggle in Algeria'.

The truth, however, was rather different. Nasser's role in the Algerian unrest was at most peripheral and, if any external sources of support mattered to the FLN, then Morocco and Tunisia were much more important. Perhaps there was another reason why Nasser loomed large in the imaginations of many Frenchmen: the language and tempo of debates in the National Assembly and between ministers suggests that, in their imaginations, some, perhaps many, of them were re-enacting memories of Munich, Hitler and *la Résistance*. It was probably also easier for them to blame Nasser for the troubles rather than to admit that the root of Algeria's problems lay at home.[121]

Above all, another defeat, so soon after the loss of Indochina, was unthinkable for the French. Just a few years before, they had been prepared to use savage force in Madagascar, partly to exorcise the feelings of shame and humiliation that followed the fall of France in 1940. Now, little more than two years after the fall of Dien Bien Phu, they would be prepared to take drastic measures, within Algeria and beyond, to avoid a further defeat.

By this time, the French and the Israelis felt sure that they would soon have an excuse to wage war on Egypt. On 28 July, Nasser had stunned the world by announcing the nationalisation of the Suez Canal Company, which was owned by British and French shareholders. Because around half of British and French oil supplies made their way through the waterway, his sensational act was an act of both supreme defiance and extreme provocation: this economic leverage seemed to mean that, as Eden put it, he would have his 'finger on our windpipe'. What was more, it was always possible that Nasser could use his grip on the Canal as a bargaining chip over Algeria, refusing French cargo the right of passage unless Paris struck a compromise with the FLN. Nasser was desperately close to giving his enemies in London and Paris the pretext for conflict that they wanted.[122]

Over the preceding few weeks, the French had decided that, if they were to act against Nasser, then another ally, alongside Britain, would be indispensable. Israel could work in conjunction with France and offer the French armed forces vital bases in the region. And as the meeting at St Germain progressed over that September weekend, another proposal was aired. Might Israel not only act with the two European powers but make the first move against Egypt, thereby giving them an excuse to intervene? If the collaboration between them remained a closely guarded secret, then France could present its own intervention as an effort to separate the two sides and keep the Canal open.

The members of the Israeli delegation hid their glee. They knew that they could make the most of French support and strike a hard bargain to obtain more of the arms that they desperately needed. And they knew that an attack on Egypt would perfectly suit their own ends. One such aim was to free the Strait of Tiran, blockaded by Egypt since the previous September. But the ultimate goal was to deal Nasser's army a pulverising blow before it became too powerful, and to carry out regime change in Cairo. And when, in Tel Aviv, the Israeli leader David Ben-Gurion later heard about the meeting's progress and the French offer, he was ecstatic. 'This is the birth of the first serious alliance between us and a Western power,' he exclaimed. 'We can't not accept it!'[123]

There were, however, differences between the two sides. Israel

wanted the French to win the approval of the Americans. The Jewish state depended heavily on Washington's support and could not
afford to sacrifice it. But the French insisted. This was an operation
that they wanted to undertake, and felt that they had to undertake,
independently of the United States. The Americans could not be
trusted, in the opinion of Mollet and Pineau, because they were in
deference to the oil lobby, which wanted closer links with the Arabs.
As the French representative at the United Nations, Maurice Couve
de Murville, had argued from the start of the Suez crisis on 28 July, the
Americans seemed to be interested only in adopting the independent
role as 'mediator', not in supporting their two European allies. The
American diplomat Robert Murphy had made it clear, almost as soon
as Nasser had made his announcement, that military intervention was
out of the question, not least because the Western powers had to carry
world opinion behind them. But with Israel's support, and perhaps
even if the British decided not to get involved, France could consider
attacking Egypt without even consulting Washington.[124]

The French continued to mistrust American policy towards north
Africa. Paris was well aware that, for both the United States and the
Soviet Union, north Africa had an enormous strategic importance.
The United States, in French eyes, had a vested interest in pushing
them out of this region and staking its own national flag. The Americans, after all, had moved straight into Indochina after the French
withdrawal from south-east Asia, and from the early 1950s NATO
had funded the refurbishment of Bizerte and Mers-el-Kébir bases, so
it therefore appeared likely that they would do the same elsewhere in
north Africa. It seemed quite possible that, if the civil war in Algeria persisted, then Washington could get involved, perhaps trying to
broker a peace deal that would give America a foot in the region at
the expense of its traditional masters.

The worst fears of French diplomats had been realised in 1954, when several countries in the developing world had put forward a resolution at the United Nations General Assembly that was highly critical of French actions in north Africa. To their fury, the American delegation refused to veto it. Feeling sure that this was a sign that Washington had its own designs on the region, the French worked hard to find allies in Latin America to contain *le clan anglo-saxon* and create a 'Latin–European–Arab' bloc that would 'outmanoeuvre the "Anglo-American groups"'. And when, in 1955, Mexico and Columbia supported French attempts to keep Algeria off the UN agenda, French diplomats were jubilant.

This meant that, to attack Nasser and defend Algeria, the French were increasingly interested in looking away from the United States and turning instead not just to Great Britain but to Israel. It was no coincidence that some of the strongest proponents of a Paris–Tel Aviv axis were also highly critical of the United States. For example, Abel Thomas, a senior and highly influential official in the Defence Ministry, was deeply suspicious of and hostile towards America and later instigated, together with Bourgès-Maunoury, the development of a French atomic bomb that would make France more independent of the United States. Later, as Prime Minister, Bourgès-Maunoury regarded the Americans as more of a 'menace' to French interests than the Soviets, and his relations with Secretary of State Dulles, who he regarded as mercurial and a stooge of the pro-Arab oil lobby, were particularly cool. In his eyes, a closer relationship with Israel not only helped France to move away from the United States but, if necessary, enabled it to act independently of the British. If London refused to strike Nasser, perhaps losing its nerve at the last minute and bowing to American pressure, then France could conceivably go it alone with only Israel at its side.[125]

As the delegates moved closer to a deal at St Germain, Bourgès-Maunoury shared a sense of satisfaction with his Israeli counterparts. This was a moment he had long waited for.

It is not clear exactly when the 42-year-old Defence Minister had first started to feel deep feelings of empathy with the Jewish people, but it is possible that these feelings were a consequence of his own wartime experiences. A brave soldier, he had commanded an artillery battery in the summer of 1940 and, before being captured, had faced a ferocious onslaught from General Heinz Guderian's invasion force. Equally, during his time in captivity he may have witnessed violence or atrocities that enabled him to empathise with the plight of the wartime Jews. After his escape from the clutches of the Germans and his subsequent passage to Britain, he went on to pursue a distinguished career with the Resistance, and at this time he would certainly have witnessed or heard more about Nazi horrors: by the time he parachuted into the south of France as a divisional leader, codenamed 'Polygon', a good number of his com-patriots would have already died either under torture, by suicide, using their cyanide capsules, or to German bullets. If such experi-ences helped engender sympathies for the Jewish people, they also gave him a taste for conspiracy and covert operations, and rendered him, in the view of British Foreign Minister, Selwyn Lloyd, 'prone to secrecy'.[126]

In Bourgès's eyes, Israel was a 'beacon of democracy' in an Arab sea of despotism and violence. He was, wrote his friend, the Israeli minister Shimon Peres, 'a man of courage … who did not hide his pro-Israeli leanings'. Above all, he regarded the country as France's natural ally in the Middle East and felt that its support was vital if France was to maintain its territories and influence there. His views on the Algerian revolt were certainly clear. As he had told the National Assembly on 12 October the previous year, the white population of Algeria, *les pieds noirs*, was too deeply rooted, too numerous and too vigorous to ever form part of a new nation under the same banner as *les indigènes*, the Muslim population. He added that:

The leaders of certain Middle Eastern countries, in their bid to disguise the wretched state that their own people live in, are trying to
divert popular anger – anger that their own people have every right
to feel – into a cult of racism and nationalism. This is the classic
tactic of totalitarian regimes under pressure ... calls to open revolt
and to murder are constantly made on the airwaves; and there is
a constant flow of material aid and psychological warfare. Young
Algerians have gone to Cairo to study but were instead placed
in military training schools and trained for rebel war by *les chefs
du terrorisme*.[127]

Bringing the Israelis to Paris and signing them into an alliance for
war was the culmination of years of effort on his own part, and by his
protégés within his ministry, Louis Mangin and Abel Thomas. He
had always been thwarted by the determined resistance of the Foreign
Ministry but now, finally, his pro-Israeli faction had won the day.

His victory certainly marked a sharp change of policy. The French
government had officially recognised the Jewish state only in May
1949, a whole year after its birth. France, noted the Israeli Prime Minister Moshe Sharett, was 'cold and calculating' towards Israel, whereas
the United States was really the country's most natural, important
and reliable ally. Then, in 1950, the French government joined Britain
and America in signing an international agreement, the Tripartite
Declaration, that emphasised their commitment to peace and stability in the Middle East, and their opposition to an arms race there.
This agreement imposed an arms embargo on Israel, as well as on
the Arab states, and was viewed in Israel as unmistakable evidence
of Western hostility towards the Jewish state.[128]

Israel's critics in Paris were concentrated in the Quai d'Orsay,
where the Arab world was widely viewed as France's natural ally. This
was partly because of the Arabs' vast oil reserves. France, which had

no reserves of its own, was hugely dependent on oil imports and Paris could not afford to lose the goodwill of any Arab exporters. Nearly all of its supplies came from the Middle East, rendering its economy and standards of living extremely vulnerable to any disruption, whether it was accidental or deliberate. Well aware of this vulnerability, French officials such as the Finance Minister, Paul Ramadier, drew up contingency plans to prepare for worst-case scenarios. Any disruption would also have destroyed French independence and national pride, not least by driving it into the arms of the United States, which had far more tankers at its disposal as well as its own oil supplies.[129]

Paris did not want to stir any anger in its north African colonies by forging close ties with a state, Israel, that was viewed with so much bitterness and which was the subject of so much intense controversy: there was widespread fury in the Arab and wider Muslim world about the expulsion of hundreds of thousands of indigenous Arabs from Palestine to allow for the creation of a Jewish state in May 1948. The French also maintained a very close relationship with Syria, which they had ruled under a League of Nations mandate from 1923 to 1943 (see Chapter 1). The Israeli and Syrian armies were clashing repeatedly along their shared border, and Paris was concerned that any conflict between them could unseat its ally in Damascus, Colonel Adib Shishakli, and allow a much less compliant leader to seize power in the Syrian capital. Above all, argued French Arabists like the conservative politician Antoine Pinay, it was quite possible that the Russians would recognise and seize an opportunity, offering arms and security guarantees to the Damascus regime.

But in the course of 1954 and 1955, Israel's sympathisers in Paris made renewed efforts to support the Jewish state. The reason was not that Israel represented an important and fast-growing commercial market in the Middle East. So did lots of Arab countries, with much bigger populations. Instead, sympathisers like the politician Édouard

Depreux regarded Israel as a natural ally against the Algerian dissidents. The rebellion was starting to spin out of control, and although French soldiers were arriving there en masse they were still unable to quell the uprising. Pierre Maillard, a senior official in the French Foreign Ministry, had pointed out to the Israeli delegation that the ties between their two countries were based 'solely on the blood spilled in North Africa and [was] bound to change at any minute'. And Israel's ambassador to Paris wrote back to Tel Aviv describing how 'the Algerian struggle has put a card in our hand and aroused a wave of admiration for Israel among wide circles in France'.[130]

In Paris, there was a cross-party consensus that no French government could afford to lose control over a region that was, constitutionally, an integral part of France. Algeria's electorate was represented in the National Assembly in the same way as the metropolitan *départments* and the sentimental ties between the two ran deep, since by 1954 Algeria had become home to nearly one million French-speaking settlers, many of whom had ancestral ties that stretched back more than a century.[131] 'Algeria and its inhabitants are an integral part of France ... as much as Provence or Bretagne', argued one its governors, Jacques Soustelle, with a passion that was felt by so many of his compatriots. It was also regarded as a gateway to France's colonies in west Africa, which were also integral to its sense of grandeur as well as to France's national security and economic well-being: many Frenchmen saw an axis between 'Paris, Algiers and Brazzaville'.[132]

But there was a growing realisation in Paris about the scale and severity of the uprising in Algeria. To begin with, the violence had not been a major concern for French officials, who were preoccupied with events in Indochina. 'We thought it could be quickly suppressed like the Constantine rebellion of 1945,' admitted Paul Grossin, the head of the foreign intelligence service, the SDECE, in a reference to the revolt in Sétif nearly a decade before. 'It was only towards the

end of 1955 that we realized it could not be put down by local authorities.' In February 1956, the new Prime Minister, Guy Mollet, had
made a desperate last-ditch attempt to find a peaceful solution to
the crisis, appointing a liberal, General Georges Catroux, as Resident
Minister. But his hopes were very short-lived. Catroux's appointment
provoked ferocious protests from white settlers and Mollet backed
down, replacing Catroux with Robert Lacoste, who was deemed to
be much more of a hardliner.[133]

To establish a regional ally and suppress the Algerian uprising,
Israel's supporters in Paris had long argued in favour of arming the
Jewish state, even if this meant violating the terms of the Tripartite
Agreement and therefore risking a major row with the British and
Americans. In the summer of 1955, a furious diplomatic argument
broke out between the British and French governments over the fate
of a batch of disused tanks that a private French company had shipped
to France and then secretly, and illicitly, exported to Israel. Whitehall suspected high-level complicity: 'the French firm has deceived
everyone but they have some friends at court somewhere,' wrote an
alarmed London official on 18 July, while his counterpart at the British
embassy in Paris noted that 'the French were very slow in providing
us with any concrete information and there is a distinct possibility
that there has been some underhand work between the Société Aéro-
Marine and various French authorities'.[134]

London was particularly concerned about French efforts to sell
to Tel Aviv a number of sophisticated Mystère jets, which were so
advanced that they would have outclassed anything the RAF had
in the Middle East region. 'It is now known that Israel has placed a
firm order for 15 Mystère IICs, with an option on fifteen more' and
that 'twelve Israeli fighter pilots have been training on Mystère in
France and will be fully trained by September of this year', wrote a
Whitehall official, K. H. Jeffery. But the French Foreign Ministry

stepped in to block this and other deals, and would only offer other, less important, aircraft to Israel.[135]

Besides the deteriorating security situation in Algeria, there were other, more incidental, pressures that may have been pushing France towards Israel. The British ambassador in Paris, Sir Gladwyn Jebb, thought he detected a degree of pique in some French officials, who felt sidelined by the British and Americans in what they, the French, regarded as their own sphere of influence.[136]

In 1954, London and Washington had orchestrated a top secret initiative, Project Alpha, which was designed to redress Palestinian grievances and finally resolve the Arab–Israeli dispute. Paris, however, was kept in the dark. 'Failure to take the French into American counsels about Alpha might give rise to further anti-American sentiment which was already bad as a result of happenings in North Africa,' noted Robert Hadow, an official in the Foreign Office's Levant Department, in a top secret memorandum on 3 August 1955.[137]

Because Alpha had infuriated the Israelis, French officials detected a political void into which they could step. The British ambassador wrote to Tel Aviv in 1956:

> It is significant that in June of last year at a moment when relations between the United States and Israel were as cool as they have ever been, the Chief of Staff of the Israeli Defence Forces was officially invited to France and decorated ... immediately after he had been refused the invitation to the United States for which he had been angling.

These French efforts, he continued, 'have borne a good deal of fruit' with close defence ties and purchases.[138]

In September 1955, a dramatic development helped Israel's supporters gain the upper hand over their critics. Alarmed by reports that the French had signed an arms deal with Israel the previous year, Nasser had started negotiations with the Czech government, which was acting on the Kremlin's behalf. In other words, Egypt's deal with the Czechs was, in effect, a deal with the Soviet Union. Even amongst some Arabist desk officers in the Quai d'Orsay, there appears to have been a sharp change of sentiment. In January 1956, Pierre Maillard, the head of the Levant desk, told the Israeli ambassador that Israel now had new supporters in Paris because of the Arabs' 'blind hatred of the Jews'.[139]

The tempo of Franco-Israeli relations now changed. Within just weeks, sources loyal to Jordan's armed forces, its 'Arab Legion', obtained intelligence about a huge new arms deal between the two countries. A 'new agreement for supply of a large quantity of arms to France [is] due to be signed at about the end of September', cabled the British embassy in Amman in a top secret dispatch. 'The equipment [is] thought to include King Tanks, armoured carriers, 105mm guns and a "large number" of Mystère Mark IV ... the Arab Legion considers these to be "primarily offensive" weapons'. The deal was being negotiated in Paris, continued the highly secret report, by the head of the European section of Israel's Foreign Ministry, an individual called 'Nagger', and Baron Rothschild was 'alleged [to be] involved as negotiator and subsequently as guarantor of long term payment'.[140]

Rumours of the deal quickly circulated, and within days the Quai d'Orsay admitted that negotiations with Israel had taken place although it hotly denied that any deal had been signed. But their denials were, quite unintentionally, misleading. On 25 October, Moshe Sharett had secretly met Prime Minister Edgar Faure and presented him with a long list of the top quality arms that his generals needed. To his astonishment, Faure had nodded his assent almost at once. Two weeks later, Shimon Peres signed a separate deal with the French Defence Ministry. Throughout all this time, however, the Quai d'Orsay was kept right out of the picture, infuriating its officials when word broke. The deal was postponed after Operation Kinneret, an Israeli attack on the north-eastern shores of the Sea of Galilee in Syria in December, which deeply alarmed the French, who were concerned about how the arms deliveries might destabilise the wider region.

In Tel Aviv, Western diplomats noticed the shift in the direction of French policy. In January 1957, the British ambassador to Israel, Sir John Nicholls, wrote a secret dispatch to the Foreign Secretary, John Selwyn Lloyd, in which he emphasised how quickly relations between Israel and France had changed. Two years before, he wrote, the French had conducted

> an irresponsible policy in supplying arms to Israel behind the backs of the Tripartite Declaration. At that time [it was] a mere trickle and I doubt whether it represented a definite policy on the part of France other than a desire to play a role in the Middle East and develop a small but useful market.

But, he continued, 'as French difficulties in North Africa increased, the advantages of strengthening Israel against the Arabs loomed larger in the mind of the French government, more particularly when it became clear that the Egyptian government was actively supporting the North African insurgents'.[141]

Nicholls noted other motives behind the emerging alliance. Israel, he thought, had become a pawn in France's Great Game with the two 'Anglo-Saxon' countries:

> I believe that the principal aim of French policy in Israel is to secure enough influence to justify France's claim to a substantial, if not equal, share with the United Kingdom and the United States of

America in developing a joint policy towards the Middle East as a
whole. A secondary purpose may be to establish a special position
in Israel as compensation for France's loss of influence and prestige in Syria and the Lebanon.

However, he pointed out that the alliance was essentially superficial and lacked any firm foundation. It was based ultimately on a
shared mistrust, even hatred, for Nasser, and Israel was in any case
'too dependent on the US to be able to turn her special relationship
with France to any lasting political use'.

But whether it was destined to last in the long term or not, France
now had Israel at its side and was in a position to strike at Nasser.

CHAPTER 6

SUEZ, NASSER AND ALGERIA

Although it had begun as a series of isolated outbursts of violence, orchestrated by perhaps just a few hundred lightly armed insurgents, the Algerian revolt was escalating. This was partly because the flames of Arab anger were fanned by heavy-handed French tactics, such as the use of the *ratissage* ('search and destroy') operations, during which whole villages were burnt and suspects, guilty or otherwise, were tortured and shot. Such brutality aggravated nationalist sentiment and created a vicious ever-spiralling cycle of atrocity and reprisal. Individual acts of violence, such as the killing of more than a hundred Europeans near Constantine in August 1955, horrified French public opinion, and more troops were rushed into the territory, bringing the total to nearly 200,000 by the year's end. But still the conflict grew worse. In the year that followed the incident, the number of significant clashes between insurgents and the security forces had shot up tenfold.

In Paris, the new Prime Minister, Guy Mollet, had won power with promises of a new, more conciliatory approach to Algeria. But he quickly started to take a harder line and announced his intention to send even more reinforcements to Algeria, bringing the number up to half a million, and looked for more foreign support. France's relations with Israel had wavered after the attack on Syria in December 1955, but Algeria was in flames and the French were becoming desperate. In Paris, the Cabinet decided to lift its embargo on arms exports to Israel.

It was not just in Algeria that the French feared Nasser's influence. They were concerned, too, about the future of their other African colonies. The Egyptian leader, who had espoused nationalism ever since 1942, when he had bitterly opposed British rule in his own country, had also made clear that he could not be indifferent about the 'sanguinary and dreadful struggle now raging in the heart of Africa'. He had met a number of African nationalist leaders at the Bandung Conference in April 1955, when he had not only forced the Algerian issue onto the agenda but called for a united struggle against 'imperialism' in general. And he also allowed nationalist organisations from Guinea, Nigeria and Kenya to open offices in the Egyptian capital.

French suspicions of the Egyptian leader had been dramatically heightened after the SDECE carried out a daring operation. Since the outbreak of the Algerian war, the spy service had been keeping a very close eye on the Egyptian embassy in Paris, suspecting its attachés of liaising with Algerian nationalists who were based in the capital. But now the French spies devised a more ambitious plan to break into the building, crack a safe and photograph secret documents. The operation had started well but, when a security guard unexpectedly appeared, two of the agents were forced to jump for cover and hide behind a cache of papers. They waited, silent and motionless, for an opportune moment to disappear, but their hearts sank as the long hours passed by and dawn eventually broke. Now that the working day had begun, they would not have a chance to slip away until the following night. But the mishap had a silver lining. A few feet away from where they were hiding, an official appeared and placed some documents on a desk in front of them, all of which gave details of Egyptian payments to FLN operatives in France. Amazed by what they had found, the agents were able to surreptitiously slip away from the embassy compound. They then returned the following day, posing as workmen, and stole the documents.[142]

In October, the SDECE also organised the interception and seizure of a former British minesweeper, the *Athos*, as it made its way from Alexandria to Algiers. Months before, the French spies had been tipped off about both the ship and its cargo – the Italian secret service had informed them that a Milanese company had supplied 2,000 rifles to a dubious Middle Eastern purchaser – and immediately activated a well-organised network of agents to keep a constant watch. The cargo, when it was uncovered, seemed to provide conclusive proof about Nasser's complicity in the Algerian rebellion.

Mollet's spies also orchestrated all manner of 'dirty tricks' against Nasser, feeling sure that he was the sponsor of Algerian violence. A black radio station was set up in the south of France, broadcasting inflammatory propaganda to the Egyptian people, as well as a number of coded messages – 'Ali asks Salahaddin to wake up the seven sleepers in the magic cave' – for undercover agents. A hired hit man, codenamed 'Steamboat', slipped into Egypt and took a shot at Nasser from a distance, narrowly missing him. Two agents carrying explosives were landed on the Egyptian coast by boat but had to abandon their operation when they realised they had been detected, while other assassination attempts were aborted because the Egyptian intelligence services managed to track down and eliminate the French and British networks. A number of operations were also carried out to obtain information about Nasser's movements as well as his support for the FLN, although not all were successful. On one occasion, SDECE agents intercepted a closely guarded diplomatic bag that was being sent from the Egyptian embassy in Paris back to

Cairo: inside they found a note from an Egyptian intelligence officer, describing his own success at intercepting a French diplomatic bag that was being sent from the French embassy in London to Paris.[143]

Mollet could not destroy Nasser without the assistance of a reliable ally, and in February he agreed to supply Israel with a vast supply of weapons: this was the transfer of arms that the Arab Legion's spies had detected. At the same time he lobbied to bring an end to the international embargo on the supply of oil to the Jewish state. The Quai d'Orsay was also being increasingly sidelined, removing the biggest single obstacle to a closer alliance with Israel. Soon the Foreign Ministry's René Massigli was replaced at the UN offices by Louis Joxe, while in 1956 Maurice Couve de Murville, deemed to be an Arabist, was also moved from Washington, where he had acted as the French ambassador since the previous year, to Bonn. But still the Israelis wanted to bring France yet closer, and allow their friends in Bourgès-Maunoury's Defence Ministry to win the upper hand.[144]

From his own contacts in Paris, and from the information given to him by Mossad, Shimon Peres saw an opportunity. He knew that India had recently cancelled an order for 200 Mystère jets and reckoned that the French government would be desperate to find a substitute customer. And he was aware that Mossad had superb contacts in the Maghreb. The intelligence services of both countries already had a good relationship since over the previous few years Mossad had been organising the mass exodus of north African Jews to Israel, and he saw scope for expanding and capitalising upon this association. Algeria presented a golden opportunity to make Israel useful to France and to win a new friend that could offer huge amounts of weaponry as well as economic and diplomatic support. He advised Ben-Gurion to step up intelligence surveillance of FLN activities.

In the spring of 1956, Israeli intelligence succeeded in intercepting a number of messages that the FLN had sent from its offices in Cairo to its agents in Rome and Switzerland. These were hugely valuable to Paris because they revealed details about the movement of several FLN leaders. The chief of Israeli intelligence, Colonel Yehoshafat Harkabi, immediately recognised the importance of the information and informed Governor Lacoste about what he knew. Within hours, Mollet and the SDECE chief, Pierre Bouriscot, were also informed. The French wanted to know more.

Relations between the two countries now took another important step further forward. At the end of June, another highly secretive top-level meeting took place. Dayan, Peres and Harkabi, and a defence official called Yosef Nachmias, flew secretly into a minor aerodrome outside the capital, using false passports and disguises, and met their French counterparts at a chateau at Vémars, near Chantilly outside Paris.

As the meeting got under way, General Dayan expounded Israel's case. Every victory that Nasser won against Israel, he argued, would be a blow to French rule in Algeria. Israel's central objective was the downfall of Nasser's regime and it needed French support to pursue that end. In the meantime it could provide them with all the intelligence they needed to prove that Nasser had strong, secret links with the FLN. He added that it was only a matter of time before the Russians got involved in the region and started to destabilise it, allowing Communism to prosper: Soviet agents had already been showing a lot of interest in the Egyptian naval base at Alexandria. Then he threw down the gauntlet. Would France be willing to join ranks and fight against Nasser?

Dayan's claim about Nasser's involvement with the Algerians was in fact largely bluff. He was deliberately exaggerating the scope, or even the existence, of this 'intelligence' in order to win French sympathy and its arms. But his tactic worked.[145]

Dayan and his three colleagues were stunned by the cooperative attitude of Bourgès-Maunoury and the other French officials, who offered them more Mystère jets and another huge quantity of arms. But the French did want something in return. First of all they produced a list of possible targets that they wanted Israel to strike: these were broadcasting stations in Cairo and Damascus, as well as an FLN camp on the Libyan coast. France would provide any intelligence information and arms the Israelis needed, but wanted Dayan's men to carry out the attacks so that it could plausibly deny its own involvement. Paris also wanted Israeli intelligence information about the FLN and, in particular, about Nasser's links with the organisation. Over the next few weeks battle plans against both Egypt and Syria were drawn up while France and Israel established channels to share intelligence. At the same time, the French hastily made preparations to spirit the tanks, warplanes and artillery into Israeli hands.[146]

Over the summer, the idea of a joint Franco-Israeli attack against Egypt gained momentum in Paris. During a meeting in Paris on 27 July, just hours after the big announcement in Cairo, Bourgès-Maunoury had suddenly dropped a question that amazed Shimon Peres. 'How much time would Israel need to cross the Sinai peninsula and reach the Suez canal?' But the Defence Minister was, at this very early stage, one of the very few individuals in the French capital who was contemplating joint action: in the middle of August, British and French generals met to draw up contingency plans for a joint strike, but they made no mention of possible Israeli collaboration.[147]

It was only on 31 August that Israel was informed of the British–French invasion plan, 'Musketeer', and invited to join. Bourgès-Maunoury had been the first to suggest involving Israel in the attack, and his proposal had fallen on the receptive ears of a French high command that needed as many allies, particularly one as capable as Israel and as geographically close to Suez, as it could muster. A flurry of meetings followed before delegates from the two countries agreed at the St Germain conference that they would, if necessary, fight a war together and that Israel would provide an excuse for Western inter-vention. Detailed plans were now drawn up and preparations made for 'Operation 750' – the French codename for the joint venture with Israel. The two armies exchanged liaison officers and set up joint commands. The French poured more arms and supplies into Israel to equip its army, while Ben-Gurion offered the French the use of Israeli bases, which would be vital if the British, who planned to use Cyprus as a forward base, decided to back out at the last minute.[148]

The French were desperate to press ahead with their plans to strike Nasser. Pineau had just received another highly classified intelligence report that seemed to show that the Egyptian leader planned to para-chute arms supplies into rebel-held areas near Aurès in Algeria. The Foreign Minister went on to advocate a domino theory, according to which a defeat over Suez would have all manner of consequences. 'We have only a few weeks (!) to save North Africa', Pineau told Dulles in London, 'and the loss of North Africa would then be fol-lowed by that of Black Africa and the entire territory would rapidly escape European control and influence.'[149]

The full extent of the Franco-Israeli cooperation was kept secret, not just from the United States but even from the British. 'They did not tell us of the extent of collaboration with the Israelis,' noted Selwyn Lloyd, who was under the impression that Paris was only supplying Israel with a limited number of Mystère jets. 'They told us very little about the military cooperation which was already tak-ing place between Israel and France.' The French had also kept their plans entirely secret from Washington, in case the Americans tried to step in the way. Algeria, felt the French, was their business: if the United States became involved in the Suez affair, then it was one step away from embroiling itself in the Algerian civil war.[150]

This was a curious state of affairs. Paris was collaborating with the United States in Operation Straggle, a British–American plan to strike Syria and keep it out of Soviet hands. In this particular case, the need for American support outweighed the threat that the Soviets seemed to pose. But in the case of Suez, the dangers that Nasser seemed to present to French interests in Algeria were deemed to outweigh the risk of a dispute, or even outright diplomatic confrontation, with the Americans.

The French had not only long lost hope of Washington lending its support against Nasser but wondered if the Eisenhower administration secretly harboured some anti-French motives. 'We are wasting our time talking to the Americans,' bemoaned Christian Pineau to the British ambassador, Sir Gladwyn Jebb. 'Our two countries should now go firmly ahead on our chosen path.' Then, at a press conference on 2 October, Secretary of State Dulles had seemed to disparage British and French efforts to find a diplomatic solution that would have put pressure on the Egyptian leader. He also distanced the United States from its two Western allies: on 'the so-called problem of colonialism,' he told his audience, 'the United States plays a somewhat independent role.'[151]

Dulles's concern may have been, as Mollet thought, to placate the American oil lobby, which was anxious to win contracts in the Arab world. But the Secretary of State also saw the risk of Washington siding with a colonial power and, by doing so, alienating African and Asian countries, notably India, whose support he was most eager to enlist against the Soviet Union.

Whatever his motives, Dulles's statement created a furore in both France and Britain. 'If the Suez Crisis had taken a bad turn,' argued Roger Massip, the highly influential editor of *Le Figaro*, 'it is because the support of our American friends has been completely denied to us from the beginning.' The sheer strength of the reaction, across the political spectrum in both countries, shook and alarmed American commentators, who noted how 'American policy-makers are now reaping a bitter harvest of Allied anger and ill-will ... Britain and France are feeling emotions and making charges that are without precedent in the last ten years.' The remarks confirmed the worst fears of Guy Mollet, who had been in 'a highly emotional state' as he informed the American ambassador, Douglas Dillon, that France had a strong sense of being abandoned by Washington.[152]

In French eyes, American motives seemed highly suspect. Paris had been desperate to keep Algeria off the agenda of the United Nations and wanted American diplomats to use their considerable weight to lobby on its behalf. But when these hopes were dashed and the General Assembly discussed the matter and laid down a resolution, infuriated French leaders pointed a finger at the Americans. At the same time, wrote Under Secretary of State Herbert Hoover, the French also blamed America for the fall of Indochina and for another territorial loss. This was the Saar region, on the border between France and West Germany. It had been ruled from Paris since 1945 but was about to vote to determine its own future and looked set to become German territory. In Paris, Ambassador Dillon also noted a 'dangerously sharp rise in anti-American sentiment because of what the French public believes our North African policy to be', while the former President, Vincent Auriol, publicly called on the Americans to 'cease their intrigues'.[153]

Dulles's remarks helped to stir strong anti-American sentiment in Algeria as well as on the French mainland. In Algiers, alarmed officials at the US consulate noted a dramatic increase in anti-American feeling, and alleged that *les colons* were actively exploiting these 'anti-colonial tendencies'. Governor Jacques Soustelle virtually ceased to have any contacts with the consulate, and in the Algerian city of Bone, French officials tried to impose an unofficial embargo on American consulate buildings, warding off any visitors who tried to making their way there, even if they were on consular business.[154]

Many French officials also suspected Washington of looking for an excuse to get their own foothold in north Africa at their expense. The Tunisian leader, Habib Bourguiba, certainly played on these fears when he offered the Americans use of the naval base of Bizerte as soon as the French pulled out. Paris also consistently asked the United States to recognise the primacy of French influence in the affairs of a post-colonial Maghreb, which Washington refused to do. The French were well aware that north Africa had been the staging post for the Allied invasion of continental Europe in the Second World War, and that it would have a comparable strategic importance in the event of a conflict with the Soviet Union.[155]

But there was now another reason why Paris was so keen to maintain its grip over its remaining colony in north Africa, and why it was afraid the United States might secretly harbour its own designs on the region. At a formal dinner in Paris, late one evening in March 1956, the British ambassador, Sir Gladwyn Jebb, heard a startling revelation from Bourgès-Maunoury. Jebb knew and liked the Defence Minister, rating him to be 'one of the most trustworthy characters in French politics', and judged that his words needed to be taken seriously.

Astonished by what he had heard, Jebb sent an urgent telegram to London the next day. 'French experts had now proved the existence of immense oil deposits in Algeria to the south of Tunisia and just north of the Fezzan on the borders of Libya,' Jebb wrote back to London. 'They were so enormous,' he added, 'that if properly developed they might even replace the Middle East as a source of oil for the West.' The downside for the French would be that 'the natural terminus for a pipeline would be at Tripoli' and there would also be a huge development cost, particularly in such a relatively remote and difficult environment.[156]

The Foreign Office immediately investigated the report and turned to the British–Dutch firm Shell for information. Shell had a minority stake in an exploration company that was working in the region, and at Whitehall's request one of its geologists, Dr W. F. Nuttall, flew to Algiers to find out what truth the reports might have. He reported back on 26 April. To be quite sure, he concluded, a lot more drilling was needed. But nonetheless, he continued, 'there are good chances of deeper oil levels being found and commercial production being discovered. The geological structure is favourable … and promising … and there may be other areas in the same vicinity suitable for oil accumulation.'[157]

Shell's experts did more digging around and discovered that three months beforehand the exploration company had struck oil at a drilling site on the Algerian–Libyan border. More was to follow, in the region of Laghouat, on 12 June. Natural gas had also been found in Algeria two years before, at Djebel Berga, near In-Salah.

Within France the discoveries prompted a huge wave of interest about the Sahara. It was 'essentially a land of minerals', wrote Jacques Soustelle, 'and modern techniques [can] transform what was a natural barrier into an economic and social link between Europe and Africa'. France, it seemed, would at last have natural resources that would allow it to compete economically with Great Britain and the United States, and in a single stroke remove its dependency upon foreign sources of supply. 'The Sahara', as the leading historian of the oil industry writes, 'became a magical word in France' that was synonymous with French grandeur and hope for the future. No longer would the French economy be dependent on the supply of oil by what appeared to be 'an Anglo-Saxon monopoly', composed of companies such as Royal Dutch Shell, the Anglo-Iranian Oil Company and Mobil Oil.

The discoveries of oil and gas hardened French resolve not to give ground in north Africa: even French Communists, who were instinctively sympathetic toward the struggles of colonial peoples, were lukewarm towards the increasingly vocal claims for Algerian independence, regarding it as a real threat to the standards of living of ordinary French men and women. The British government was also aware that 'the increasing discoveries of petroleum and natural gas in the Sahara and the strategic location of Algeria add to the complexity; the French appear determined to maintain control of the development of the Saharan economy regardless of what *modus vivendi* eventuates'. But at the same time, French suspicions were rife about the designs of foreign powers, particularly the United States. The State Department in Washington protested that 'rumours of US intentions to replace France in North Africa or to gain control of Saharan resources are utterly without foundation'.[158]

Criticism from Washington about the *Athos* affair had infuriated opinion in France, heightening suspicions that the Americans had their own colonial motives in north Africa. But there were also other causes of tension. In particular, the US government had opened an embassy in Tunis on 5 June, causing deep anger in the French capital. The French were in the process of granting Tunisia its independence and wanted the Americans to approach them first and acknowledge their own 'pre-eminence' in Tunisian affairs before they established their own consulate there. The American action, continued officials at the Quai d'Orsay with a most diplomatic choice of term, was 'inopportune'. But the American Secretary of State John Dulles made things even worse when he informed Mollet that the American administration would negotiate its interests in Morocco directly with the Sultan and circumvent Paris altogether.

French allegations and suspicions about the motives of American oil companies in the region soon made things worse still. When the French authorities investigated Ahmed Ben Bella's documents, they found his correspondence with these companies about leases and exploration in the region. In French eyes, this 'proved' that

Washington had a motive in supporting Algerian independence. At the same time, an American resolution in favour of an immediate ceasefire was easily carried at the UN. The Under Secretary of State, Herbert Hoover, earned many plaudits in the Arab world, but Louis de Guiringaud, the French delegate in New York, was outraged, angrily protesting that France was being treated like some of the world's worst regimes and insisting that the United Nations had no right to get involved in a domestic matter.

Determined to maintain their own grip on Algeria and fight off any American interference, the French now held one more high-level, and highly secretive, conference, this time at Sèvres outside Paris, which was necessary to conclude the finer details of the plan, and to let the British put their own viewpoint forward.

The arrival of the Israeli delegation at Villacoublay aerodrome, on the morning of 21 October, followed the familiar pattern of the two earlier conferences at Vémars and St Germain. The air force person-nel who manned the control tower were to be informed at the last minute of a 'Tunisian delegation', and would not be given any chance to see their visitors close up. But to the anguish of Abel Thomas, the Defence Ministry official who was organising the venture, thick fog stopped the plane from landing. Frantic efforts were made to find other landing sites around the capital and, later than planned, the jet finally touched down at Brétigny, south of Paris. Thomas ordered the staff not to divulge the arrival of the plane, and the identity of the 'Tunisians', to anyone. His efforts did not go totally unrewarded. Later that day one of the papers, *France Soir*, published a newsflash about the 'secret arrival' in the French capital of Habib Bourguiba, the Tunisian statesman.

Just days after the Sèvres conference, the highly secretive plan was put into action. On Sunday 28 October, Israeli forces launched a fast, aggressive campaign in Sinai, providing France and Britain with an excuse to launch their own attack, which began three days later, around the Canal. During the seven-day war that followed, three French air squadrons were based in Israel and flew missions from Ramat David, Lod and Kfar Sirkin, dropping supplies to Israeli forces and often carrying Israeli navigators, who sent and translated radio signals to and from ground forces. Secrecy was paramount – the collaboration with Israel was meant to be a secret as closely guarded during the war as before – and French pilots were forbidden to communicate with their operational headquarters in Cyprus, since any radio messages would have been immediately picked up by American or Soviet eavesdroppers.

Similar efforts were made by the two French officers, Colonel Simon and Captain Guerrin, who led and organised France's covert naval support for Israel. These two commanders, however, were the only French sailors who were not left bemused by the dramatic events of 28 October. The rest were given their orders only after arriving in Israel and knew nothing about the secret collaboration between the two countries. When they were given orders to assist the Israelis, incredulous French officers asked their superiors to confirm and verify what they were told.[159]

Above all, the French and the British were concerned to keep their collaboration with Israel a secret from the Americans. The three warring parties had been alarmed by the arrival of the US Sixth Fleet in the Mediterranean. It was closely monitoring developments in and around Suez, ostensibly to safeguard the lives of American nationals. American surveillance of the operation probably explains why *Cressant*, a French destroyer that was anchored at Haifa, refused to pursue an Egyptian ship after it attacked the Israeli port: instead the *Cressant* gave chase and then suddenly stopped and withdrew a few miles from harbour. Had it persisted, the Americans would quickly have detected its presence and figured that it must have been based at an Israeli port.

For the French, as much as for the British, the Suez operation was a major disaster. By the time a ceasefire came into effect on 6 November, Nasser's status and prestige amongst his fellow Arabs had soared, because he had stood up to two Western powers and withstood their onslaught. France's grip over Algeria was undermined because the rebels witnessed the humiliation of their colonial master. The canal remained under Nasser's control. There were other, much more important, targets that the French could have focused their resources upon, notably the tightening of Algeria's borders, through which many of the FLN's supplies moved, rather than concentrating, to the point of obsession, on a figure of relatively marginal importance.

The operation also sent relations between France and the United States crashing down to a new low. The Americans had not only failed to support the Suez operation but actively undermined it, effectively imposing sanctions on their two European partners by obstructing and refusing emergency funding to fill the huge financial void created by the flight of international lenders. So soon after the loss of Indochina, many French people began to seriously question where American sympathies really lay, and openly doubted the value of the NATO alliance.

The episode also pushed London and Paris much further apart: Mollet and his commanders wanted to ignore the UN resolution and carry on with the fight against Nasser and seize both the Canal and Cairo. In London, however, there was little such belligerence, prompting an infuriated de Gaulle, in opposition, and others to condemn British unreliability. After the Suez episode, the British also moved much closer to Washington, becoming more reluctant than before to act independently of American wishes. The French, however, turned to other European countries to find new allies – the Suez crisis drove forward the creation of the Common Market – and to the development of an independent nuclear deterrent to make themselves more secure. 'The Entente Cordiale broke over Egypt', as one historian of the episode has pointed out.[160]

Over the coming weeks, relations between the two capitals deteriorated even more. In January it emerged that the Free Trade Union Committee, an organisation that was funded by the American government, had lent a vast subsidy of 40 million francs to several trade unions in Morocco, Tunisia and Algeria. The committee wanted these organisations to form an international league of Arab trade unions that would be based in Cairo. But in France this was viewed not just as an unnecessary American intrusion in French north Africa but also, because of the Egypt connection, as a deliberate provocation. A new wave of anti-American feeling swept through the country. In the streets, there were reports of French filling stations refusing to sell petrol to American tourists and of Parisian taxis turning American customers away. The press was full of vitriolic headlines, and in debates and discussions apologists for the United States were shouted down. Paul Devinat, a French politician with pro-American sympathies, said the situation was 'deteriorating with a rapidity which he, as a political veteran, would not have believed possible'.[161]

This of course caused deep alarm in American political circles. In the National Security Council, the diplomat Allen Dulles expressed concern about the 'acute rise in anti-Americanism in France in recent days'. In Paris, the American ambassador urged President Eisenhower to show support for its Western ally because 'France's membership in Nato is no longer by any means assured', while other diplomats emphasised that 'comprehension and sympathy for US policies are zero', even in political parties that were usually pro-American.[162]

The French government acknowledged, however, that some effort had to be made to patch up relations with Washington. France, after all, still needed American cooperation to confront the Soviets. At the end of February, Mollet and Pineau arrived in Washington to repair the political damage inflicted by the Suez operation. They also wanted to build closer links with the Arab world and to guarantee the flow of oil through the Suez Canal.

John Selwyn Lloyd, Guy Mollet, Sir Anthony Eden and Christian Pineau discuss the Suez crisis, Paris, 16 October 1956.

Around the same time France's alliance with the Israelis started to wane. This was partly because the country now entered a period of extreme political instability – it had three prime ministers in the nine months between June 1957 and March 1958 – and this played into the hands of the policy-makers in the Quai d'Orsay, who stepped into the political void and took a more pro-Arab line. In both countries, advocates of a Franco-Israeli alliance were pushed to the political fringe. A chapter in the story of France's struggle to retain its grip over Algeria had come to a close.

But France still had its colonial territories south of the Sahara. It now focused its attention on maintaining its imperial grip in Africa and warding off an 'Anglo-Saxon' threat that was not always imaginary.

CHAPTER 7

GREAT POWER RIVALRY IN AFRICA

B y the summer of 1958, the French were fighting for their lives
in Algeria, deploying increasingly desperate and brutal tactics
to suppress the nationalist uprising. With France in political crisis,
President René Coty asked Charles de Gaulle, now sixty-eight years
old, to act as the head of a government of national safety. He had
accepted the offer on the condition that he could establish a new
constitution, one that would bestow far greater powers upon the
presidency at the expense of the 'excessive powers' of any elected representatives. The Fifth Republic, the new constitution that enshrined
this strong presidential executive but a relatively weak parliamentary
legislature, was about to be born.

But it was not just French Algeria that was under intense nationalist pressure. De Gaulle was well aware that it was only a matter
of time before France's African colonies would want to go the same
way as Indochina, and demand their own independence. But this
posed a clear political challenge because he had always argued that
the colonies were integral to French grandeur and its status as a

world power. 'Unless France felt she were a "world power",' he told Secretary of State Dulles, 'she would degenerate internally.' It was no coincidence that, just weeks after a major and highly publicised trip to west Africa in August 1958, de Gaulle wrote to President Eisenhower and the British Prime Minister, Harold Macmillan, proposing a joint Anglo-American-French directorate of NATO that would be responsible for the security of the free world: it was almost as if his colonial experience had inflated his view of his country and its role, or that he wanted to assert France's global role while it still possessed its African territories.[163]

The association between the greatness of France and its empire was not just a matter of territorial possession but also reflected the colonies' natural resources. If France retained its imperial grip then it could exploit those resources and overseas markets, which would fuel its economy and, by extension, bolster its international status and reduce its dependency on the United States and Britain. Cameroon had aluminium, Gabon boasted oil, Senegal harboured phosphates and Niger possessed uranium. All of these were hugely important for the French economy.

Oil was a particularly important colonial asset. The French mainland had no indigenous petroleum resources, yet the vital strategic importance of oil had been clear ever since the First World War. One incident in particular had seeped into the French national consciousness: over several tumultuous days in September 1916, a vast fleet of Parisian taxis had rushed tens of thousands of soldiers to reinforce the Western Front as it came under intense German pressure. As a historian of the energy industry has written, the drivers and the barrels of oil that powered their taxis 'had saved Paris and also demonstrated what motorized transport would mean in the future'. Oil was synonymous, in other words, with national security. Crucially, however, de Gaulle was aware of the sheer technical and logistical difficulties of developing Saharan oil, which had just been discovered, and this meant that alternative sources would remain as important as ever.[164]

A secure flow of oil from the colonies also meant keeping 'Anglo-Saxon' influence at bay. This was because, in the years that followed the First World War, American energy companies had started to exercise an increasingly tight grip on global production. In the 1920s, Standard Oil of New Jersey controlled more than half of France's petroleum supplies, rendering the country vulnerable not just to price shocks but also to political exploitation: in other words Washington was in a position to hold Paris to ransom. The time had come, decided the great French statesman Raymond Poincaré, to create an 'entirely French' oil company that was 'controlled by France' and to find and exploit reserves 'in France, in the colonies and in the protectorates'.[165]

But the attitudes, policies and designs of the United States seemed, in de Gaulle's eyes, to considerably aggravate the daunting challenge of reconciling growing nationalist sentiment with France's own interests. Both the Americans and the British seemed to have their own anti-French agenda in north Africa, and to be intent on replacing French colonialism with their own.

The French were on the defensive. Anglophone cultural influence was already seeping into France's former protectorate, Tunisia, which had only just won its independence: the President, Habib Bourguiba, had just introduced educational reforms which made compulsory five years of English language training, alongside French and Arabic. When de Gaulle heard that Bourguiba, who he disdainfully called 'the American', had asked the French government to supply English language teachers, which were in very short supply, he flew into a terrible rage. If the 'Anglo-Saxons' could do this in north Africa then, in de Gaulle's eyes, they could do it elsewhere.[166]

Someone who particularly provoked French ire was the American diplomat Robert Murphy. This was partly because, during the Second World War, he was suspected of harbouring pro-Vichy sympathies, but also because of his unhelpful stance during the Suez crisis. He was, in the view of the Prime Minister, Michel Debré, 'generally contemptuous of our country'. When, in April 1959, French officials met their American counterparts in Washington to discuss north Africa, he quickly aroused their suspicions. Murphy had emphasised that 'the loss of North Africa to Soviet control would outflank Europe and it is doubtful whether the free world would survive such a disaster'. The presence of so many military bases there was a reminder of its strategic importance, he continued, 'and if we could secure the friendship and cooperation of the inhabitants of North Africa this would also have a favourable influence on the political position of the West in the Middle East and in Africa South of the Sahara'. In general, the region had 'a major bearing on US security interests … and the bases that we maintain there will remain for some years important factors in our military strength'.[167]

The strength of national indignation was clear. American diplomats noted:

> There is French resentment concerning the activities of the FLN representatives of the United States [and] some suspicion that the United States actually intends eventually to supplant French influence in North Africa. In any event, the French will continue to blame the United States for their own failures in North Africa.[168]

The French ambassador in Washington, Hervé Alphand, asked Dulles to make a public statement that the United States neither had any designs on north African oil nor any wish to replace France in north Africa, and to acknowledge that France had 'leading interests' in the region. But no such statement was forthcoming. Matters were made worse when Washington refused to take France's side in its disagreements with the Tunisian and Moroccan governments. Alphand angrily pointed out to his American counterparts that President Bourguiba had stopped food supplies from reaching French troops in Tunisia, expelled French residents and closed several French consulates in the country. But when he demanded American support he got none: Washington would not put any pressure on the Tunisians and admitted that, if the matter went to the UN Security Council, it would be obliged to take a position against France, even if that had 'a very adverse effect on US–French relations'. In Tunis, US officials were even more direct, pointing out that Bourguiba's actions manifested the 'sovereign rights of the Tunisians'.[169]

Franco-American tension now caused a political crisis in Paris. A draft of a letter from President Eisenhower to the Prime Minister, Félix Gaillard, was leaked to the French press. Highly critical of the French position towards Algeria, the letter created uproar in the National Assembly, whose members brought down the Gaillard government on 14 April. Aggravating the tension even more, Murphy publicly declared that France should negotiate directly with the FLN, implying that Washington now sympathised with the nationalists. His declaration prompted an immediate rebuke from Alphand, who demanded that Dulles make an immediate revocation to avoid 'incalculable consequences'. For several tense weeks, Paris was rife with rumours of an imminent army coup, led by generals who were deeply inimical towards Algerian independence. 'I shared the general excitement,' wrote one American visitor to Paris, 'momentarily expecting a military coup and watching with my friends for an airdrop in the Place de la Concorde.' Such tensions spilled over in an acrimonious meeting between President de Gaulle and John Dulles in Paris on 15 December 1958.[170]

Events elsewhere in the world were aggravating Franco-American tensions. In July 1958, the American government had intervened in a political crisis in Lebanon, dispatching a force of marines to Beirut. Given their historic links with Lebanon, the French were deeply angered that neither Washington nor London, which sent its own force shortly afterwards, had consulted them. Almost immediately, the Foreign Minister, Maurice Couve de Murville, issued a formal protest to both governments, warning of possible 'consequences' for the NATO alliance. In France, the episode not only heightened anti-American sentiment but rendered its national influence in Africa, where it held its last vestiges of colonial influence, all the more important.[171]

In fact, the Americans were in an impossible position. On the one hand they had watched nationalist sentiment in the Maghreb and sub-Saharan Africa grow and wanted to establish close relations with the individuals who they regarded as the next generation of leaders. But if, on the other hand, these aspirations were thwarted then there was a real chance that the colonial peoples could turn to the Soviets, or to other extreme ideologies, for support.[172]

De Gaulle and his chief adviser on African affairs, Jacques Foccart, were concerned that a French withdrawal from the region would create a political void into which either Communists or 'Anglo-Saxons' could step. There was a real chance of a 'Communist conspiracy' in sub-Saharan Africa being undertaken by organisations like the *Rassemblement Démocratique Africaine*, which had close links to international Communism. If Moscow's sympathisers made ground in just one of these former colonies, then Communist forces could establish a base from which to attack others, perhaps oil-rich countries like Nigeria or the diamond-wealthy regions of the Congo.

It seemed equally possible that, if France withdrew, then *les anglo-saxons* could start to move in, staking out their commercial interests and buying influence with their vast financial assets. Foccart's writings, his memoirs in particular, certainly reveal a strong preoccupation with the threat that he felt American political and economic power posed to French interests.[173]

The French were also afraid that these two apparent threats could merge and interact. It was possible that the Americans and British might fear a Communist takeover somewhere in the world and then take pre-emptive action, intervening before the Soviets were likely to do so. It seemed vital for the French to take an assertive, proactive role in Africa if they were to avoid being pushed out of the region altogether. In 1959, the Eisenhower administration appeared happy to stand back and allow the French to exert a ruling hand over their colonies, keeping Communism at bay. But de Gaulle and Foccart knew that this policy could change at any time if France was seen to be soft on Communism or when, after the Presidential elections due the following year, there was a change of administration.

A senior official in the SDECE spy service, Colonel Maurice Robert, noted this 'américano-soviétique' interplay. 'As long as France was in a position to protect its sphere of influence from Soviet penetration then the Americans didn't show much enthusiasm for getting involved,' he recalled. 'But if they perceived any weakness or any retreat ... then they would deploy their personnel and resources and get involved there before the Soviets did so.' America's Cold War mentality, he continued, merged with other interests: 'sometimes they didn't wait (for any Soviet provocation), such was their haste to buy up the natural resources of some countries.'[174]

To ward off these various threats, Foccart harboured his own vision of a 'third way' that would help France maintain its influence in post-colonial Africa and maintain its ranking in a world that was now dominated by 'Anglo-Saxons' and Communists. This approach lay in between these two alternatives and, more generally, between out-right independence and old-style colonialism. It was this third way, later to be termed *la Françafrique*, that represented a solution to 'the

Africa dilemma'. If nationalist sentiment became overwhelming and its colonies did become independent, he argued, then France could still exert its influence. Independence could be made conditional upon a commitment to various agreements that would give France a right to intervene and guarantee the colonies' security, to station its troops on local soil and provide 'technical advisers', material and training to their armed forces. And, even if they were independent, the colonies could still belong to *une zone franc*, underwritten by a central bank in Paris and sharing a common currency. Another fundamental condition was that France would have exclusive rights to buy natural resources at subsidised prices. And behind the scenes, French 'advisers' often pulled the strings of power. 'French officials in [the] background and sometimes quite openly are giving guidance to constituted governments, helping government officials prepare documents for them, and frequently making decisions for them,' noted American diplomats in the region.[175]

The clash between France's own vision of *la Françafrique* on the one hand and the 'Anglo-Saxons' on the other soon erupted in two places, Guinea and Cameroon.[176]

In a referendum held on 28 September 1958, the Guinean people had voted overwhelmingly for independence. Guinea was the only country, out of the thirteen African colonies where referenda were held, that chose to go its own way rather than to remain under French sovereignty. De Gaulle was sure that its new President, Ahmed Sékou Touré, had instigated and encouraged this electoral outcome. Touré had made a series of speeches, all of which were highly charged with a strong nationalism that was designed to stir up anti-French sentiment. Denouncing any constitution that failed to guarantee Africans their 'legitimate and natural right to independence', Touré had asserted that 'we prefer poverty in liberty to riches in slavery'.[177]

Touré was, in the words of a Western observer, 'skilful, adroit, clever and affable, a good speaker and well turned-out'. But although in some ways de Gaulle admired the Guinean, regarding him as 'young, brilliant and ambitious', he was dismayed by the outcome of the referendum and deeply insulted by an incident that had taken place during his visit there. This happened when he had arrived to address Guinea's National Assembly but had been drowned out by the shouts and cries of an anti-French crowd. Feeling sure that the demonstration was orchestrated, de Gaulle had left the podium and cancelled a dinner with the President.[178]

Behind the scenes, Foccart worked hard to smooth things over but de Gaulle would have none of it and immediately deemed Guinea to be a threat to his country's interests in the wider region. The French administrators withdrew from Conakry, hoisting down the Tricolour, removing and burning documents, and even ripping out telephone wires from their compounds. They vowed that Guinea would not receive any more aid and ordered a cargo ship filled with huge quantities of grain to steer away from the country. Cranes at Conakry port disappeared, building equipment was sabotaged and huge sums of money were diverted out of the country. Some French businessmen were bitter about de Gaulle's approach, arguing unsuccessfully that the drive for independence was inevitable and that France would do better to work with the new regime and to maintain as many business links as they could.

There was now a huge power vacuum in Conakry. In Paris, questions were immediately asked about who was going to fill it. To begin with, the two 'Anglo-Saxon' countries seemed clear contenders. It seemed significant to the French that a British dependency, Ghana, had indicated its willingness to provide newly independent Guinea with economic aid. In the eyes of a French official in Conakry, this revealed 'the desire of London to try and extend its influence into Guinea'.[179]

French officials also eyed newly arrived American representatives in Conakry with suspicion. For example, the young George Lambrakis, who had already encountered French hostility in Indochina, was deemed to be not only 'a laid-back individual who could have been Graham Greene's model as "the quiet American"' but also 'one who is full of the most absurd and deeply held prejudices against French colonial rule'. The French official also added that 'the studies that this son of Greek immigrants took at John Hopkins and Princeton Universities don't seem to have endowed him with the general culture that would allow him to make a criticism of the information he receives'.[180]

But in the months that followed independence, Paris seemed to detect a change of attitude. 'American opinion regards anti-colonialism as a "good cause" and actively acts as its advocate but it is also afraid of communist infiltration into new African states … and reluctant to subsidise economies that are not self-sufficient and badly run,' wrote the French ambassador to Washington. As a result, he continued, 'the Americans are starting to acknowledge the downside of taking a knee-jerk, narrow-minded anti-colonial policy'. The Americans also expected

> *les anciennes métropoles* [Britain and France] to continue to intervene in the matters of those colonies. In this respect, the case of Guinea marks an interesting change of approach and perhaps might even start a sensible change of policy on one of the issues that separates [the US] most sharply from its traditional European allies.[181]

The reason was that Sékou Touré had quickly started to turn to the Soviet Union and its eastern European allies for support. In February 1959 he had struck a trade deal with Moscow, while whole teams of east European medical and technical experts arrived in Conakry in the weeks that followed: some were medics, others foreign-language teachers, while a team from Hungary also arrived to help the process of 'political indoctrination'. At the end of March, a huge consignment of Czech arms arrived at Conakry on board a Polish transport ship, causing alarm in neighbouring states Liberia and Ghana, as well as in Paris. So many arms arrived, reckoned French officials, that the Guinean Army simply wouldn't be able to make use of them.[182]

Sékou Touré may have been lured eastwards out of conviction, for despite his claims about Guinea's neutrality and independence he had Marxist sympathies. But it may have been simply because, in the desperate days that followed independence, the Soviets made the first, and the most generous, move to support his country. Quick to spot the political vacuum and well aware of Guinea's natural resources, notably its aluminium, Moscow had offered to print a new Guinean currency to replace the French franc. 'Great efforts are now being deployed by the communist countries to woo Guinea and there is a real need to stop her from slipping into communist clutches,' wrote the French ambassador to Washington.

From the spring of 1959, Paris turned to London and Washington for support against the Soviets. 'We want to stop Guinea sliding on a slippery slope towards exclusive relations with the East,' ambassador Jean Chauvel wrote from London. In April, British, American and French representatives met secretly in Washington to discuss the strategic challenges that they faced in the wider African continent and weighed up the possibility of devising a common defence plan. The French were cautious, however, about how much attention they gave Guinea in particular: they didn't want the two 'Anglo-Saxon' nations to be 'judge and jury of our policy towards Guinea and of our negotiations with Sékou Touré'.[183]

Because relations between Conakry and Paris were so strained, London was in a better position to steer the Guineans westwards and the French turned to the British to help them. In the second half of 1959, the British government stepped up its efforts to establish closer relations with Guinea, providing technical assistance and English-language teaching as well as signing a trade deal that agents from eastern Europe worked hard to sabotage. But this was done in close collaboration with Paris: 'the French were consulted in advance and raised no objection to Her Majesty's Government's proposal,' wrote the British ambassador in Washington in a highly secretive memorandum that was leaked to the French officer based in the United States. At the same time, an American economic mission led by ambassador John Morrow, arrived in Guinea to draw up an economic assessment of the country and its needs. A delivery of 5,000 tons of rice and 3,000 tons of wheat followed soon after, welcomed by a French official who judged it to be 'politically beneficial (because) it offsets the delivery of Czech arms'.[184]

But still Sékou Touré looked east. On 18 September, the French ambassador in Moscow noted with alarm the departure of a Soviet delegation for Conakry, and the presence of Guinean officials at a Communist conference in Tashkent. 'It has come to us from a very good source', he wrote back to Paris, 'that Guinean representatives had expressed very hostile feelings towards France and denounced the Community [of colonial states, proposed by de Gaulle] as a sham intended to keep the Africans enslaved by colonialism.' The following month Ambassador Alphand noted that Guinea was still turning to Moscow, expressing exasperation that American aid was subjected to so many legal restrictions. The State Department, added another French observer, had a 'relaxed' approach to Guinea, which contrasted with the inroads that Communist officials and agents were making at every level in Conakry, not least in their infiltration of the government apparatus. And when, in November, Sékou Touré visited Moscow on a nine-day trip, greeted with splendour and espousing strong Marxist sympathies, it seemed the battle had been lost.[185]

But even at this moment of French cooperation with the 'Anglo-Saxons' against a mutual enemy, the French still regarded both Britain and the United States as a potential threat. There was also a danger that the Americans might make a move of their own to keep Moscow out: 'The Americans did not want to let the Soviets get one up on them' in this region, recalled Colonel Robert, who was the head of the SDECE's station in Dakar, 'and we had to be on our guard against an American encroachment in our zone of influence'. Soon Touré started to flirt with both the Soviet Union and the United States. Finding the Soviet representatives arrogant and contemptuous, he turned increasingly westwards and made trips to Washington. There was now a real danger that he would ally himself with both Nasser and the Ghanaian nationalist leader, Kwame Nkrumah, and rally anti-French sentiment elsewhere in the colonies. De Gaulle gave Foccart and General Grossin the order to get rid of Touré.[186]

De Gaulle entrusted the SDECE and Jacques Foccart with the task of overseeing, organising and orchestrating regime change, and Grossin in turn gave his regional station chief, Colonel Robert, a carte blanche to carry out regime change as he thought fit.

Robert's first task was to headhunt and then recruit agents who lived and worked in the country, and who were in a position to closely inform him of what was happening there. Much of the agent-running was undertaken by the press attaché at the French embassy in Conakry, Captain Boureau, who used bribes, persuasion and promises to recruit informers. Most important of all, ran the instructions given to Boureau, was the task of finding individuals who knew about Touré's attitude towards the Communist world and the United States. If there was any sign that Touré was leaning towards either of them then it would be necessary to identify his key advisers and offer them bribes to deal with French companies instead. To get this information, the SDECE infiltrated its agents into Conakry's main hotels, where foreign envoys and visitors nearly always stayed.

A big part of this particular plan was to target and win over Bangouri Karim, who was an economic adviser to the President and later became a minister for mines and industry. 'I was recruited by the French services through Jacques Périer, who represented the former French trading stations,' he later admitted. 'In July 1959, I met him at home in the Avenue Raymond Poincaré to make my first [intelligence] report,' he continued. 'The secret instruction ... was to enter the government ... and to carry on the work for French dominance in every sphere, particularly in economic, cultural and political matters.' Within a few months, Foccart and his deputies had a network of informers, drawn mainly from businessmen and administrators, at their disposal.[187]

The French agents tried all sorts of other tactics to destabilise the Touré regime. Another SDECE officer, Colonel Beaumont, organised an operation to print large quantities of the local currency and then flood the country with the forged notes. For a time it worked, causing panic and hyperinflation in the capital, but still the regime survived. General Grossin's agents also worked hard to isolate the Guinean leader, even sabotaging his private aircraft just hours before he was due to fly to London for talks with the British Foreign Secretary. But de Gaulle and Foccart wanted a more audacious plan and to organise something more hard-hitting.

In December 1959, the SDECE readied itself to mount a coup. From neighbouring countries, its radio operators had over the preceding weeks established contact with some of the Fulani and Peul people who were deeply opposed to Touré's rule, and who had enough arms to mount an insurrection. French undercover soldiers had then journeyed into the mountains, around Fouta Djallon, to assess their strength and motivation, and reported back to the

SDECE that there was a real chance of success. The French spies then arranged for large caches of arms to be hidden at several locations along Guinea's borders with Senegal and Ivory Coast, where the French could move them without any real chance of detection.

The coup was all set to go ahead in the closing days of 1959 but was postponed at the last minute when Touré's own agents got wind of the plot. Part of the problem, conceded Colonel Robert, was his agents' abysmal lack of security. At Dakar these 'over-confident' special-force soldiers had even hired some cars in their own names, giving their ranks and units to the garage, and word had quickly reached the local police. But the SDECE's generals still wanted to have another try, and four months later they gave the operation a green light once again. But this time everything went wrong. Touré's security services uncovered another plot that his enemies had, by chance, launched at just the same time. News of the security crackdown caused the SDECE's protégés to panic and flee. Arrests followed and the arms caches were discovered. France had suffered a humiliation. Still Touré clung on to power.[188]

But it was not just upon Guinea that the eyes of Jacques Foccart and Paul Grossin were fixed. Although every French African colony other than Guinea had voted to remain under French rule and *la communauté*, this state of affairs did not last long. Just months later, Mali had suddenly proclaimed its right of national independence and, true to his word, President de Gaulle had respected the wishes of its people. All the other colonies in west and equatorial Africa now followed.

What now happened in Cameroon revealed how the old colonial master could still make its presence unmistakably felt, although covertly and surreptitiously. It was here, too, that events seemed to be confirming all of the worst French fears about 'Anglo-Saxon' encroachment into their empire.

The French had acquired their stake in Cameroon only after the

First World War. It had been a German colony since 1884 but in 1922 a League of Nations mandate had allocated the territory to both Britain and France. The British Cameroons were divided between Northern and Southern Cameroons, while French Cameroon, a vastly bigger area, formed one entity that was ruled from the capital Yaoundé.

After the Second World War, growing nationalist sentiment started to prise France's strong colonial grip off its own Cameroonian territories. A nationalist party, the Union of the Peoples of Cameroon (UPC), was founded in 1948 and soon attracted a strong following. It wanted an immediate reunification of British and French Cameroonian territories followed by independence.

The French were deeply alarmed, not least because the UPC had close ties with English-speaking African nationalists in Ghana, who were fighting against British rule but whose rise to power threatened to spread Anglophone culture throughout French west Africa. The UPC was also well versed in the elevated language of universal rights that Roosevelt had popularised: its spokesmen lobbied hard in the offices of the United Nations and claimed to have numerous supporters who would sponsor an anti-French resolution in the General Assembly.

The French also knew that the 'Anglo-Saxons' and the Soviets would have good reason to establish themselves in Cameroon. Petroleum had been discovered in neighbouring Gabon in 1951, when a French drilling team had struck a small but promising reserve that was located north-east of Port-Gentil. Other discoveries now quickly followed and by March 1957, when a tanker set sail from Cape Lopez to Le Havre with the first-ever export consignment of local oil, a drilling boom across the wider region began.

Because petroleum exists in vast underground basins that cover huge areas, French geologists knew that if oil was present in Gabon then it would in all likelihood exist in Cameroon as well, for Port-Gentil was only 200 miles from the Cameroonian border. If France lost its grip over an independent Cameroon, then rival countries would be quick to step in to search for oil and exploit any reserves that were found. The most likely contenders were American oil companies, which were already active elsewhere in the Middle East and Africa, or the British–Dutch giant Royal Dutch Shell. In 1957, prior to Gabonese independence, Shell and the American oil company Mobil had already formed joint ventures with their French counterparts, which needed foreign expertise to extract offshore oil. All these ventures, including the proceeds of the profits, fell under the control of France, because Gabon was, at this time, one of its colonies. But if Cameroon, or any other colony, won independence, then the French would have no such control.[189]

In 1954, Paris dispatched a hardline administrator, Roland Pré, to the Cameroonian capital to maintain French rule over its colony. But Pré could not stop a rebellion from breaking out in the port city of Douala, and his heavy-handed approach probably provoked it. Government soldiers, acting under the orders of French Army officers, opened fire on protestors. Martial law was imposed and the UPC was outlawed, prompting its exiled leaders to unleash a guerrilla war against their colonial masters.

Paris was concerned that the UPC's new leader, a charismatic and popular young doctor called Félix-Roland Moumié, would steer his country well away from France. Foccart and de Gaulle needed safeguards, and just before Cameroon won its independence on 1 January 1960, representatives of the two countries struck a secret deal that gave France a right to intervene and guarantee Cameroon's right of self-defence. They also ensured that they handed over power to a new leader, 35-year-old Ahmadou Ahidjo, who was sympathetic to French interests.

The French were particularly concerned that British influence in the region would grow. They knew that the people of British-controlled Northern and Southern Cameroons, who were also heading towards independence, had been promised a referendum to determine their future: they could either join Nigeria, which was still a British colony, or newly independent Cameroon.

If the people voted to join Nigeria, then some senior French officials feared that an emboldened Nigeria would carve out a much wider sphere of influence at France's expense. 'We can foresee a resurgence of Anglo-French rivalry abroad – traditional but anachronistic,' wrote one French intelligence chief, as Cameroonian independence loomed. Adding that Whitehall would continue to pull the strings of power in the Nigerian capital even after independence, he voiced his fears that Nigeria 'would seek to absorb the cotton-rich areas of the Chari-Logone basin in Chad. The influence of an independent Nigeria, an enormous block of 34 million people, will have a decisive effect on the future of Cameroon.' He lamented the fact that London was not more cooperative:

> If the British cast aside their selfish ends … and instead agree to work in solidarity with their European partners, then the French and English can easily work together to the benefit of the West and of Africa. But if the Colonial Office persists in pursuing its policy of seizing more territory from France's own domain, then Nigerian–Cameroonian relations don't look good.

For the same reasons, continued the official, the decision of Southern Cameroons to secede to French Cameroon was 'a failure' for British policy, one that London will regard as 'the outcome of French dirty tricks'. In a worst-case scenario, he added, the British would want 'to maintain the state of insecurity in [the province of] Bamileke, while allowing terrorist bands to maintain their bases deep inside

south Cameroon; and ultimately to break up Cameroon, while allowing north Nigeria to take over its "brother country" in Northern
Cameroon'.[190]

French suspicions were hardly alleviated by intelligence reports of
American and Czech weapons leaving Rotterdam on board a British ship called the *Katha*, and heading for west Africa, 'destined for
the Cameroonian subversives'. Other French spies noted how 'the
British authorities are using terrorist actions as an excuse to expel
activists in favour of Cameroonian unification'.[191]

But Paris was also concerned about Communist infiltration, and
the SDECE carefully monitored the movements of African nationalists in and around Communist Europe. One intelligence report made
a careful note of Moumié's 'pro-Communist sympathies', while in
August 1959 another pointed out the presence of two Cameroonian
nationalist officials, Isaac Tchouliba and M. Nikabor, in Moscow,
where they met members of the Soviet press as well as senior party
officials. During their visit, the cause of Cameroonian independence
received a lot of attention in the Soviet press, which condemned the
country as a place of 'bloody struggle, mass executions, arrests and
tortures' by the 'forces of colonialism'.[192]

In the months that followed independence, Foccart watched
Moumié's power grow and that of the first Cameroonian President,
Ahmadou Ahidjo, wane. Fighting broke out in the south of the
country between UPC supporters and the newly formed, French-
trained Cameroonian Army. But the government forces were on the
defensive and Ahidjo soon appealed for French support. De Gaulle
wavered but Foccart's pleadings won him over and within weeks a
sizeable expeditionary force, composed of several infantry battalions,
tanks and fighter planes, was secretly moved to the region. At the
same time, Foccart leaked stories to the press about Moumié's supposed Soviet links, hoping that such reports would win a sympathetic

ear in other Western capitals. 'Responsible for most of the slaughter are the exiled leaders of a dissident political party ... led by Dr Félix-Roland Moumié, who has been issuing Czech pistols to Bamileke tribesmen', ran *Time* magazine shortly after independence. 'Just back from Moscow, Moumié operates from his refuge in nearby really independent Guinea.'[193]

The opening salvos of France's secret war in the south of the country were now fired by a former *résistance* fighter, Colonel Alexandre du Crest de Villeneuve. But he did not last long, judged by his superiors in Paris to lack the aggression necessary to wage an effective anti-insurgent campaign. Another, more suitable senior commander was appointed to replace him, a veteran of both Indochina and Algeria called General Max Briand. In both arenas of war he had acquired a reputation for raw brutality, and the top brass in Paris knew that he would use similarly heavy-handed methods in Cameroon. They were not to be disappointed. Over the following few months, his soldiers combed vast areas in search of insurgents, notably the Sanaga maritime, Mungo and Bamileke, and used the same tactics of burning villages, deporting and torturing suspects. Meanwhile, Paris provided Briand and his men with all the equipment they needed.[194]

One of the eyewitnesses was a Western journalist who professed to feeling 'revolted by the innumerable abuses of the veritable Gestapo regime, which was rapidly installed after independence'. He mentioned 'the sinister torture camp of Manengouba [where] nameless horrors took place'. In a chilling description, he described how:

> Some nights, one heard the howls of the wretches; during the day, the lorries came up the road filled with men in chains. Around three in the morning, it was the creaking and grating noise of the military lorry going to the cemetery where a team of prisoners buried the dead, naked and bloodied – unfortunates who had been tortured

to death, and sometimes still breathing ... I couldn't eat, or work
or sleep ... there have been massacres, summary executions, even
hostages executed ... it is estimated that 3–4,000 is the number of
persons who have been deported.[195]

While Briand's men were ravaging regions of Cameroon, General
Paul Grossin's intelligence agents were closing in on Moumié. They
knew that, over the previous few years, he spent much of his time
in a compound in Conakry, but to their frustration they were well
aware that he was virtually untouchable there. Not only was his
compound heavily guarded but any operation against him would
have been immediately jeopardised by Touré's hypervigilant security
network. There were, however, two vulnerabilities that the French
intelligence officers pinpointed and which they wanted to exploit.
One was Moumié's fondness for foreign travel, for he enjoyed moving around the world to meet sympathisers and potential supporters,
especially when there was the added prospect of entanglements with
foreign prostitutes. The other was his poor health. French spies discovered that he had a liver disorder and knew he would be receptive
to any treatment from a respected Western clinic.

In the summer of 1960, the SDECE recruited a highly experienced veteran of special operations, William 'Big Bill' Bechtel, to deal
with Moumié. Bechtel, who had acquired a reputation for daring
and bravery in both the French Resistance and as a Special Forces
operative in Indochina, now acquired a new, fictitious identity. With
forged documentation, 'Big Bill' would pose as a Swiss journalist
and use the influence of a Western prostitute, Liliano Ferrero, to
win an introduction to the UPC leader. Then he could recommend
a specialist doctor in his 'native' Geneva who could diagnose and
treat his disorder. When Moumié arrived in Geneva, Bechtel would
have an opportunity to poison his drink, killing him with a carefully

measured dose of thallium that would leave virtually no trace in his bloodstream. And if this slow-acting poison was administered just before he left Switzerland, then there would be no chance of getting a proper medical examination, let alone a warrant for Bechtel's arrest, since there was a dearth of respected doctors in the Guinean capital.

Over the following weeks, Bechtel and Moumié met several times and established, as the SDECE handlers hoped and expected, a good rapport. Moumié started to trust his new friend and accepted his advice. In early October, he flew to Geneva to discuss his health with Swiss doctors and the French plan kicked into action.[196]

One Saturday night, Bechtel and Moumié sat down together at a restaurant in the city centre. Not long after they had ordered their meals, a waiter informed Moumié that there was an urgent phone call for him. Moumié was bewildered because he hadn't told anyone where he was going that evening but nonetheless got up and left to take the call. The ruse had worked brilliantly because, while his back was turned, Bechtel slipped a capsule of thallium into his aperitif.

Just a minute later the UPC leader returned to his seat, complaining that the call must have been an error or a prank, because the line was just dead. To Bechtel's horror he pushed aside his aperitif and reached instead for a glass of wine. But during their main course the French assassin found a moment of opportunity and slipped another dose of the poison into his victim's wine.

Bechtel's jubilation, however, was short-lived. He was shocked to see Moumié now reaching for his aperitif. If he drank that then he would have double the dosage of thallium, one from the glass of wine, the other from the aperitif, meaning that he would die more quickly than he was supposed to and pass away not in Guinea but Switzerland, where doctors would search for a cause of death. They would not be likely to overlook such a high dosage.

With enough presence of mind, Bechtel could have knocked

over the aperitif, 'accidentally' spilling it to prevent such a mishap from occurring. But it was too late. The next day, his victim was in agony and was taken immediately to hospital. He died several days later, well aware that he had been poisoned but not living quite long enough to see the results of the blood tests that doctors carried out. On 29 October, two weeks after the restaurant meal, the Swiss police decided that Moumié had been murdered and started investigating the true identity of the mysterious 'Swiss journalist' who had accompanied him. Bechtel had long disappeared, crossing the border back to France almost as soon as he left the restaurant, but for French intelligence it was a hard blow. True, its agents had eliminated a key enemy, but they had aroused enormous suspicion amongst neighbouring governments about their nefarious activities.[197]

Hitherto, policy-makers in Paris had fought to maintain a grip over former colonies that had voted for independence but which, in French eyes, properly belonged under the thumb of their former colonial masters. They were deeply conscious that, at some future point, the United States or Great Britain could easily start to exert their own influence and push France out. But up until this time, very few American politicians, diplomats or businessmen had ever shown much interest in the African continent, which was considered to be of peripheral interest compared with the real showgrounds of Cold War competition – Asia and the Middle East. In 1959, State Department officials had met a French delegation, composed of Hervé Alphand and Louis Joxe, and made clear that north Africa was much more important to Washington than sub-Saharan Africa. 'The US regards the European powers', the Americans had told their visitors, 'as best equipped for the leading role' in Africa.[198]

But thousands of miles from the war zones of Cameroon, where the French Army, little noticed by the outside world, had been brutally suppressing insurgents, a young, fresh-faced politician was rising fast. And his ascendancy was to have important consequences for French policy in Africa, and elsewhere. He was John F. Kennedy, who on 8 November 1960 had defeated his Republican rival, Richard Nixon, in the American Presidential election.

At their embassy in Washington, French diplomats had been carefully monitoring the contenders in the race to succeed Eisenhower in the elections. They had first noticed Kennedy several years before, when he had made speeches that were strongly anti-colonial in tone. As early as 1951, a French intelligence report had noted with alarm that Kennedy had drawn up plans to visit Indochina. The report pointed to some 'regrettable' remarks he had made about France, in particular his allegation that its contribution to Western security had been lacklustre, and noted his 'anti-colonial' prejudices. 'He is known for his random spirit and his lack of maturity', ran the memorandum. Six years later, in July 1957, he ventured similar sentiments before the Senate, where he strongly criticised the French war in Algeria. Put forward in highly elevated and idealistic language about 'man's desire to be free', and the importance of meeting the 'challenge of imperialism', the senator's 1957 speech condemned the Eisenhower administration for failing to give the Algerian conflict the attention which he felt it duly deserved. America, he argued, had to 'support an international effort to derive for Algeria the basis for an ordinary achievement of independence'.[199]

As he was sworn into office, Kennedy called, in truly idealistic language, for 'the nations of the world' to confront 'tyranny, poverty, disease and war'. His election to the White House in 1960 was now set to bring these transatlantic tensions to boiling point far more quickly than anyone in Paris, or elsewhere, probably realised.

CHAPTER 8

COMMUNISTS AND ANGLO-SAXONS IN AFRICA

Early in 1961, a young Frenchman stepped off a transport plane in a remote town in central Africa. Wearing civilian clothes and clutching a small suitcase, he could in ordinary times have been taken for a businessman or possibly even a tourist who was drawn to an unusually far-flung destination.

These were not ordinary times, however, and the young man, just thirty-two years old, was not an ordinary traveller. Gilbert Bourgeaud was better known by his *nom de guerre* 'Bob Denard', although during his subsequent, illustrious career he was also known as 'Saïd Mustapha Mahdjoub', 'Antoine Thomas' and 'Jean Maurin', amongst a number of other fictitious identities. What had brought him here to Elizabethville in the Congo was a craving for the excitement, honour and importance that he felt an active military life offered. As a child, growing up in a village near Bordeaux, he heard numerous tales of adventure and derring-do from his father, who was a warrant officer in the French colonial service and who lived and worked, and fought, in China. Then, when he was just eleven years old, he witnessed first-hand something of the reality of battle and invasion, watching streams of German soldiers and columns of their armoured cars and tanks moving into the towns and cities of France. 'They appeared magnificent to our kids' eyes,' he later told a biographer. 'We looked on enviously as they played war games in the dunes.'[200]

By the end of the war, Denard was so keen to serve in the military that he lied about his age, telling the recruitment officers in the French Navy that he was a year older than he really was. He spent the next eight years on board a number of small ships, sailing the world, patrolling dangerous parts of French Indochina, and winning promotion to a low-grade supervisory role. But he is not known to have even heard a shot fired in anger, and this was scarcely the life of adventure that he had dreamed of. He returned home to France in 1954 and was implicated in a plot to assassinate the Prime Minister, Pierre Mendès France, before taking up a series of menial, tedious and poorly paid jobs. He was in debt but continued to dream of a life of action.

Five years later, in December 1960, his luck changed when he saw an advert in a newspaper. 'A mining company in Katanga is recruiting security officers, preferably ex-military' ran the copy. Denard did not wait long. Within a fortnight he had left his job and was on his way to the remote province in south-east Congo.

Tall, well-built, colourfully dressed and sporting a large moustache, Denard certainly cut an impressive figure as he stepped onto the airfield outside Elizabethville. He had been recruited as a humble infantryman by the senior officer in charge, Colonel Roger Trinquier, and was full of ambition to rise higher.

Trinquier and Denard were both working on behalf of a French government that was deeply concerned not just about Communist infiltration into Africa but also the real threat of an 'Anglo-Saxon' presence, one that would challenge and supplant its own. The Democratic

Republic of the Congo had won its independence from Belgium the previous year, in June 1960, and the Americans felt that there was a power vacuum that the Soviets could fill. They would have to get there first before Communist forces did.[201]

This was a country that had always been rife with ethnic divisions and tensions, and from the moment of independence these rivalries started to drive it apart. A tribal leader in Katanga, Moise Tshombe, quickly declared the province's independence. He set up his own rival Katangese government, based in Elizabethville, and urged the major regional powers, France, Britain, the US and South Africa, to recognise his new state and fend off the inevitable, savage counter-reaction from the Congolese government led by Patrice Lumumba.

Tshombe's declaration was of real strategic importance. Katanga was a big producer of highly prized resources, including copper, cobalt and manganese. If Tshombe broke away, then he would be taking a great deal of the country's mineral wealth with him.

Confronted by this crisis almost as soon as it came to power, the new Kennedy administration decided to oppose Tshombe and instead support a broad coalition that was run by moderate politi-cians, including Lumumba. This was part of a wider approach that the new President wanted to pursue elsewhere on the continent, one that would support the drive towards decolonisation and 'allow each country to find its own way'. It was a risky approach because there had long been concern in Washington about Lumumba's socialist policies and his apparent sympathy for the Soviet Union.

But Kennedy and his Secretary of State, Dean Rusk, also calcul-ated that a broad-based coalition government represented the best chance of reaping popular support and keeping the Soviets out. A failure to reintegrate Katanga into the Congo would lead to a 'Soviet onslaught', felt Rusk, and 'would mean civil war and the ensu-ing chaos on which the Communists have capitalised in other parts of the world'. He also wondered what might happen to American commercial interests if Tshombe broke away. Congo's oil business, a vast distribution network composed of pipelines, gas stations and storage facilities, was controlled by an international consortium in which American business was well represented. Mobil had a $12 million investment in the Congo, nearly all of which was concentrated in Katanga, and its stake, along with that of another American company, Texaco, amounted to around 40 per cent of the market. Katanga also had vast deposits of copper, and this would allow Tshombe to manipulate the global market price if he wanted to.[202]

The Kennedy administration had supported a United Nations mission to establish this coalition government. 'The alternative', argued Dean Rusk, 'would have been violence and chaos and a ready-made opportunity for Soviet exploitation.' But in Paris, President de Gaulle and Jacques Foccart were both well aware of just how valuable Katanga's assets actually were. Over the preceding few years, French companies had started to send out geologists to the region to assess the quality of its uranium deposits. If they did not intervene then it seemed certain that their foreign rivals would do so.[203]

French oil companies had been excluded from the international oil consortium that been operating in the country over the previous fifty years. At the outbreak of the Katangan crisis, this consortium sided with the central government. By backing Tshombe instead, the French found a commercial opening.

But French interest in supporting Tshombe was not just about winning material prizes. France had enough of those in its own former colonies. De Gaulle and Foccart were also concerned about keeping the Americans out of a continent that they regarded as their own *domaine réservé*. The Congo was French-speaking, and an American presence there would be an unmistakable challenge to *la francophonie*. Lumumba had been murdered in custody in Elizabethville in January so there was no immediate likelihood of Soviet involvement, but the United States had forged close relations with two Congolese leaders, Cyrille Adoula and Joseph Mobutu, and these links threatened to give the Americans a foothold in the very heart of French-speaking Africa. This gave Foccart and de Gaulle one reason to look to Tshombe as a prospective ally.

Jacques Foccart wanted to fight American interference in the 'largest country of francophone Africa', regarding any such involvement as a clear 'victory' for American interests at the expense of French. Others shared his concern. 'We didn't want to let Francophone Africa slip into American hands,' pointed out Colonel Maurice Robert, 'nor abandon it to Soviet designs.' The Americans were at this stage 'locked in a deadly rivalry' with Moscow, he continued, 'and wanted to prepare for a future in which they would have a strong presence in the African continent, and where France would be relegated to a more modest position'. Even if the two countries shared the same anti-Communism, he said, 'our interests sometimes conflicted and there was economic competition ... and suspicions and tension between us'.[204]

As a result, de Gaulle lambasted the United Nations mission, viewing it as a fig leaf for American ambitions, and withheld French subsidies. 'The UN is a scene of disturbance, confusion and division,' he told a press conference, 'and it carries to the local scene ... the individual partiality of each of the states which send their contingents.' He denied the United Nations permission to fly its planes over French territory to the Congo and persuaded former colonies to impose the same restrictions. He told Maurice Couve de Murville that it was 'important not to yield France's established position in Africa in the name of Western partnership'. French officials now pointed out that, under treaties of 1884 and 1908, France had a preemptive right to the Congo in the event of the King of the Belgians renouncing his sovereignty over the area: if Belgium was quitting,

France, and not the Congolese, had first right of refusal to this vast region.[205]

His fears were confirmed in March, when Jacques Chaban-Delmas, the President of the National Assembly, met the newly-elected American President at the White House. The United States, Kennedy had suggested, was well qualified to become the prominent Western power in Africa, even though its new role would be at French expense. 'There are,' he added, 'some countries in Africa which mistrust France but trust the United States, which has no colonial past. A co-ordination of policies between the two countries could take advantage of this privileged position of each of them.' But Kennedy had not revealed the full extent of his interest in Africa and ambition to supplant French influence. He failed to mention that he had even asked the State Department's Bureau of Intelligence and Research to investigate French objectives and strategies in Africa, and to assess how the United States could challenge them. An Africa expert, Donald Norland, was headhunted as a case officer to undertake such a study.[206]

On 31 May, de Gaulle and Kennedy met for the first time when the American President stopped off in Paris on his way to Vienna for a major summit with his Soviet counterpart, Nikita Khrushchev. He had been well briefed about the Africa issue before he arrived. Just two weeks before, a presidential briefing paper had emphasised that 'France acknowledged the primary US interest in the Far East and Latin America, but criticised US diplomatic initiatives in south-east Asia and Africa – both of which they felt were areas of French primary responsibility. Therefore, they believed the US should coordinate policy and defer leadership to Paris.'[207]

Kennedy was greeted by vast, cheering crowds as he was driven from the plane at Orly airport towards the Élysée. Onlookers crammed up against the security fences that surrounded the base and climbed onto the top of neighbouring buildings to get a view. As soon as his elegant

wife, dressed in navy blue, came into view they broke into an adula-
tory, rhythmic chant, *Vive Jacqui! Vive Jacqui!* Just sixteen years after
the Second World War, memories of the liberation, and America's
leading role in ending the war, were immensely powerful and moving.
Genuinely touched by the outpouring of emotion, Kennedy made a
simple, but moving speech, paying homage to France's 'leadership in
Europe and Africa' and to 'the grandeur of her mission in carrying
the torch of liberty to new nations throughout the world'.

The Kennedys meet Charles de Gaulle in Paris, 31 May 1961.

Kennedy and de Gaulle now met in private and, although their tone was calm and friendly, tension soon started to break through. The French leader talked down to his visitor, who was young enough to be his son, and corrected some of the remarks he made. Then his concerns about France's role in Africa became clear. He emphasised that the world needed to be divided into zones of influence and that, to an important degree, the fate of the African continent should remain France's responsibility. Privately, le Président noticed how his counterpart 'is resolved to make his career in the service of liberty, of justice and of progress. It is true that, persuaded of the duty of the United States and himself to redress grievances, he would be led at first to interventions which calculation did not justify.'[208]

By this time de Gaulle had already authorised the use of force to support the Katangese rebels. The SDECE station in Dakar liaised closely with the French consulate in Elizabethville, which acted as a staging post to supply Tshombe with large quantities of arms, weapons and cash. Senior military officers, most of whom were smarting with bitterness at their defeat in Indochina, were offered the opportunity to 'make themselves available' for service in Katanga, and encouraged to recruit sympathisers into the rebel army from the ranks of the French military. By the time Denard arrived, there were already twelve French officers in Elizabethville who were training the Katangan soldiers and leading them from the front.

Colonel Roger Trinquier had also been a senior officer in Indochina and Algeria, where he had acquired a formidable reputation as a thinking soldier with an abundance of new ideas about how to fight, and fight against, insurgencies. At the time of Congolese independence he had been based at barracks in Nice, where he had been deeply restless after spending so many years on active service. It is likely that Foccart or one of Grossin's SDECE officers had put his name forward to Tshombe and recommended him as the right man to defend Katanga from encroaching armies. However he was recruited to the cause, Trinquier was offered the role of commander of the Katangan armed and police forces. He accepted without hesitation, claiming that the Minister of Defence, Pierre Messmer, had given him strong support for doing so. He went there full of ideas and high hopes about creating a 'people's army' of Katangan villagers who could rise up against the UN peacekeepers and win the province back under Congolese control. At the same time he and his fellow officers subsequently resigned their commissions so they could fight in Africa without formally implicating Paris, although he was in constant touch with the French consulate in Elizabethville.[209]

Trinquier did not last long in the Congo, quickly becoming disillusioned by the restrictions and impracticalities of fighting a war in this remote region. But in the chaos and confusion of the weeks that now followed, Denard soon got noticed by the senior French commander, Lieutenant Colonel Roger Faulques, who replaced Trinquier. And when, in September 1961 and again in December the following year, the UN-led forces launched a series of ferocious attacks against Elizabethville, Denard made his name, fighting bravely and holding out for much longer than most before having to beat a retreat with what was left of *les affreux* ('the terrors'), as the foreign mercenaries called themselves.

A year later, Denard's reputation grew even more. Faulques had now left the country and Denard was in charge of the small band of foreign mercenaries, who had now been squeezed into an enclave around the town of Kolwezi. He was popular with his men, exerted a natural charisma and, by now, was experienced in battle.

Meanwhile, de Gaulle's suspicions of Washington and its covert motives in Africa were growing. Within just months of coming to power, the Kennedy administration had started to drastically increase American involvement on the African continent. Now there was a

US diplomat in almost every African state – previously it had been common practice on the continent for an ambassador to be responsible for several African countries – and Washington had also initiated an aid programme to all twelve of France's former colonies in the region. Perhaps most grating and threatening to the French, however, was Washington's promotion of the English language. French officials lobbied hard to bar English language teachers, working for the US Peace Corps, from entering their former colonies, and when their efforts failed they did everything they could to make their jobs as difficult as possible. Scarcely could there have been a greater challenge and affront to *la francophonie*.[210]

Franco-American relations were reaching another nadir. Deeply concerned that de Gaulle might strike a deal with the Soviet Union and orchestrate a campaign against America, Kennedy instructed the CIA to bug the Élysée. One of *le Général*'s closest advisers was also recruited as an informer. Some commentators speculated that, as Algeria moved towards and then won outright independence in July 1962, anti-Americanism had become the President's new 'emotion' that underwrote nearly all of his policies. Others thought that de Gaulle was 'obsessed with the Americans', while the President himself publicly declared that 'France is violently opposed to the blatant American imperialism now rampant in the world. France will continue to attack and to oppose the United States in Latin America, in Asia, and in Africa.' It was not just in these regions: two years before, he had rejected British entry into western Europe's Common Market on the grounds that it would lead to a 'colossal Atlantic Community dependent on and led by America, which would soon absorb the European Community'. His veto meant, in the eyes of the British Prime Minister, Harold Macmillan, that 'French domination of Europe is the new and alarming feature'.[211]

But de Gaulle also knew that France needed the United States, and

Washington's own assessments of French policy acknowledged this: a State Department report summarised the state of Franco-American relations in these terms: 'To the question "Can we do business with de Gaulle?" one is inclined to respond, after this catalogue of disagreements, in the negative. But at the same time we are prompted instinctively to say, "But we must!"'[212]

By early 1964, American influence in Africa was still growing, watched by wary French officials. In particular, the rise of the Congo's new leader, Joseph Mobutu, was a source of real concern. 'The strength of American influence on Mobutu worried us,' admitted Colonel Robert, 'and it was unacceptable to us that the head of the country should be so completely subservient to Washington, as he seemed to be.' But the next battleground between France and the United States was not the Congo; it was a small, undeveloped west African state with a meagre population but vast natural resources of oil, manganese and uranium.[213]

After winning its independence in 1960, Gabon had retained very close links with France. Many people regarded its President, Léon M'ba, as little more than a puppet of Jacques Foccart, who was rumoured to have engineered his electoral victory by making a number of very generous bribes. An adviser to M'ba's Cabinet was a Frenchman called Monsieur Pigot, and a fellow national, Marcel Vitte, was an adviser to the Ministry of Education. 'Gabon's resources of petroleum and minerals had considerable potential,' recalled Colonel Robert, 'and France protected its economic interests there.' Algeria's independence had forced Paris to look to west Africa for secure oil supplies, and Gabon and Guinea had vast resources.[214]

France's grip over the country was so strong that, paradoxically, it even encouraged some American companies to bid for contracts there. Gabon needed their investment and skills to develop its infrastructure and resources, and by 1963 several US oil and steel companies had established themselves in the country. At the same time, the American ambassador worked hard to forge contacts with politicians across the political spectrum, some of whom were M'ba's enemies, while members of the US Peace Corps arrived to build schools and hospitals throughout the country. Suddenly America was getting a bit too close to the Gabonese.

Then, in January 1964, Gabon was thrown into a state of political chaos when an increasingly autocratic M'ba suspended parliament. His enemies quickly plotted their response. Shortly after midnight on the morning of 18 February, they stormed the presidential palace and placed M'ba under arrest. At the same time, their soldiers seized several key strategic points, such as the airport, radio stations and important highways. A small French contingent, composed of several dozen men, was based outside the capital but was not in a position to challenge the much larger force that confronted it. The SDECE's liaison officer raced to the palace to see what was happening, but was immediately arrested and then tied to a chair to stop him from escaping. The top brass announced that Jean-Hilaire Aubame, M'ba's most bitter political rival, was now the country's new leader. The French had always kept a finger on the pulse of local politics but somehow they had failed to see how strong M'ba's enemies were.

As soon as news broke in Paris, in the early hours, Foccart arranged an emergency meeting that included his two SDECE chiefs, General Grossin and Colonel Robert, his deputy René Journiac and Guy Ponsaille, an official who was very familiar with the people who were implicated in the coup. Also present was Pierre Guillaumat, a minister with expert knowledge of France's energy policy. 'We had an important stake in Gabon's petroleum,' recalled Robert, 'and this explains Guillaumat's presence at this late night meeting.'[215]

Foccart was sure that the Americans had orchestrated the coup.

He knew that some of Gabon's new leaders had met with American representatives and officials, notably the US ambassador, Charles Darlington, who was a former official in Mobil. In his eyes these meetings were proof enough of an American connection, and he and his fellow officials in Paris ordered a military response. Elite soldiers, based in Dakar and Brazzaville and under the command of General Louis Kergaravat, immediately prepared to fly to Libreville to topple the new regime and put M'ba back in power. Paris had not intervened the previous year when Togo had descended into chaos following the assassination of President Sylvanus Olympio, or in Congo-Brazzaville when its leader Fulbert Youlou had resigned. Gabon, however, was different, partly because it had superb natural resources but, more importantly, because it also had links with Washington at a time of resurgent American interest in the African continent.[216]

On the morning of 19 February, just one day after the coup, several French transport planes arrived suddenly and unexpectedly at the airport, and as Kergaravat's men stormed onto the tarmac, local soldiers ran and disappeared. The French contingent raced unchallenged towards the capital, and just hours after he had been toppled, M'ba returned to his presidential palace, accompanied by a detachment of French soldiers.

This time the French were going to take no chances. They strengthened the French garrison that was stationed permanently at Camp de Gaulle barracks just outside the capital, ready to scramble to the palace at very short notice if the French ambassador ever requested their intervention. At the same time, the SDECE disseminated rumours and allegations in the state-controlled media that the CIA had orchestrated the unsuccessful revolt, and that Ambassador Darlington and the Peace Corps had been working on the agency's behalf. French expatriates also boycotted American enterprises and the American embassy was bombed.

After the coup, the French found correspondence between Aubame and Darlington that was, in their eyes, very close to incriminating. Shortly before the coup, Darlington had promised strong American support if Aubame ever became the Gabonese leader, although this was hardly proof that the Americans had actually instigated or backed the coup. But the French were sure the Americans were ringleaders and their suspicions fell on one of M'ba's chief rivals, Jean-Marc Ekoh. 'According to our information,' alleged Colonel Robert, Ekoh sought 'to seize power with the support of the Americans... [and] established numerous contacts with them'. The SDECE responded by blackmailing Ekoh, while Robert met a CIA official in Paris and warned the agency to stay out of Gabon.[217]

Colonel Robert had a scathing view of what the Americans were doing. Washington was playing a double game, he claimed. Officially the Americans were distancing themselves from France's former colonies, but in practice, he continued, they were driven by commercial interests to exploit local resources and to sell arms. He also detected a certain jealousy towards France on the part of both America and the Soviet Union. Either way, Robert argued, the United States was getting involved in a continent that it was completely unfamiliar with, and as a result it was 'taking at face value the claims and arguments, completely unfounded and ungrounded, that were aired by opponents [of existing regimes] who needed foreign support'.[218]

The intervention in Gabon formed part of a more aggressive style of French diplomacy that asserted itself elsewhere, notably in Laos and West Germany. France 'seeks to move forward in Europe and Latin America at US expense' while Washington was increasingly tied down in Vietnam, President de Gaulle told an American journalist. The anti-American tone of his speeches now became markedly more heated. During a tour of South America in the summer, he openly attacked 'hegemonies' and argued that 'we cannot accept that some

states should establish a power of political or economic direction outside their own borders. All and every hegemony must be banned from
our world.' France had to fulfil her 'exalted and exceptional destiny'
by steering her own independent course between two rival power
blocs. He went on to echo these sentiments continually in the months
ahead. In particular, de Gaulle feared that his decision to withdraw
France from NATO in March 1966 would provoke retribution from
the United States. He became increasingly mistrustful of American
motives, and suspected that the CIA was involved in all manner of
scandals that rocked France in these final years of his presidency.[219]

Several years after Kennedy's assassination in November 1963,
rivalry in 'Black Africa' between France and the 'Anglo-Saxons' once
again came to the fore. This time the setting was Nigeria, which
had won its independence from Britain in 1960. It was here, like the
Congo, that the French briefly came close to fighting a war by proxy
with Britain.

CHAPTER 9

BIAFRA: THE LAST ANGLO-FRENCH WAR?

Around midday on 28 July 1969, several light aircraft suddenly streaked at very low altitude over a town in southern Nigeria. Painted green on top and sky blue underneath, they had escaped detection along their way and slipped unchallenged through their enemy's defences. They now swooped fast and low over their targets, located a short distance outside the town, and fired several rockets before disappearing quickly out of view. No one was hurt but the lightning-fast attack inflicted considerable damage, setting several buildings ablaze.

Brief though it was, the bombardment on Kokori escalated Nigeria's bitter and bloody civil war. News of the incident sent shock waves through the highest echelons of the British government. The Prime Minister, Harold Wilson, was immediately alerted, and hours later the matter was discussed in London by the Joint Intelligence Committee and the Cabinet.[220]

The reason was that Kokori lay in one of Nigeria's main oil-producing regions. It was where, a decade before, the British–Dutch energy giant Shell had discovered a major field that soon began to produce 50,000 barrels of oil every day, all of which was pumped into a series of pipelines that flowed southwards to the main exporting terminal at Bonny Island. This attack was bad enough, but any more such assaults, warned the British High Commissioner in Lagos in an urgent, top-secret message, could have 'disastrous consequences on the Shell/BP export capacity'. International investors would take fright and the flow of oil to the British market could be seriously disrupted. The economic cost to Shell and BP, and to Britain and Nigeria, might be huge.[221]

But there was another, wider dimension. British officials felt sure that the planes had been armed and then supplied to the attacking force – secessionists who were fighting for the freedom of the region of Biafra – by the French government. The Swedish police had informed them that these planes were adapted for military use at several airfields outside the French capital, and the British in any case also had their own intelligence reports on the matter. It was, in other words, 'a situation in which French rockets fitted in France were used to attack British oil installations'. But officials in London were also convinced that French support for the Biafran cause was motivated largely by anti-British feeling. Nor could they rule out the possibility that Paris had ordered or instigated the attack on Kokori.[222]

Not surprisingly, the media quickly picked up the story. By this time, one British tabloid declared, the Biafran war had been transformed 'into a giant post-colonial battle between Britain and France for political and economic dividends in West Africa as a whole'. Just briefly, over those difficult summer weeks, any references to an 'Anglo-French war' must have seemed more than just media hyperbole. The British government was already strongly supporting Lagos with military equipment and now stepped up its involvement. In London, Prime Minister Wilson authorised further sales of valuable

British military equipment and allowed 'a qualified retired officer' to travel to the front line 'to advise [Shell] on passive air defences', although in Lagos the British High Commissioner urged him to go even further and take more drastic measures. The British and French governments, in other words, were close to waging a proxy war.[223]

Nigeria, like so many other African states, had always been rife with ethnic, religious and tribal diversity and tension. In 1914, during the days of British colonial rule, a legendary explorer and colonial administrator called Frederick Lugard had amalgamated the northern and southern regions into one artificial, federal entity, but this had done nothing to heal the underlying tensions. In particular, the Igbo people, who were predominantly Christian, had long complained about discrimination and harassment by northern tribes, most of whom were Muslims.

Charles de Gaulle (second from right) and Georges Pompidou (second from left) meet Harold Wilson (right) and his wife in Paris, 1965. Within three years, the Biafran crisis had caused major Anglo-French tension.

Such pressures had boiled over soon after Nigeria won independence from British rule in 1960. In the summer of 1966, General Yakubu Gowon's federal army killed thousands, perhaps tens of thousands, of innocent Ibos and orchestrated large-scale pogroms against them, driving many more of their number, perhaps as many as a million or more in total, out of the north and back to their homelands in the south-east. At the same time, the Igbo began to weigh up the case for establishing their own, independent state, based in the region of Biafra, and on 30 May the following year their leader, Colonel Odumegwu Ojukwu, publicly declared Biafra's independence. For many years, successive Igbo leaders had regarded the establishment of a federal Nigeria as the best answer to discrimination. Now, after the pogroms of 1966, secession seemed to many of them to be the only solution.

Ojukwu had been educated at Oxford and was the son of a Nigerian millionaire who had been knighted by the British government. He was a clever and astute politician who worked hard to win sympathy in the Western world. Within days of making his announcement, he appealed to policy-makers not just in London and Washington but also in Paris for support.

In the Élysée, President de Gaulle and the *éminence grise* of French power in Africa, Jacques Foccart, had been closely following developments in Nigeria and tried to determine what interests, if any, France might have in its rapidly escalating civil war. Should they recognise Biafra as an independent state, or even give Ojukwu their active support? Or should they support a federal solution, as the British appeared to be doing, or perhaps follow the United States by adopting a neutral position?

For its first year, the Biafran conflict won little interest in Paris, and the French government even honoured some defence contracts with the federal government. But Ojukwu's agents were allowed to set up an office in the French capital under the guise of the 'Biafra Historical Research Centre', to headhunt mercenaries and to liaise directly with Foccart. At the same time, the French authorities allowed the two veteran commanders of Katanga, Roger Faulques and Bob Denard, to help organise the mercenary operation. Judging from the sizeable numbers of recruits who made their way from France to Biafra over the coming months, comprising a force of around eighty men, Faulques and Denard had excellent contacts as well as plentiful supplies of money. 'Without telling me explicitly,' recalled one of the freelance soldiers of fortune, the headhunters gave me the impression that they were 'semi-officially mandated by de Gaulle'. The mercenary operation became a fiasco, however, when the soldiers-of-fortune suffered losses at the city of Calabar, in southern Nigeria, and beat a rapid retreat back to France.[224]

But on 31 July 1968, President de Gaulle issued a public declaration of support for Ojukwu's cause for the first time, although, unlike the leaders of Gabon and the Ivory Coast, he did not now formally recognise an independent Biafran state. France, he declared at a press conference, 'has helped Biafra within the limits of what is feasible. It has not carried out the act that would be decisive – the recognition of the Biafran Republic – for it believes that the birth of Africa is, above all, a matter for the Africans.' He also openly acknowledged France's humanitarian support for Biafra. But he had by this time probably also decided to deploy similar tactics to those he had used in the Congo, giving covert and discreet military support to Biafra. The reason for this underhand approach was simple. If the Biafrans lost their war, then he could plausibly deny French involvement. But if Ojukwu won, then France would have a new ally. This was a policy that was shaped by the Élysée, not by the French Foreign Ministry, whose advisers appear to have been relatively sidelined. Quite why de Gaulle and Foccart took this decision to support Biafra remains unclear, but it is possible that the leader of the Ivory Coast, Félix Houphouët-Boigny, who was a close ally of Ojukwu from the onset of the Biafran crisis, exerted a strong influence over them.[225]

It is true that if Ojukwu had won his war then he would almost certainly have rewarded his supporters with lucrative oil contracts and preferential treatment. These would hardly have been opportunities that France could ignore. British diplomats noted that French support for Biafra coincided with diminishing oil prospects in the Sahara, and judged that this was probably spurring them to look elsewhere for openings. 'French companies are having an increasingly difficult time [in Algeria],' noted one official. 'If, as we believe, they would like to diversify out of Algeria, Nigeria would present attractions for obvious geographical reasons.' France, it seemed, was 'scheming for oil supplies' and by 1967 French companies were searching hard for Nigerian petroleum.[226]

But there was as much oil outside Biafra as there was within, and French oil interests could equally have pushed de Gaulle and Foccart to side with General Gowon, or to take a strictly neutral position in the conflict. Instead of giving military support, they could have decided to provide only humanitarian aid to the Biafrans while making efforts to broker a ceasefire and sponsor talks between the two sides. This would have been a much safer course of action than supporting the Biafran struggle, which risked provoking retaliation from the federal government. On the eve of war, French companies had a strong commercial stake in the Nigerian market, where they competed with British, American and other foreign rivals. But by backing the Biafrans, de Gaulle and Foccart knew that they risked sacrificing these commercial interests because the federal government would probably retaliate against French companies. And if the war proved to be protracted, or if the Biafrans lost, then France risked losing out on an oil boom that Nigeria's eastern and mid-western districts had been experiencing over the preceding two years and which American companies were already starting to exploit. Nigeria was in any case one of the biggest and fastest-growing markets in sub-Saharan Africa.[227]

Something more important than oil was at stake. This was clear to British officials, who noted how de Gaulle's pro-Biafran position had 'caused discontent' amongst all the French-speaking African leaders other than those of Gabon and Ivory Coast. 'It would be irrational,' they concluded, 'to sacrifice the sympathies of ten states for the sake of potential oil successes.'[228]

Instead, the most convincing explanation of French policy towards Biafra is that it was motivated by a visceral Anglophobia. A divided Nigeria would have served French interests better than a federal one because, if it remained united, it would form a vast geographical, demographic and economic Anglophone entity that could easily dominate the entire region. Nigeria had no traditional allegiance to France but had instead been part of the British Empire ever since the mid-nineteenth century. This meant that a federal Nigeria could, in the years ahead, easily become a base from which 'Anglo-Saxon' cultural, political and economic influence could seep into France's neighbouring strongholds, notably Cameroon, Central African Republic, Chad and Niger. This was the same attitude and approach that French officials had shown at the time of Cameroonian independence (see Chapter 7).

De Gaulle never publicly admitted this, but British officials could certainly find no other convincing explanation for his position. 'Nigeria cut across the now almost mystical concept of "francophonie",' judged one analyst at the British Foreign Office. The French President was 'hoping that Nigeria, as a very large Anglophone British creation, would break up and cease to be a potentially major African power which would dominate the small Francophone states around her'. This prospect seemed to inflame a deep sense of French inferiority. The British official continued:

> We seem to be getting back into the bad old days of 1898 and 1899 – of Fashoda and the rival parties of French and British officers going round Borgu planting the Tricolour and the Union Jack at each village they came to [although] General de Gaulle himself looked back much further than that – to the seventeenth century and Cardinal Richelieu.

The French position, argued another, seemed to be the result of de Gaulle's 'absurd historical analogies' with Fashoda and other colonial rivalries in a different age. Respected French commentators thought the same as British officials.[229]

The French President certainly missed few opportunities to take a swipe at British interests, or at least his perception of them. At almost the same time that the Biafran War had begun, he had undertaken an official trip to Canada in 1967, during which he had infuriated officials in the capital, Ottawa, by making a public rallying call of *'Vive le Québec libre!'* Afterwards he told Foccart how pleased he was to have angered the British in particular, adding that 'I got out of a visit to Ottawa where I would have had to drink a toast to the Queen of England'. Soon afterwards there was unrest in Mauritius. 'Follow that closely,' he told Foccart, because 'we're going to take back from the English all they stole from us: Quebec, which is in hand, then Mauritius and then the Anglo-Norman Islands [the Channel Islands]'.[230]

Such feelings of rivalry were all the more powerful at this time because the French, too, were concerned about their grip over their former colonies. 'Soviet penetration of Algeria has shaken French complacency and they appear to be making a really major effort to restore their position,' noted one British diplomat. The Biafran War also coincided with trouble in Chad, riots in Senegal and Mauritania, and civil unrest in France, which was rocked by student-led riots in the summer of 1968. It seemed possible that the French were staking out Biafra as an area where they could exert influence to compensate for its loss in other regions.[231]

The President probably had other reasons to support Ojukwu, one of which was vindictiveness. Several years before, in 1960, the Nigerians had complained to the French government about its testing of a nuclear device at Reggane in the Sahara. Then they had expelled the French ambassador, Raymond Offroy, and imposed sanctions on the movement of French planes and ships. In Paris, these protests were regarded not as anti-nuclear but as anti-French and anti-colonial. De Gaulle regarded this as a contagious attitude that could easily contaminate the wider region. Lagos was, in other words, *un pôle d'attraction naturel* for anti-colonial sentiment throughout the neighbourhood. Another possible motive for supporting Biafra was to check the rise of Islam: 'the French', felt one British official, 'have always grossly exaggerated this Islamic bogey' and were perhaps fearful that the Islamism of the northern tribes could spread elsewhere in Africa and challenge their post-colonial influence.[232]

Needless to say, de Gaulle's talk about respecting Biafra's 'right of self-determination' raised eyebrows because, like so many political leaders, *le Président* had a very selective view of such a 'right', picking and choosing those who merited his sympathy. He had spoken out in favour of self-determination when France had nothing to lose and perhaps something to gain – in Latin America in 1964, Cambodia in 1966, Canada and Poland in 1967 and Romania the following year – but then orchestrated, or overlooked, its bloody suppression in places like Damascus and Sétif when he deemed it to be in French national interests to do so.

Nor had de Gaulle said anything about the flow of arms that Foccart and one of his chief intelligence officers, Jean Mauricheau-Beaupré, were already running from Libreville and Port-Gentil to Biafra. From his semi-permanent posting at the French embassy in Libreville, Mauricheau had been working closely with several officials, including the defence attaché Colonel Merle, the SDECE representative Philippe Le Terron and a mysterious Frenchman called Pierre Laureys, to supervise the airlift of large quantities of arms and ammunition. Meanwhile, in Paris, the SDECE had also started to unfold a media campaign on Biafra's behalf, constantly spinning stories of Nigerian 'genocide' to the press. Such a term may or may not have been an exaggeration – many people argued that the killing of the Igbo people in 1966 merited such terminology – but it was still a 'shock word', admitted a senior SDECE officer, that the agency was exploiting to raise public awareness about the situation in Biafra.[233]

Strictly speaking, the French did not give any arms to the Biafrans, for they were keen not to spark any unnecessary dispute with the British and with Nigeria's other foreign supporters. Paris instead flew arms and supplies to their strongest ally in west Africa, President Houphouët-Boigny of the Ivory Coast, whose transport planes then moved them on from Abidjan to Biafra. The supplies that reached Biafra were in this respect Ivorian rather than French. By February 1969, the French were delivering around 150–200 tonnes of supplies to Biafra every week, flown from restricted areas of airports that armed French security officials made 'exceptional efforts' to hide from prying eyes. 'French support for Biafra', noted British officials, 'and the arms airlift organized with the help of the French and her African friends are the main things keeping Ojukwu and his secessionists going.'[234]

Maintaining the flow of supplies was no mean feat, particularly after the fall of the highly strategic city of Port Harcourt to the federal army in May 1968. From this moment on, the Biafrans were left with only one main runway, which was at Uli, several hundred miles from the coast. In the early stages of the war, this was not a destination for the faint-hearted, since it was at this time little more than a widened country road that ran through the bush. Bordered by high elephant grass, pilots had hardly any spare space on either side of each wing as they came into land. Night landings were particularly dangerous, since the rebels used the headlights of parked cars to guide in the pilots. These lights were difficult enough to see at the best of times, but the rebels deliberately used them only at the last possible moment in case they were seen by any federal aircraft circling above. To the relief of pilots, however, the airstrip was upgraded as the war raged on.

Indispensable to the French effort were the flights undertaken by various international aid agencies, including Caritas International, a Catholic relief organisation that had been formed solely to alleviate the Biafran emergency. Some of the arms were packed in unmarked crates and hidden alongside medical equipment and emergency supplies of food and clean water. Equally, these aid groups made good use of the flights that Mauricheau had organised. 'Many people thought it was wrong for us to have anything to do with a gun-runner,' one of the Caritas workers, Father Dermot Doran, later admitted. 'But our view was that we were determined to get relief in whatever way it was done. People were starving and we wanted to help them.' The Reverend Nicholas Stacey, a director of Oxfam's operations in the region, noticed that the local Jesuit priests were also in close contact with their brethren in France, who used their own influence in every section of the French government and military to lobby for support.[235]

De Gaulle and Foccart also did all they could to help others to intervene on the Biafrans' behalf. In the later stages of the war, they

liaised closely with the politically isolated South African government, which was keen to find as many allies in 'Black Africa' as it
could and which strongly supported Ojukwu for that reason: for
several months, France and South Africa used the same independent air company to fly supplies into Uli from Libreville. Another ally
was a maverick, somewhat eccentric Swedish aristocrat called Count
Gustaf von Rosen. Harbouring visions of 'transforming Africa', he
worked hard to find ways of evading sanctions and supplying the
Biafrans with warplanes that they desperately needed. Von Rosen
was also reported to have trained Biafran pilots in Gabon, something
he could only have done with French connivance.[236]

During the summer of 1969, Biafran planes struck two British-
owned targets, a timber mill at Sapele and a merchant ship at Port
Harcourt. By this time British intelligence had established a detailed
picture of how France was helping von Rosen. Its chief source of
information was the Swedish police force, whose personnel had
closely interviewed two employees of an aviation company, based in
Stockholm, that had supplied von Rosen with several planes known
as 'Minicoms'. These were two-seater, single-engined, low-wing
monoplanes, which were originally designed as trainer aircraft but
which had proven their worth in battle during the Congo crisis several years before. They were ideally suited to the Biafran War since
they were more manoeuvrable than jets, easier to fly over relatively
short distances, and cheaper to purchase and operate. And when
they were adapted to carry bombs, rockets and machine guns, they
were almost as lethal.

On 27 April, ran the intelligence reports, five Minicoms had flown
from Sweden to different airfields in France – Toussus-le-Noble near
Paris, Brétigny and Cazaux – where they were inspected by teams of
engineers who then carried out a series of modifications that enabled
them to carry rockets. Two weeks later, the planes were dismantled,

packed into crates and flown by transport aircraft firstly to Portugal and then to Abidjan and Libreville. Von Rosen was now ready to strike Kokori and other oil installations, all of which were central to Biafran objectives because the federal government relied upon oil revenues to sustain its war effort.[237]

It had become obvious to Whitehall officials that 'the Biafran aircraft are deliberately trying to kill expatriate staff' and that 'French weapons are now being used to strafe British civilians'. Others concurred with the judgement. 'We now had proof that the rockets used were of French manufacture,' noted a British official. 'If this sort of thing [continues], the knowledge that French rockets were being used against British [and also American and Dutch] commercial installations in Nigeria would spread.' This would lead, he continued, to 'anger with the French' and 'it would be hard to avoid great damage to Anglo/French relations'. It was, as a result, 'a potentially explosive situation'. The British now stepped up their flow of arms to Nigeria, delivering large consignments of anti-aircraft weapons and authorising several RAF personnel to visit Nigeria to advise its forces on how to upgrade their defences. Like the French, they tried to plausibly deny their own involvement by flying supplies via third parties, sending them to NATO's depots in western Europe before forwarding them into the hands of Gowon's forces.[238]

It was at this time, during the summer and early autumn of 1969, that the British and French government came close to fighting a war by proxy as the Minicoms continued to target Western oil installations and other businesses. The British government stepped up its clandestine supplies of large quantities of shells and bullets, which were 'loaded secretly at Gatwick [airport] after dark' under a 'Top Secret' classification. Millions of rounds of ammunition, large quantities of light anti-aircraft guns and Saladin armoured vehicles made their way to Lagos, while a British government minister, Lord Shepherd, admitted that 'we have been supplying Nigeria with pretty well all its military equipment'. London had supported Gowon's forces from the outset of the conflict, perhaps because it genuinely feared that Biafran secession would encourage other regions to do the same and thereby 'Balkanise' an entire continent, or else because it wanted a swift end to a conflict that would otherwise put the substantial interests of British oil companies at risk. But now, as British oil installations came under pressure, the relationship between London and Lagos moved a step closer.[239]

By this time, the civil war had created serious Anglo-French tensions. There were hopes in London that de Gaulle's resignation as President on 27 April would bring about a major change in foreign policy, but these hopes were dashed as his successor, Georges Pompidou, continued to express his support for Biafra and as Foccart continued to exert influence, despite being briefly out of office. The French, noted senior British officials, were 'leading a campaign of hatred against Great Britain in both Africa and Europe, accusing it of allowing atrocities to take place in Nigeria and encouraging Nigeria to attack defenceless targets'. In particular, they continued, 'a good many French officials [for whom] the memory of Fashoda, as told in the French history books, is still green ... think we are constantly leaking information damaging to France in Africa or designed to modify French policy against their will'. French officials seemed to think, for example, that the British were trying to stir up ill-feeling between Paris and African capitals by providing the Africans with classified information about French support for the racialist apartheid regime in South Africa.[240]

British officials did raise such matters with their French counterparts but made little progress in resolving them. This was partly because Paris steadfastly refused to admit its support for the rebels, but also because the British did not want to jeopardise their prospects for joining the European Economic Community, which France could continue to veto if it chose. Both acknowledged a shared interest in promoting stability in Africa but, as one official pointed out, 'the French representatives did not succeed in removing our suspicions that French policy in Africa is born in part of a desire to discomfort us'. The British accused the French of failing to pressurise Ojukwu into negotiations and compromise, allowing the war to descend into a bloody stalemate that threatened to drag on indefinitely. Conversely, Paris accused Gowon and his British supporters of being untrustworthy aggressors whose promises of respecting Biafran autonomy were hollow.[241]

In the tense summer weeks that followed the attack on Kokori, British diplomats worked hard to limit the political damage. It was necessary, one senior official wrote, 'to keep the temperature down and to avoid criticizing the French directly'. Eventually, British officials decided to give the French Foreign Minister, Maurice Schumann, 'a short sharp representation which would leave him with a sense of some shock and which might offer the hope that he would be prepared to call M. Foccart to order'. There were also sharp exchanges between British and French government officials at international summits, while London pressed Lagos to impose economic sanctions on French businesses that were operating in federal territory.[242]

But by now the Biafran struggle was nearing its bloody end. Towards the end of December, Gowon's army launched a powerful offensive that drove through Ojukwu's defences. Within just weeks, federal forces had captured nearly all of his remaining territory, including the airstrip at Uli, his last link with the outside world. Ojukwu had no choice but to surrender and flee into exile. France had lost its secret war.

Meanwhile, a whole decade after Guinea had declared its independence and, by doing so, infuriated General de Gaulle, the French secret services were still working hard to find ways of toppling the troublesome President Sékou Touré. Their agents searched for weaknesses in Touré's security and power base that they could exploit.

Unseating Touré had become all the more important because, over the preceding few years, there were signs of growing American interest in Guinea. 'The Americans', pointed out the SDECE's chief officer in Africa, 'had openly manoeuvred to take our place in Guinea. They had started to put forward numerous business proposals and to set up local businesses or invested in existing ones.' In particular, American trade delegations had organised and sponsored a technology fair in Conakry, which the SDECE tried to stop foreign companies from participating in. But Touré's relations with Washington were unclear: the SDECE was unsure if the Americans regarded him as a potential ally or as someone who they could topple and replace. When the French spies discovered that Touré was sponsoring an anti-American resolution at the Organisation of African Unity, one that was openly critical of Kennedy's handling of race relations in the United States, it seemed more likely that Washington would want a more compliant leader in his place. Either way, from the French perspective the Guinean leader had to go and be replaced by someone who was sympathetic only to France's interests.[243]

The SDECE's chance came in the late 1960s, when it discovered that Touré was supporting the independence movements in the neighbouring states of Guinea-Bissau and Cape Verde. The Portuguese had established their own foothold in the Guinea region in the fifteenth century, whole centuries before the French had done so, and were now fighting tooth and nail to retain their grip on these colonies in the face of sharply growing nationalism. Touré deeply sympathised with the anti-Portuguese insurgents and was probably suspicious of the Portuguese presence in his own backyard, fearing that the French could potentially exploit it. Above all, he hoped that a Portuguese retreat would create an opportunity that he could seize, allowing him to annex their former territory.

Looking for a breakthrough, the SDECE started to cooperate closely with their counterparts in the Portuguese intelligence agency, exchanging information and determining ways of undermining their common foes. They knew that, in Conakry, Touré often hosted leaders and representatives of the anti-Portuguese independence party, the PAIGC (Partido Africano da Independência da Guiné e Cabo Verde).[244]

In particular, two undercover agents noticed that there were a good many Guinean members of the PAIGC who resented Touré's interference in the affairs of Guinea-Bissau and Cape Verde. It was with the aim of exploiting such differences that the French and Portuguese now collaborated on another joint venture to unseat the President. Operation Sapphire was designed to exploit these rifts and embolden a political rival in Conakry to mount a coup and oust Touré.[245]

The idea was far-fetched but, after so many years of failing to unseat their arch African rival, the French operatives were prepared to try it anyway. From their inside sources they discovered the names of thirteen PAIGC members and four of its senior officials who were interested in setting up their own rival Guinean organisation and mounting a coup against Touré. The French even made contact with Samba Djalo, the PAIGC's spy chief, who nodded his approval at suggestions of pushing Touré out.

During their secret dialogue, Djalo seemed to confirm French fears about 'Anglo-Saxon' designs on Guinea, for he informed the French spies that there were others who were also planning on toppling Touré. He disclosed that he had met three foreign representatives shortly before, one of them a Canadian who had offered $20 million to mount a coup against in Conakry. Djalo was well aware of Guinea's highly valuable natural resources and he had no doubt that the visitors were not really Canadians but Americans who were working for the CIA. If the French did not get rid of Touré, in other words, then there was a real risk that the Americans would do so and establish a base in a region that France regarded as its own sphere of interest.

On 4 April 1974, the SDECE officer responsible for the operation drafted a report that summarised the plan. At the beginning of May, the leaders of the planned coup would meet in secret in Brussels and in African capitals to be briefed on the details of the operation. From the end of May, the two spy agencies would then start to move arms, radio transmitters and supplies to a secret base camp, which would be established in a Portuguese-controlled area of Guinea-Bissau. After this, French Special Forces would give the attacking force intensive military training. Then, either towards the end of June or in July, the attacking force would launch their assault on the capital, moving at night, and, as soon as they had accomplished their objectives and won control of the capital, the coup leaders would fly into Conakry and declare a state of emergency.

But just three weeks after the document was written, there was a coup in Portugal and the new government in Lisbon promised Guinea and other colonies full independence. Fittingly, the PIDE chief who had helped to plan the attack on Touré, Barbieri Cardoso, fled from Guinea-Bissau and headed for France, taking up residence in Paris.

The French had once again failed to oust Touré.

CHAPTER 10

AFRICA, AMERICA AND THE FRENCH NUCLEAR BOMB

After de Gaulle's resignation from office in April 1969, Jacques Foccart continued to exert his influence over France's former African colonies. And one of his priorities was to ensure that these colonies continued to supply France with one of its most highly prized commodities – uranium.

This was vital to the development of an atomic bomb. The French government had started to research atomic energy before the end of the Second World War, but in 1954 Prime Minister Pierre Mendès France had taken the decision to develop a nuclear weapons programme. His successors continued with the project and it was then pushed much further forward during de Gaulle's presidency.

The bomb's advocates argued that it offered a much more reliable guarantee of national security than conventional defences: in 1940, after all, the supposedly impregnable Maginot Line had failed to protect France from the onslaught of Hitler's tanks. But they also argued that France needed to have its own independent nuclear deterrent rather than rely upon the hollow promises made by a foreign power.

France had been a member of the NATO alliance since 1949 and was therefore supposed to fall under the American nuclear umbrella. But any French faith in America's security guarantees was badly shaken during the Suez crisis. On 5 November 1956, Moscow seemed to threaten a nuclear attack if the French continued with their assault against Egypt. Panic-stricken, Paris had turned to the Americans but found their pleas ignored.

The bomb, often referred to in France as the *force de dissuasion* or *force de frappe*, also bestowed prestige and status. It was no coincidence that the nuclear programme had been instigated just months after the fall of Indochina. And as the empire came under increasing nationalist pressure, French interest in the bomb grew. Nuclear weapons would give France membership of an exclusive 'club' of very select nations – the United States, Great Britain and the Soviet Union – that enjoyed unique status and influence. 'A great state that does not possess them does not control its own destiny,' de Gaulle once remarked, adding that, without this capability, France would become a political satellite of the Americans. It was to maintain France's independence, and also to lodge a protest about Washington's policy to Algeria, that, soon after becoming President, de Gaulle not only withdrew the French Mediterranean fleet from NATO's command but also denied the Americans permission to base nuclear weapons on French territory.[246]

One of the crucial ingredients of any nuclear project is uranium, a radioactive metal that comprises the fissile material of a warhead. There were several countries in the former French Empire that possessed vast deposits of this hugely valuable material, and Paris was prepared to fight hard to maintain its tight post-colonial grip over these territories and their resources. Without these supplies, the French nuclear project was bound to remain moribund: the only other major sources of supply were in Canada, Australia and the

United States, and none of them would export their resources without firm guarantees and safeguards that they would be used only for peaceful purposes.

Mendès France, de Gaulle and other French leaders always knew that Washington would strongly oppose the French nuclear programme. A French bomb would allow Paris to be less dependent on the United States and might increase the temptation to leave NATO. In November 1956, for example, the Americans tried to inflate the market cost of enriched uranium to make it more difficult for France, and other countries, to pursue their own atomic programmes. President Kennedy was well aware of the political fallout of a French bomb and had made a speech arguing that 'we should face the fact that the fundamental purpose of the French atomic bomb is not to increase French capabilities but to increase its stature in the [Nato] Alliance. The French bomb is aimed toward Washington rather than Moscow. This is an odd way to run an alliance.' Such sentiments reinforced a French perception that the bomb was 'an Anglo-Saxon' club, even if by this time the Russians had developed their own.[247]

Gabon, where considerable deposits of uranium had been discovered, was one place of particular importance to the French atomic programme. In 1951 the French Bureau de Recherches Géologiques et Minières (BRGM) had carried out a major survey there, lured by a number of very promising geological reports. In particular, its geologists discovered considerable deposits of uranium north of Moanda, where valuable deposits of manganese, used for the production of steel, had also been found. In 1960, France granted Gabon its independence, but in return demanded a monopoly over these uranium deposits, which were subsequently mined by a company, Compagnie des Mines d'Uranium de Franceville, that was partly owned and funded by a subsidiary of the French Atomic Energy Agency. To stop France from developing the bomb, and to starve it of the raw materials of a nuclear programme, Kennedy had sought to establish an American presence in Gabon and may have orchestrated the coup that briefly toppled the strongly Francophile leader, Leon M'ba (see Chapter 9).[248]

But after the assassination of President Kennedy, American interest in the African continent waned. President Lyndon B. Johnson, like Eisenhower, considered the continent to be a region of marginal concern and instead prioritised the Middle East and south-east Asia. But the French government could still not afford to look away from any sources of uranium. It could not allow the Americans, or the Soviets, to win too much influence in uranium-rich states, or to forfeit control over the raw materials of its nuclear project.

It was these concerns that underwrote a French intervention in the African continent that took place in the autumn of 1979. In the first two weeks of September, around a dozen Western oil workers arrived in the Central African Republic. All of them were working on behalf of Royal Dutch Shell, which six years before had won an exploration permit to search for oil and gas in the republic. And all of the employees stayed in the capital Bangui, readying themselves to head off into the remote regions of this vast country, covering nearly a quarter of a million square miles, which geologists had deemed to be worthy of close exploration.

Had the republic's security officials been more vigilant, however, they might have wondered why so many oil workers should arrive at once. There was usually just a trickle of employees coming and going because Shell's interest in the country was only small scale and low key. This, by contrast, was a relative influx.

The truth was that, although the employees had official passes and documentation, they were in fact agents of the SDECE. In effect, they were a fifth column that had arrived in Bangui to provide Paris with up-to-date reports about the state of affairs in the capital, and to prepare the ground for an imminent French-led military assault. A military coup was about to get under way.[249]

The man who had incurred the displeasure of the Élysée was 58-year-old Jean-Bedel Bokassa. Some months before, President Valéry Giscard d'Estaing had decided that Bokassa had to be removed from power. A new leader would be imposed in his place, one who the French could keep more closely under their thumb.

It is often said that the driving force behind this coup was 'the Diamond Affair'. President Giscard, according to this version of events, wanted to topple Bokassa even before he made awkward revelations against the French President, who was alleged to have accepted a number of hugely valuable gems from the African leader. Giscard, claimed the weekly newspaper *Le Canard enchaîné* shortly after the coup, wanted Bokassa deposed so that incriminating documents, which proved this top-level corruption, could be removed. But it has never been proven that these 'diamonds' were more than industrial grade: 'Bokassa had tiny industrial diamonds and what he had were of no value,' the spy chief Alexandre de Marenches asserted. Besides, any documents in Bokassa's possession would also have been of equally dubious value and their veracity easily refuted while any gems were quietly disposed of.[250]

A more convincing explanation is that France's leaders feared foreign intervention in a country that was thought to harbour large uranium deposits. Bokassa was becoming too close to the Libyan leader, Colonel Gaddafi. But in the circumstances of the moment, it also looked as though Gaddafi was moving towards another country – the United States. Relations between Washington and Tripoli were later to crash: this happened in December 1979, when the American embassy in Libya was attacked and burnt by a mob and Washington deemed Gaddafi to be a 'state sponsor of terrorism'. But over the preceding months there was a real chance of a rapprochement between the two countries.

Since becoming President in January 1966, Bokassa had been a close protégé of the French government, which bestowed upon him its full support. He was, felt Jacques Foccart, 'a very pro-French military man' who was, in return, fiercely loyal to de Gaulle. During the 1968 student protests in Paris, when de Gaulle's power came under intense pressure, Bokassa even wanted to play his part in defending him: very late one night, he arrived at the French ambassador's residence in Bangui, armed with grenades and a machine gun, and informed the astonished diplomat that he was all ready to take Paris by storm and rescue *le Général* and save the capital from the grip of the demonstrators. But he was much closer to President Giscard, who at one point proclaimed himself to be a 'friend and family member' of the African dictator and who shared with him a love of hunting. Paris was even prepared to turn a blind eye to the stories of the dictator's savage barbarism, as well as his shocking extravagance. The republic was stricken by wretched poverty but in December 1977 Bokassa spent huge sums of money on his own 'coronation', a lavish two-day extravaganza.[251]

This was the high point of Giscard's efforts to assert French interests on the African continent. More and more African states were attending the annual Franco-African summit meetings, and Giscard sometimes claimed that France spearheaded a 'Eurafrican' entity that excluded, and challenged, both the United States and the Soviet Union. At the same time there was a new spirit of *activisme* in Paris, which dispatched arms and troops to support the governments in both Chad and Zaire (formerly the Congo), notably at the mineral-rich town of Kolwezi in May 1978. France had just experienced thirty years of prosperity, known as *les trentes glorieuses*, and wanted a more assertive role to reflect its 'feel-good factor'.

But no amount of French wishful thinking could hide the fact that, over the previous three years or so, Bokassa was behaving even more erratically than before. In particular, he was looking towards the Libyan leader, Colonel Muammar Gaddafi. Bokassa knew that Gaddafi was a beneficiary of a dramatic rise in the price of oil and was therefore a potentially very generous donor, one who could subsidise his own extravagance, particularly in the event of a disagreement with a future French government that may not remain as sympathetic. In September 1976 Gaddafi invited Bokassa to Tripoli to mark the seventh anniversary of the Libyan leader's coup and accession to power. Keen to make a good impression, Bokassa had converted to Islam and even changed his name to 'Salah Eddine Ahmed Bokassa'. It made no difference, however, because the Libyan leader failed to offer any firm financial commitment. And perhaps finding Islam's prohibition on alcohol too stringent – Bokassa was a notoriously heavy drinker – he soon reverted back to Catholicism.

By this time, the republic was also thought to be rich in uranium resources. In the early 1970s, teams of French geologists working for the BRGM had visited the Bakouma region and judged that the area potentially held important uranium resources that could be commercially exploited. The French informed Bokassa but he denied them permission to start excavation. Nor would he agree to the sale of his country's raw stocks to Paris at subsidised prices. Giscard sent one of his cousins to meet with Bokassa and to persuade him otherwise.[252]

But in 1979 the SDECE discovered that Bokassa was once again reaching out to Tripoli. Bokassa, the French spies heard, was even interested in leasing the republic's military bases, notably its air strips, to the Libyans if Gaddafi paid the right price.

Gaddafi was interested in the republic for a number of reasons. He regarded Central Africa as lying within Libya's natural sphere of influence and was interested in developing his own nuclear bomb, for which the republic's uranium deposits would be indispensable. He was also keen to flex muscle in the affairs of his southern neighbour, Chad, and knew that the republic's strategic position would be hugely instrumental in helping him do so. In the event of a war against Chad, he would then be able to attack his enemy on two opposing fronts.

But it was not just Libyan interference in the Central African Republic that France would have feared. Just briefly, in the summer of 1979, it also seemed possible that the Libyans might bring the influence of another country along with them. This was not the Soviet Union, with which Gaddafi had distinctly unsettled, and often very cool, relations. It was instead the influence of the United States. For in the late 1970s the relationship between Libya and United States was shifting subtly – or so it seemed in Paris.

Relations between Tripoli and Washington had crashed soon after Gaddafi seized power in 1969, but the two countries needed each other. The Libyans wanted American arms and trade, and had placed a number of orders, all of which were blocked by the State Department, for aircraft and industrial machinery. In 1977 Gaddafi had sent a number of trade delegates to the United States, who claimed to have 'succeeded in establishing new relations with Americans', and encouraged their American counterparts to make return visits. At the same time, US oil companies started to buy increasing quantities of Libyan oil and cast an avaricious eye to the commercial opportunities that Gaddafi's vast reserves of petroleum offered. Equally, American defence chiefs wanted to stake their claim to a giant military base from which Gaddafi had ejected the US Air Force in 1970: overlooking the Mediterranean, the Wheelus Air Base remained as strategically important during the Cold War as it had been to the Germans and Italians in the Second World War. At the very least, Washington would have wanted to lure Libya away from the Soviet Union.

In the summer of 1978, Libyan officials pulled a long and complex string of acquaintances to make contact with American businessmen.

One of them was Billy Carter, the younger brother of the American President, who was invited to Tripoli. Carter Junior made his first visit in September, during which time he toured a succession of farms, factories and schools and accepted a number of gifts. At a drinks reception, when the Libyans raised the matter of buying American transport planes, Carter allegedly replied that he would 'do something about it'. Four months later, in January, the Libyans made a high-profile return visit to the United States, touring the Carter family peanut farm and appearing on popular televisions shows. Billy also stopped off at the White House and continued to raise the matter of the C-130 transports with officials.[253]

The French government could hardly have missed this Carter–Libya connection, which attracted huge media interest. It knew that, in November 1978, Washington had decided to authorise the export of Boeing 727s to Libya and then, two months later, three 747s. True, the President and his national security adviser, Zbigniew Brzezinski, had publicly distanced themselves from Billy's trip, but such statements seemed hollow when Gaddafi had two things – oil and military bases – that were of such obvious importance and value to Washington. So when, on 16 July 1979, Billy made a television appearance and announced his intention to attend Gaddafi's tenth anniversary celebrations in Tripoli, which he had been invited to, the broadcast must have rung alarm bells in Paris. If Bokassa became more dependent on Gaddafi, then it must have seemed in Paris that the Americans would have a pathway into the Central African Republic.

British diplomats had picked up other indications that changes were afoot. 'I had noted several recent indications that the Libyans were making another attempt to place US/Libya relations on a better footing,' noted the British ambassador to Washington. In particular, the Libyan Foreign Minister had visited Washington shortly before 'and had let it be known that his government was interested in improving its dialogue with the US'. On 25 October 1978, the *Christian Science Monitor* also noted that 'even while denouncing the United States, Libya is quietly extending an olive branch to this country ... and [is] receptive to a more normal relationship with the United States'. And when, in the summer of 1979, Gaddafi announced plans to drastically increase oil production, American energy companies knew that enormous contracts would be on offer. At the same time he told visiting British diplomats that he wanted better relations with Washington.[254]

It was no coincidence that at exactly the same time, over the summer of 1979, the SDECE's case officers devised a plan to oust Bokassa. First of all, they decided to portray France's intervention as a humanitarian one. French troops were going to intervene, the message would run, to safeguard the lives and well-being of the republic's citizens. This was an easy story to sell because in April the emperor's guards had brutally suppressed a street protest by local children, opening fire and killing around one hundred civilians. Throughout the summer, more horror stories about Bokassa's behaviour appeared in the press, most of which concentrated on his drunkenness and, much more spuriously, about his supposed cannibalism.

The spies also had at their disposal someone who was suitable to step into the Emperor's clothes. Despite its support for the Bokassa regime, the French government had allowed David Dacko to live in Paris for the past year. In this time they had always maintained cool and distant relations with the former President, but all that changed in late August 1979, when the SDECE received intelligence that the Emperor was about to make a visit to Tripoli to finalise his growing relationship with Libya. They wanted to strike while Bokassa was out of the country.[255]

Late in the afternoon of 19 September, several French agents escorted Dacko from his Paris flat into an ordinary, unmarked car, which was waiting for him in the street outside. Dacko was now driven to the airbase at Dugny-Le Bourget, outside the capital, where he boarded a government-owned passenger jet and within half an hour had flown off, unnoticed by the press and the general public.

Meanwhile, at Bangui, the SDECE agents who had arrived several days before, posing as oil workers, received a message on their hidden radio sets. Dacko's plane was on its way and would touch down at 9.30 p.m.

They moved fast, putting their prearranged plan into practice. Because the airport was still under the control of Bokassa's men, the agents had to surreptitiously make their way onto the airstrip and light it up with special flares. But they had to move at just the right moment, just as the plane approached in the distance, to avoid being noticed by the airport authorities and alerting the guards.

The transport plane touched down and the soldiers, carefully briefed about the airport's layout, ran towards the control tower and a nearby garrison. They surrounded both buildings, and General Bozize, the garrison commander, ordered his men to put down their weapons. In the space of just fifteen minutes, the French had the airport under their control. Another two transport planes, carrying a 300-strong French military force, now landed, sealing off the road that led from the airport to the capital and then racing towards the country's government-controlled radio station. It was here, just before midnight, that Dacko made his own official statement on national radio, pronouncing 'the fall of the Emperor Bokassa the First' and 'appealing to France to send troops immediately to ensure security in our capital'. Meanwhile, at N'Djamena airport in neighbouring Chad, a senior French commander received the order to move his highly trained soldiers to Bangui to seize and seal the airport. The fighting force touched down soon after, just before 3 a.m., and immediately raced towards the capital. They were all surprised, and hugely relieved, by the almost complete lack of resistance they encountered along the way. Despite his delusions, the Emperor Bokassa plainly had almost no popular following. By this time Dacko had also been making rapid progress. Escorted by a strong contingent of French Special Forces, Dacko's limousine had headed away from the airport towards the capital. Using loudspeakers, one of the soldiers shouted that 'We have the money Bokassa stole from you'. He waved wads of cash and pointed to several large bags that were loaded with notes. The ploy worked. At every checkpoint and roadblock along the way, the guards quickly dropped their weapons and Dacko's limousine was waved on. By dusk, less than twenty-four hours after he had touched down, the capital had fallen. France's daring operation had paid off.

The vast riches of the African continent also lay behind the deposition and death of an African leader called François Tombalbaye three years before the coup in the Central African Republic. Once again, the 'Anglo-Saxons' were in the background.

Tombalbaye had become Chad's first leader after it won independence in 1960. The French struck the same secret deal with his government as they did with their other former colonies, giving it exclusive developmental rights to vital resources, but in the years that followed they became convinced that Chad had few if any resources of value. In 1966, for example, the Bureau de Recherches Pétrolières concluded that there were no oil deposits worth exploiting. Infuriated by the lack of any French interest, Tombalbaye turned instead to an American company, Continental Oil, and offered it exclusive prospecting rights. Continental's geologists argued that Chad was full of promise, not least because its immediate neighbour was oil-rich Libya, and quickly sent exploration teams into the country. Two years later, the Americans struck oil in Chad and prepared to start commercial drilling.

In Paris, these developments were watched with alarm, disappointment and fury. Michel Debré, the Minister for Foreign Affairs, considered Tombalbaye's links with the United States to be 'a true insult'. An American presence in Chad would not only deprive France of the resources that it felt entitled to but would also give Washington a presence in a country that was bordered by three of France's former colonies – Niger, Central African Republic and Cameroon. If the Americans established a cultural influence there, then Chad would, in French eyes, stand alongside neighbouring Nigeria to form a vast Anglophone power bloc.[256]

But the Stars and Stripes did not fly for long in Chad. In April 1975, before Continental Oil had a chance to exploit the country's oil, Tombalbaye was ousted by an army coup and shot dead. Few disputed that the old colonial master had a hand in the operation. A veteran French soldier, Colonel Camille Gourvenec, who was a head of both the Chadian intelligence service and its national guard, doubtlessly watched the developments with a sense of satisfaction.

The French had a long association with Chad and could not afford to let it slip out of their hands. This was not just because of oil. 'French troops aren't there for any economic motive – the country is one of the poorest in Africa and Paris is regularly forced to give it financial support – and there is no sentimental tie,' argued one French newspaper in 1969, although it downplayed the importance of petroleum. Chad also had an important strategic position. 'Located at the intersection of east and west Africa, and of Muslim and Black Africa, it acts as a bridgehead, a listening post and a frontline of radical sentiment,' pointed out one analyst. Paris was desperate to 'maintain a central link in Francophone Africa, given Chad's central position in Black Africa', knowing that any rebellion there would prove 'contagious' and spread elsewhere.[257]

If, as seems highly likely, this coup was French-inspired, it probably did not involve the SDECE, which was at this time under the directorship of a leader, Alexandre de Marenches, who had strong pro-American sympathies. After taking over the SDECE in 1970, he had sacked a great many officers who he suspected of harbouring anti-American views, and at the same time, he collaborated closely with the CIA. It was instead more likely to have been the work of the 'Africa Cell' that was so closely linked to the Élysée. For whatever de Marenches's personal leanings were, there were other policy-makers in Paris who remained much less sympathetic towards *les anglo-saxons*. This emerged less than three years after the Bokassa coup, as Britain fought Argentina over the Falklands Islands.

CHAPTER 11

MRS THATCHER'S 'VICTORIAN WAR': FRANCE AND THE FALKLANDS

On Thursday 10 June 1982, a top secret telegram was brought to the urgent attention of the British Prime Minister, Margaret Thatcher. It bore alarming news. Three days before, ran the 'UK Eyes Alpha' message, a British intelligence operative had caught sight of three warplanes, manufactured in France but bearing Peruvian markings, outside Dassault-Breguet's factory at Bordeaux-Mérignac airport in southern France. The 'contact' had also noticed a number of Peruvian personnel at the premises. Then, the following day, a Peruvian transport plane had paid a quick visit to the airport. In a very limited space of time, it had touched down and picked up a cargo, the contents of which were unknown.

The planes, which were the latest version of Dassault-Breguet's Super Étendard fighter-bomber, bore Peru's national insignia on their wings and undercarriage. But the government in Lima had never ordered these aircraft. 'We have no record of an order by Peru for Super Étendards,' the telegram pointed out. Nor did its armed forces use them. This covert activity, suggested the intelligence source, 'all added up to a possible circumvention of the French arms ban to [the] Argentines in the guise of a delivery to Peru'.[258]

Such a revelation could hardly have come at a more tense time, because Britain was at war with the likely end-users. And Margaret Thatcher, her Cabinet, commanders and general public, were well aware how much damage the Super Étendard could inflict on any enemy force. Boasting a range of around 400 miles – although it could do more if refuelled in the air – and using a highly sophisticated radar system, it was capable of locating and attacking an enemy target over long distances. Then, once it had found its target, the Super Étendard could launch the single most feared weapon in the Argentine arsenal. This was the AM39 missile, better known as the 'Exocet'.

The 'air-to-surface' Exocet was designed by its French manufacturer, Aérospatiale, to strike and destroy even the biggest and most heavily guarded warships. When it was fired from the Étendard, it fell like a stone for about ten metres before its booster rockets suddenly flared into life, propelling the missile at ferocious speed towards an enemy ship. Then it skimmed just a metre or so above the sea as it shot forward, perhaps over a distance of up to thirty or even forty miles, and used its own radar and computer-guidance to identify and 'lock on' to its prey before slamming into it with a hugely potent explosive force.

The missile's sheer destructive power had become terrifyingly clear on 4 May, when a Super Étendard had fired a French-supplied Exocet at HMS *Sheffield*, a British destroyer operating in the South Atlantic. The Argentine pilot had used his specialised training to head towards the British ships at a daringly low altitude, rendering his plane extremely difficult to detect. Then, at a range of several miles, he had fired two missiles. One missed its target but the other scored a direct hit that killed twenty men and injured another twenty-four.

The ship smouldered and finally sank, and a shocked and horrified British public held its breath as the war for the Falklands continued.

But at almost exactly the same time that the intelligence operative in Bordeaux had made his alarming discovery, the British embassy in Lima also picked up another disturbing report. The French government, the diplomats found out, had agreed to release eight Exocet missiles to the Peruvian government but had not determined a delivery date. There was a real possibility, in other words, that someone in Paris had quietly authorised an early delivery, and that the Peruvian transport plane had collected this deadly cargo from Bordeaux.[259]

On that June day in 1982, Mrs Thatcher and her most senior advisers had carefully deliberated the meaning and significance of the intelligence reports before them. Ever since Argentina and Britain had gone to war over the Falklands Islands two months before, President François Mitterrand had promised the British leader that the French government would impose an immediate, although temporary, ban on arms exports to Argentina. But now France's main defence exporters, which were state-owned and closely monitored by government agencies, appeared to be supplying extremely valuable arms to a Latin American country that was not known to have ordered them. Before the crisis began, Aérospatiale had supplied Argentina with five of these deadly missiles, and perhaps more were now on their way.

Like every crisis, the Argentine invasion of the Falklands Islands on 2 April was sudden and unexpected, even if, after the event, it also seemed to have been curiously predictable. Ever since he had taken the reins of power in Buenos Aires the previous December, General Leopoldo Galtieri had been determined to step up diplomatic pressure on Britain over the future of the islands, claiming that the 'Malvinas' had always belonged to Argentina. They had been unjustly seized by British sailors in 1833, he argued, and the Union Jack had therefore never had any right to fly there. A long succession of regimes in Buenos Aires had made such a claim, but in the spring of 1982 Galtieri and his Foreign Minister, Nicanor Costa Méndez, had started to lobby particularly hard to attract more international interest and sympathy over the matter. But although the Argentines had warned Britain that they meant business, and even flown their warplanes provocatively over the islands, the invasion in early April nonetheless took Mrs Thatcher's government wholly by surprise.

Keen to prove her mettle, the 'Iron Lady' had immediately ordered an armed response, and within just three days British commanders had assembled a large task force which on 5 April set sail from Portsmouth, undertaking a 6,000-mile journey to the South Atlantic to confront the invaders. Composed of more than 100 ships, which were carrying nearly 30,000 troops, the task force was an impressive sight, and large, cheering crowds had flocked to the Portsmouth quayside to wave off the two big aircraft carriers, *Hermes* and *Invincible*, as they set sail.

British government ministers and their military chiefs all hoped that they would not need to use force and that the mere threat of war would prompt Galtieri to withdraw his forces from the Falklands. But if the crisis continued then there was a huge risk of serious British casualties or even outright military disaster. British resources were stretched to breaking point and the Argentines, particularly their air force, might strike lucky: if a single Exocet missile hit one of the two carriers then the task force would suffer massive losses, which would force London to abort the entire operation. Britain would be humiliated and Margaret Thatcher, having badly misjudged the mission's viability, would have had to take responsibility for the fiasco and resign.

Fortunately, however, the British government did have foreign friends to count on, including the French President, François

Mitterrand. The morning after the invasion he had phoned Thatcher to declare his support and sympathy for Britain and for her personally. He was the first foreign leader to do so, and his message touched the Prime Minister deeply. 'I shall never forget that quick, timely and energetic gesture,' she later said.

François Mitterrand and Margaret Thatcher, 1981.

Mitterrand promised to place an immediate embargo on the supply of French arms to both Argentina and to Peru, whose government could easily forward them into Galtieri's hands. After the sinking of the *Sheffield*, he also ordered military chiefs to dispatch a squadron of Super Étendards to a British airbase so that RAF pilots and aviation experts could get a closer idea of what confronted them. Given the huge battlefield capabilities of the Exocet, and the material sacrifices that the embargo would place on French defence manufacturers, the President was immediately fêted in London, in the words of the British Defence Secretary John Nott, as Britain's 'greatest ally'.[260]

It helped matters that Mitterrand had a close rapport with the British leader. Despite his notorious womanising, he was said to have been 'one of the few in Europe who treated her as an equal', which Thatcher 'appreciated'. On one occasion, he was said to have been more fulsome in his description, remarking that 'she has the eyes of Caligula, and the mouth of Marilyn Monroe'. But there were other, more compelling reasons why he lent his support. The President had once explained that he 'naturally supported Britain, which was an ally' partly because his views and attitudes, like those of his British counterpart, had been so profoundly shaped during the struggle against Nazi Germany. The two countries, Mitterrand pointed out, 'had fought in two world wars' and as a result France 'owed a real debt of gratitude to Britain'. In 1943 and 1944, he had spent three and a half months in London, having been spirited out of occupied France, and then back in again, courtesy of the Royal Navy. Britain's ambassador to Paris at the time, Sir John Fretwell, noted this 'debt' and 'warm regard stemming from World War II', which he thought also explained why 'French public opinion is broadly in favour of Britain'.[261]

Mitterrand was also well aware that he could easily find himself in the same situation as the British. France still had its own overseas territories that other foreign countries claimed as their own: the French, noted Fretwell, were 'feeling vulnerable' about their own colonial possessions and knew that an Argentine annexation of the Falklands could easily encourage other would-be aggressors. An example was Madagascar, which, since winning independence in 1960, had continued to proclaim a right of possession over a number of French territories, notably Mayotte and Réunion in the Indian Ocean. The ambassador also noted that Mitterrand wanted to be seen in London and Washington as a reliable Western ally, particularly when, as a socialist President whose Cabinet included several

Communist ministers, his credentials as a true ally of Britain and America had sometimes been called into question. He knew that the support of the two Anglophone nations was too important to risk a serious rift.[262]

But, as the top secret telegram of 10 June suggests, France's relations with Britain and Argentina during the Falklands crisis were in fact much less straightforward than the President's official position would suppose. French defence contractors gave covert support to the Argentines with the complicity of some government officials – exactly who and how many remains unclear – harbouring, in all likelihood, a degree of anti-British sentiment. And towards the end of May, Anglo-French relations were plunged into their deepest crisis since 1945, when Mitterrand's government looked ready to break its arms embargo to Latin America. Had the crisis continued for just a short while longer, then these tensions between London and Paris would in all probability have erupted into a furious diplomatic rift.

When the Falklands crisis began, British officials always expected to encounter some hostility from certain quarters in Paris. What they did not know, however, was how much sympathy President Mitterrand would harbour for the critics and enemies of Britain, and how tight a rein he would, or could, keep on their activities.

The most influential and important anti-British lobbyists in the French capital were representatives of the defence industry. In the words of British officials, this lobby was 'powerful and vocal, and capable of exercising strong pressure'. It had a vested commercial interest in supporting Galtieri's regime not because they necessarily wanted to see Britain being defeated but simply because Latin America in general, and Argentina in particular, was a major arms market. 'The strongest pressure on the government to break ranks with the UK', noted Fretwell, 'came from the arms lobby.'[263]

The defence industry was just one beneficiary of a wider drive that

Paris had initiated in the late 1960s to improve ties with Argentina. This may have been motivated by de Gaulle's wish to push American influence out of a region that was full of commercial potential. But the strength of such interest in the area probably also reflected the fact that opportunities in more traditional marketplaces were seen to be dwindling. 'It is perfectly acceptable for France to get involved in Central America since we cannot confine ourselves to Africa,' wrote Bernard Destremau, the French ambassador to Buenos Aires. He added that 'although this region has not hitherto been important, it had now clearly become essential ... France is also in a state of evolution and that integrates us into this strategy'.[264]

By 1980 Argentina had become France's second biggest trade partner in Latin America, and the French were the fourth biggest foreign investor there. 'The French government regards Franco-Argentine relations with the greatest importance', Quai officials wrote in 1980. During the presidency of Giscard d'Estaing, numerous trade delegations visited the country to help French exporters increase their market share, particularly in foodstuffs, petrochemicals, electronics, telecommunications, hydro-electric power and defence. Special docking facilities were even set up at Bordeaux to facilitate trade.[265]

Latin America was also a potentially huge arms market and in 1968, French defence companies started to export weapons to Buenos Aires. This was a tricky balancing act. On the one hand, if France did not supply Argentina, then other foreign countries would fill the market gap. For example, West Germany, Israel, Brazil and the Soviet Union were all showing increasing interest in the Argentine market at this time. But on the other hand, Argentina had a notoriously dire human rights record that repelled every French government: during the late 1970s, 'a brutal and often indiscriminate repression lasted over a period of four years', pointed out a Foreign Ministry document, 'and led to the disappearance of between 8–15,000 people, fifteen of whom were

French citizens'. Paris balanced these competing pressures by authorising the sale of arms that the Argentines could use to deter or repel a
foreign attack, while refusing licences for weapons 'that could be used
to maintain law and order or against (domestic) insurgents'. At the
same time, in their discussions with General Galtieri and other Argentine leaders, French diplomats did raise the fate of *les disparus* – the
thousands of political dissenters who had simply disappeared without
trace – even if Paris was nonetheless also prepared to 'ignore calls to
harden its line towards the Argentine government'. The Quai emphasised that, in all its dealings, it needed to show *une certaine prudence*.[266]

At the beginning of 1978, Giscard's government provided Buenos
Aires with a $200 million low-interest loan to buy an impressive
new armoury from French manufacturers. Contracts were signed for
thirty Exocet missiles, sixteen Super Étendard planes and 200 anti-
tank missiles as well as helicopters and rockets. On 28 June 1980, the
Argentine Foreign Minister, Carlos Pastor, also began a four-day visit
to France and discussed 'the acquisition of arms' as well as 'nuclear
installations' in his homeland, although it is unclear if this was a
peaceful, and legal, programme of civilian energy or a totally illicit
project to develop a warhead. But in the months that preceded the
Falklands invasion, French arms deliveries to Argentina were erratic
and by December 1981 only five Exocets and nine warplanes had
arrived. Paris was still determined, however, 'to maintain the strong
military links, as made evident from the imminent delivery of the
Super Étendard'.[267]

As the war for the Falklands continued throughout May 1982,
some French defence companies attempted to support and supply the
Argentines, although there is no reason to suppose that these efforts
had the approval of any complicitous, and duplicitous, government
officials in Paris. These companies had everything to gain. On the
eve of the Falklands War, Aérospatiale could sell one of its Exocet

missiles for £200,000. But just six weeks later, Argentine undercover agents in Paris were reputedly offering £350,000 to acquire a weapon that had the capability to determine the outcome of the war. At the same time, French suppliers knew that if they pulled out of Argentina then they could face retribution after the cessation of hostilities, or simply acquire a reputation for unreliability.

On 21 May, just as British soldiers were landing on the Falklands and starting to head for Argentine positions, British customs officials arrested a Dassault-Breguet employee, Jean-Pierre Leroux, who was attempting to procure, from a British manufacturer, a number of components that could be used in the Exocet. 'Cases like this – large quantity, no export licences, no indication of ultimate end user – cannot be ignored,' wrote an alarmed official in Whitehall. But Leroux's undercover operation did not appear to have any sanction from anyone in Paris, just as the British manufacturer was of course operating without the approval of the British government.[268]

Whitehall was by this stage aware that some French defence companies were exploiting the war for their own commercial ends. 'Since the onset of operations in the South Atlantic', wrote a top aide at the Ministry of Defence, 'we have had indications that the French were taking opportunities to point out to potential customers the apparent success of French equipment sold to Argentines and to run down the performance of British equipment.' Such 'French mischief-making' was perpetrated by some government-funded publications, even if Mitterrand himself and his ministers were probably unaware of it: one magazine that aired 'particularly tendentious material of this kind', for example, had 'close links with the official French arms sales machine'.[269]

This led to an alarming possibility – that those companies had a strong commercial interest in actively assisting Argentina to strike the British, using the damage as solid evidence of their weapons' superiority. If their equipment proved effective, then other countries would turn to French suppliers: destroying British ships, in other words, was a superb marketing exercise for French arms manufacturers. And this seemed all the more plausible when, on 31 May, as the British and Argentines fought increasingly bitter battles on the Falklands, the London *Daily Mail* published a startling report.

The newspaper claimed that just two days before HMS *Sheffield* was hit and sunk, a team of French technicians had given Argentine experts 'detailed instructions' on how to use the Exocet. Quoting 'private reports', the article alleged that the company had 'wanted to see the missile in action' and 'decided to send two technical experts to Rio de Janeiro', ostensibly on 'holiday'. From Rio, continued the report, 'they could have gone to Argentina' but had been stopped by the French government. Instead the Aérospatiale experts made a series of phone calls, lasting seven hours in total, from their offices in France to give the Argentines the technical support they needed. By doing so, continued the report, they had 'defied the orders of the French government, which has strictly adhered to its promise to embargo all arms deliveries to Argentina'.

The devastating firepower of the French-made Exocet missile became clear during the Falklands War, when HMS *Sheffield* (left) was sunk with the loss of twenty lives.

Perhaps the French authorities could have more closely monitored the Exocet experts, whose highly specialised knowledge would obviously have been so sought after. Or perhaps the phone calls had never taken place. But the report seemed to confirm that Mitterrand's officials were at least making a determined effort to enforce the presidential embargo, even if it might not be watertight. Whitehall distanced itself from the article, pointing out that the French government had been 'entirely cooperative and has taken a number of measures to ensure that "Aérospatiale" toe the line'. The British government was 'confident', continued a Foreign Office minister, 'that "Aérospatiale" have made no "Exocet" missiles available to Argentina since the invasion of the Falklands ... and have also suspended delivery of "Exocet" missiles to Peru for the time being, since neither we nor they can be sure Peru will not pass them on to Argentina'. He added that 'our continued representations to the French authorities have brought home to them the need to keep "Aérospatiale" under control'. However, the government response cautioned that 'we cannot be certain that they have not provided some form of technical collaboration in respect of missiles or systems already delivered. We have no confirmation of the claim in the *Daily Mail*.'[270]

In general, the French government was undoubtedly working hard to enforce the embargo: at Le Havre on 20 May, for example, its officials had intercepted and halted an Aérospatiale effort to sell eight missiles to Peru, preventing them from being loaded onto a Peruvian warship. But there were, nonetheless, specific individuals at various levels of government, within particular departments of particular ministries, who harboured sympathy for the position of the French arms industry. In some cases this may have been because in the early 1980s the French government desperately needed to redress its imbalance of payments. It was importing far more from abroad than it was exporting, and selling arms to foreign markets reaped vast earnings that helped it to undo this imbalance. But another driving force, at least as important as economic pressure, was the anti-British sentiment that existed within the ranks of the French government, its bureaucracy and its state-owned industries.

In one of his dispatches to the Prime Minister, Fretwell noted these 'currents flowing in the opposite direction'. Some of them sprang from predictable sources, such as the French Communist Party which, like its British counterpart, condemned Britain's 'colonialist' war even if its members were also wrong-footed by their bitter opposition to Galtieri's militaristic, brutal, 'fascist' regime. French Communists, the ambassador pointed out, were taking a 'stridently anti-British' tone, arguing that 'imperialism's hands are "blood-stained"' and blaming the crisis on murderous folly on the part of Mrs Thatcher'. Such opposition to Britain's 'colonial adventure' was not of mere academic importance because Mitterrand had appointed several Communists to his Cabinet, including the transport minister, Charles Fiterman, who 'had begun to feel increasingly uncomfortable' about France's official support for Britain's war.[271]

But Fretwell was also aware that not only were there 'fears that Britain was going too far and was liable to drag France into a war' but also that 'it seemed to irk some Frenchmen that "decadent" Britain was proving that it was a power to be reckoned with after all'. Doubts about Britain's policy, he continued, were 'most widespread amongst the "professionals" – politicians, journalists and civil servants'. In general, he continued, there was

> a tendency for alignments on the Falklands issue to parallel those in
> previous issues in which the French have been divided on whether
> to espouse a cause championed by Britain. One elder statesman
> told me recently that those who were against Britain in 1940 had

re-emerged against us ... this of course applies mostly on the right
wing of French politics.[272]

It was essentially anti-British feeling that explained why so many
senior French officials, notably in the Foreign Ministry, argued that
the Falklands really belonged to Argentina. Before the war, some
civil servants in Paris even wrote that 'the Malvinas are an integral
part of Argentina'. After the invasion, they reiterated their position.
'The French do not accept the British claim to sovereignty over the
Falklands', as Fretwell noted. This view was endorsed by Mitterrand
himself, and on 14 June François Gutmann, the Secretary-General
of the French Foreign Ministry, infuriated British officials by arguing for a 'face-saving formula' which was 'unacceptable' to London.
'Even if comprehensible from the point of view of their own self-
interest,' wrote Fretwell, 'the French attitude is deplorable.' But there
was no reason why anyone in Paris needed to express any views on
the matter: if they had wanted to win defence contracts in Buenos
Aires then they could have silently maintained a neutral position.
France had also taken this anti-British position on the Falklands long
before South America became an important arms market, implying
that it was not just commercially motivated.[273]

During the Falklands conflict, anti-British sentiments were soon
voiced by senior officials in French ministries. In London on 7 April,
the French ambassador, Emmanuel de Margerie, branded Margaret
Thatcher as a 'Victorian, imperialist and obstinate' individual who
had 'a tendency to get carried away by her combative instincts'. And
on 15 May, Le Figaro published several leaked documents, all of which
were internal Foreign Ministry memoranda, which caused the French
authorities serious embarrassment. One had been written on 22 April
by a very senior director in the Quai, Bernard Dorin, who labelled
the entire Falklands episode as a British 'fiasco' and ventured stinging

criticisms of Thatcher's government for ever allowing the Argentines to invade as well as for its subsequent response. Five days later, the Foreign Minister, Claude Cheysson, then penned a document which damningly referred to the 'self-importance of a great and *ancien* power [that has] a knee-jerk and fundamental sense of contempt for every aspect of the Latin people, and of untrustworthy foreign people'.[274]

During his twelve months in the role as French Foreign Minister, 52-year-old Claude Cheysson had never refrained from speaking his mind. He liked, as he freely admitted, 'to shoot from the hip' and was proud to point out that 'I have heard the president say some twenty times that I'm the least diplomatic of all the diplomatic corps'. An example of this came in the very tense and difficult hours that followed the assassination of the Egyptian leader, Anwar Sadat, when Cheysson tactlessly but unashamedly stated in public that his death would 'remove an obstacle' to the advent of peace in the Middle East.

Whitehall officials were not too surprised when news broke of Cheysson's memorandum on the Falklands conflict, since the Foreign Minister had by this stage started to argue quite openly that the conflict was a British 'colonial war'. When the conflict had started, he had initially shown a mixed reaction. On the one hand, he had condemned Argentina's 'aggression' which was 'unprovoked' by 'a very close ally', and argued that France was 'at the side of those who defend law and international agreements'. On the other hand, he was far from supportive of the British use of force to resolve the conflict, calling instead only for 'diplomatic means' to resolve an 'old dispute'. But as the conflict continued into June, his position hardened. Arguing that France had 'never recognised [Britain's] sovereignty over the Falklands', he added: 'There are limits to this conflict which I fully intend to soon make known.' He also accepted that France's relations with Latin America 'were clearly liable to be jeopardized', but that he would do everything in his power to prevent that. Within key ministries in Paris, such sentiments were rife. 'A lot of officials in Paris hated Margaret Thatcher,' admitted a former French intelligence official, although it is difficult to be sure if such sentiments were directed against Britain, women in positions of authority, or the Prime Minister and her policies in particular.[275]

In the French Foreign Ministry, such anti-British sentiments merged with commercial and economic pressures. Parisian officials, remarked the British ambassador, 'seemed to see their schemes for extending French influence in Latin America going wrong' as a result of the war. On one occasion, Fretwell was given 'a sermon by the Secretary General of the Quai about the danger of poisoning the atmosphere between Europe and Latin America if we drove the Argentines off the islands'. This in turn created a 'curious psychological climate' in Paris, where officials 'regarded a ban on arms sales as 'an exceptional favour' to the British.[276]

Such sentiments did not necessarily carry any weight, provided President Mitterrand stuck to his pro-British position and his officials also enforced and supervised his imposition of a total arms embargo on Argentina. But as the war progressed, and as Cheysson continued to press him to change course and side with Argentina, Mitterrand appeared to waver.

Towards the end of May, the war entered a critical stage. British troops were still fighting bitter battles with the Argentines, but the ships of the Royal Navy, which were transporting reinforcements and supplies, were desperately vulnerable to further Exocet attacks. On 25 May, the Argentine air force had struck a British transport ship, *Atlantic Conveyor*, with a single Exocet, wiping out in one stroke her invaluable cargo of troop-carrying helicopters.

Before the war began, the Argentines had five Exocet missiles. But by now two had sunk British ships, one had missed its target and another had been test-fired in a training exercise. With just one missile left, Galtieri's commanders were desperate to acquire more, knowing that just a handful would tip the military balance sharply in their favour.

On 29 May, Mitterrand had telephoned Thatcher to inform her that he was deliberating upon a Peruvian order for the missiles. Peru had made its request before the onset of the Falklands War and Paris had subsequently shelved any decision, refusing to grant an export licence because Peru was an ally of Argentina. Thatcher and her aides entertained no doubt about the missiles' true destination, and Mitterrand's phone call – a clear sign that his willingness to support Britain was wavering – infuriated her. France 'was now releasing weapons to Peru that would certainly be passed on to Argentina for use against us', she warned, adding that 'this would have a devastating effect on the relationship between our two countries. Indeed, it would have a disastrous effect on the alliance as a whole.' At the same time, her senior diplomatic adviser, Sir Michael Palliser, met with François Gutmann and 'made it absolutely clear to him that this was a matter of crucial importance to the Anglo-French relationship in general and to the Prime Minister's own relationship with the president in particular'. Britain's threat to sever diplomatic relations with France worked: the following day a senior French diplomat said the Peruvians would be told the weapons could not be sent for 'political reasons'.[277]

British diplomats knew that Mitterrand was being more cooperative than other French political leaders would probably have been if they occupied the Élysée. Fretwell noted that 'Mitterrand himself wavered from time to time under the various pressures', but added that 'Giscard or Chirac would have been less keen to support us at the beginning [and] would have been even less inclined to have stuck with us at the end'. However, even Mitterrand was prepared to exploit Britain's vulnerability at this crucial hour: while Britain was focused on the war, noted Whitehall officials, the French President 'chose to move against us quite ruthlessly in the Community, over the agricultural prices and budget issue; and he went on to threaten us gratuitously with a crisis over the nature of British membership'. At the same time, as the conflict continued into June he had appeared to warn that his patience was wearing thin: 'While this war must not turn into a war of revenge', he told a press conference on 9 June, 'there are limits to this conflict which I fully intend to make known at the right time, which will not be long.'[278]

Mitterrand's support had wavered, but his position remained uncertain when, just over a week later, the British embassy in Lima learnt that Paris had agreed, in principle, to deliver Exocets to Peru but had not determined a delivery date. What is clear, however, is that there were individuals within the French government who were actively supporting the Argentine war effort.

On 12 May, the British Secret Intelligence Service reported that 'a team of (French) technicians had arrived in Argentina to try and discover how the Argentines had done the job' of configuring the Super Étendards to the Exocets. Then, twelve days later, 'a further secret report suggested that SNIAS [Aérospatiale] were being foolish in observing the French embargo, since other companies, including Dassault-Breguet, were not'. The press had also picked up the story, and on 11 May, the London *Times* had reported that French personnel were inside Argentina in a 'purely maintenance role'.[279]

But after the war Isabel Hilton, a *Sunday Times* reporter, alleged that this French team had really taken a much more proactive role. Her source was an Argentine air force pilot who told her about a French technical team that had arrived, before the Falklands War broke out, at the Espora Aeronaval base in Bahía Blanca to advise and assist the Argentine military on using the Exocet missile. Composed of nine members, seven of whom were employees of Dassault-Breguet, the team had a great deal of knowledge and skills at its disposal. But in what would appear to be a clear and major breach of the government's embargo, its members had stayed in Argentina throughout the conflict and actively helped the Argentines prepare their Exocets for launch.

Hilton had been taken to meet the team's leader, Hervé Colin, who admitted that his fellow technicians had done more than just help to fit the missiles to the planes, which was something the Argentines probably had the capability to do themselves. Instead, they had carried out a number of technical tests on the missile, one of which was particularly valuable for the Argentine forces. 'The verification process involves determining if the missile launcher was functioning correctly or not,' Colin told Hilton. 'Three of the launchers failed. We located the source of the problem and that was it. The rest was simple.' But with French assistance, the Argentines were able to rectify three previously faulty missile launchers, which they then used to fire the Exocets at British ships.[280]

Years later, Sir John Nott admitted that the British Cabinet had known about the team's presence in Buenos Aires, although he downplayed its importance. At the time, Foreign Office diplomats accepted that the *Sunday Times* stories, published on 25 July and 1 August, had 'enough circumstantial evidence to give them a ring of truth'. British officials also admitted that 'it has always been something of a mystery how the Argentines managed to complete the delicate final stages of preparing the AM39s for launching. The French themselves did not think that they had the technical capability to do this.' As a result, Whitehall sought 'urgent clarification from the French government, who have denied any knowledge of such assistance and have set up a special enquiry'.[281]

On 27 July, in a joint statement, the foreign and defence ministries in Paris announced the results of the investigation that Mitterrand had personally ordered into the British allegations. Before the war had even begun, ran the statement, Dassault-Breguet had ordered the technical team not to help the Argentines in the event of an armed conflict. The ministries were also satisfied that it had followed these procedures.

But the British government admitted that this response was evasive. 'It is fair to say', British Foreign Minister, Cranley Onslow, told Parliament, 'that the French statement does not contain a detailed point-by-point rebuttal' of the *Sunday Times* article. There were several unanswered questions. Had Dassault-Breguet informed anyone in the French government about the team's presence in Argentina? How sure was anyone in France, in the government or in the defence industry, that the embargo was being respected? And why had the team not been ordered to leave Argentina, even just temporarily? Colin, in his interview, had told Hilton that no one in the French government had ever asked his team to pull out of Argentina, and the Paris statement of 27 July did not address this point.[282]

It is inconceivable that some senior officials in Paris, in the defence, foreign and intelligence ministries, and in the Élysée, had not known about the presence of the team inside Argentina. But it is likely that they nonetheless chose not to disclose the facts, despite their supreme importance, to the President. As a secret British government document pointed out after the war:

> It is quite possible that Aérospatiale and Dassault-Breguet could
> have decided ... not to send any instructions to their joint team
> in Argentina to down tools or come home during the conflict.
> We know they were very keen to see their aircraft/missiles in oper-
> ation, and have since made much of their 'success' with a view to
> boosting sales elsewhere. The French government may well not
> have had any knowledge of this, or may have preferred not to ask
> the companies too many questions.[283]

Equally, there were key individuals within Dassault-Breguet and Aérospatiale who were responsible not just for supervising their company's foreign missions but for informing the Quai's Department of American Affairs what was happening on the ground. For example, in December 1978, Jacques Bence, the head of Aérospatiale's international affairs team, had met with the Quai's directorate and informed it of several projects inside Argentina that his company was pursuing. Just over three years later, it appears that either Bence's successor, or his contacts within the Foreign Ministry, had failed to pass similar information on to the Élysée.[284]

A former chief of staff in the French foreign intelligence service later admitted that his department was fully aware of the team's presence inside Argentina, telling a BBC reporter that the DGSE (formerly the SDECE) had an informer amongst the members of the technical team who was able to give them some information about what the Argentine military was doing. Since the French were very short of inside information about events and developments in Buenos Aires, they kept the team in place. But the former spy failed to explain why his service had not flagged the issue to the Quai or directly to the President's Office.[285]

Departmental officials may have failed to disclose such vital information to the highest levels in Paris because they did not want the French defence industry to risk losing such a valuable customer. Or it may have been because they harboured anti-British feelings. As the war progressed, these sentiments may have started to merge. In particular, some senior French officials started to feel animosity towards the British over the fate of an Argentine prisoner of war, Lieutenant Commander Astiz.

Captured by British forces in the early stages of the war and subsequently taken to England, Astiz was one of the Argentine henchmen who had been implicated in the disappearance of two French nuns,

Alice Domon and Leonie Duquet. French officials were keen to question him as soon as they heard of his detainment and in the course of May they made several approaches to Britain's ambassador in France, requesting permission for a formal interview. But the Argentines protested, arguing that Astiz was a captive of the British and that under the Geneva Convention the French had no right to even meet him.

The Foreign Office regarded Astiz as 'odious' but took a characteristically law-abiding approach to the matter and informed Paris that it could not agree to its requests. But the refusal stung a number of very senior officials in the Quai, notably Gutmann, who was 'shocked to find that Britain was being so obstructive' over Astiz. In the course of May, French anger started to mount and caused diplomatic tensions. 'The French refusal to take no for an answer is awkward,' noted a senior Foreign Office official. 'Their latest response is a rather crude attempt to pressure us.' Most alarmingly, 'Gutmann came close to making a direct and overt link between the sort of help we are seeking from the French on such matters as the supply of arms by third parties and the cooperation they are seeking from us on Astiz.'[286]

Anglo-French tensions over Astiz were particularly strong just at the time that a British spy detected Peruvian activity at Bordeaux. On exactly the same day, 7 June, that French warplanes were seen with Peruvian markings, Gutmann had phoned the British ambassador in Paris to 'express concern' about the Astiz affair. And it was at the same time that the British embassy in Lima had picked up on alarming news about the delivery of Exocet missiles to Peru. This raises the possibility that senior officials in Paris were willing to turn a blind eye to Argentina's arms procurement drive, or conceivably encourage it, out of pique towards the British. Such acrimony may also help explain why, towards the end of May, the French allegedly refused requests to provide more detailed information about the

Exocet missiles that might have enabled British scientists to develop a way of jamming its radar.[287]

But it was not long before the battle for the Falklands was over. On the night of 11 June, British forces began to assault a mountain range that surrounded the capital, Port Stanley. They encountered patchy resistance and after three days of fighting the commander of the Argentine garrison, General Mario Menéndez, surrendered. In the course of this brief conflict, the Exocet had sunk three British ships – HMS *Glamorgan* had been struck on 12 June – and taken the lives of forty-six men, out of a total loss of 255.

British officials knew that they had won back the Falklands just as their relations with France, as well as their military capabilities, had reached breaking-point. 'If the conflict had gone on much longer or if the British success had been only partial,' Fretwell pointed out, then 'Mitterrand's support for Britain would probably have become more hesitant and qualified'. But though the battle was over, the war was still not quite won. After the June ceasefire, tensions between Britain and France quickly resurfaced when, on 10 August, Paris lifted its embargo on arms exports much more quickly than London had wanted.[288]

This was extremely troubling for the British. Even after the Argentine surrender, the acquisition of just a few Exocets would have allowed Galtieri's regime to launch a belated but devastating counter-attack against an enemy that had just declared victory. The British had immediately flown a number of warplanes to the main runway at Port Stanley but there was still a glaring weakness in their defences: because they lacked early-warning radar, there was a real chance that the Argentines could undertake a sudden attack on the islands, launching their missiles before the Royal Air Force even knew enemy planes were airborne. General Galtieri had not formally surrendered, even if his commanders on the ground had been forced to raise a white flag. If his regime came under heavy political pressure at home, as it did in the wake of the campaign, then he could have been sorely tempted to lash out at the British.

Whitehall was alarmed to discover, almost as soon as the June ceasefire took effect, of France's plans. 'The French have made it clear', wrote a Foreign Office diplomat, 'that they are under pressure from Argentina and Latin American countries (with whom they are keen to restore their relations) not only to resume arms supplies but to support a United Nations resolution calling for negotiations over the future of the Falklands.' Nor was it just these regimes that were putting pressure on Paris, particularly the Defence Minister, Charles Hernu. So too was Dassault-Breguet and SNIAS, which both 'strongly opposed any limitation on sales', and the leading trade unions, which wanted to boost the arms trade and reduce unemployment at a time when France's economy was stricken by recession.[289]

At some point in the weeks that followed, Paris relented. Nine Super Étendards were secretly shipped out of Nantes Saint-Nazaire in the course of November and December, while on the night of 20 November a cargo of five Exocets was also flown out of France. The French undertook 'a carefully designed military plan' to keep the operation a secret, Whitehall experts reckoned, 'to avoid British interference'. The deliveries formed an important part of a major Argentine drive to modernise its armed forces in the light of the Falklands War and the lessons it had taught them. The Argentine commanders were determined to make their forces more professional than before, and put more emphasis upon the 'quality' rather than 'quantity' of their resources. The press also reported that Paris had signed new contracts with Buenos Aires for additional planes, but these reports were not confirmed.[290]

In London, officials expressed their 'disappointment' and raised the matter at the highest level, but the sums of money involved were simply too great for the French to ignore. By October, the Argentine procurement team, led by a Captain Alfredo Corti, was reputedly offering £1 million, more than three times the ordinary market price, for each Exocet. Aérospatiale's directors had reason to feel pleased, since by this time they had a 'very full order book from other customers' after their weapons had proved their worth in the war. British commanders now rushed to upgrade their radar in a desperate bid to contain the resurgent Argentine threat.[291]

France's stance on the Falklands campaign, in other words, was much more complex than is generally supposed. Perhaps it is significant that Mrs Thatcher herself found Jacques Chirac easier to deal with than Mitterrand 'because his public actions bore a greater similarity to his privately expressed views'. And when Sir John Nott was asked if 'the French are duplicitous people', he gave an unhesitating reply: 'Of course the French are duplicitous people – and they always have been!'[292]

Three years later, French hostility towards *les anglo-saxons* once again helped to cause serious tension with other countries. When, in the summer of 1985, French secret services agents bombed the *Rainbow Warrior*, their targets were not just Greenpeace, the well-known environmental organisation that owned and operated the vessel, but 'Anglo-Saxons' across the wider region.

CHAPTER 12

GREENPEACE AND THE REMNANTS OF FRENCH EMPIRE

One Sunday morning in July 1985, a middle-aged man was taking his usual stroll around the harbour in his home city of Whangarei in the far north of New Zealand, photographing the scenery and the passing yachts, sailors and wildlife. The yachts were always an impressive and uplifting sight as they glided so silently to and from the Pacific Ocean, or when they were all moored together on the quayside. Watching them on that particular day was all the more enjoyable because the weather was pleasant, quite a bit cooler than the often uncomfortable summer temperatures of December and January.

In such relatively quiet surroundings, anything out of the ordinary quickly stands out, particularly in the eyes of an amateur photographer who had lived and worked in Whangarei nearly all his life. And as he wandered around the harbour, he immediately noticed a relative rarity – the presence of a yacht with a large French flag draped around the stern. He hadn't previously seen many French boats here, thousands of miles away from home.

Intrigued, he went closer and saw a young woman sitting on the deck. She was all alone, engrossed in a newspaper and apparently oblivious to anyone who was around her. He wanted to ask her about the journey and thought she might be grateful for the chat. Most sailors were friendly, particularly after a long trip, and spoke freely to passers-by. But on this occasion, the young woman took no notice of his approach, even though she must have been well aware that he was around. She ignored him and just carried on reading.

After several minutes, he wandered off, disappointed and frustrated at the lack of any response, as well as feeling a bit hurt and angry. A hundred or so yards away, he turned round and noticed that the young woman had disappeared into the cabin. Now there was no one on the deck at all. He stopped and waited for a bit longer and then saw two youngish men emerge from the cabin and use a small ladder to clamber their way onto the quay. He watched them walk in his direction and then continue past him, speaking in French as they did so, before meeting a third man, who was a short distance away.

He sensed that something wasn't right, though couldn't explain why, and raised his camera and pointed it at the three men. But one of them saw him do this and started walking quickly, almost running, towards him in a menacing way. The New Zealander suddenly felt a strong sense of threat, particularly as there was hardly anyone else around, and suddenly pointed his camera in another direction, making it look as though all along he had really been following the path of a bird in flight. The Frenchman now stopped and backed off. The sense of threat was gone but the middle-aged man had sensed danger and walked off, in the opposite direction, as quickly as he could. For the first time in many years, he was genuinely afraid.[293]

At around the same time, a French couple, Alain and Sophie Turenges, were checking out of a hotel in the coastal town of Paihia, a few hours' drive further north. The owners of the Beachcomber Hotel had found them to be very pleasant guests, always polite, relaxed and helpful. That morning they had enjoyed their breakfasts and then started to move their luggage out of their room and into a camper van parked outside. The manageress was a bit surprised by the large amount of baggage they were taking with them, particularly as they seemed to have more of it now than when they first arrived.

Then her dog, running around outside the hotel, jumped into the van. Suddenly Alain's whole manner changed and a look of extreme anger came over his face. He stayed calm but moved quickly to pick up the dog, a small terrier, and firmly put it back outside. Then he positioned himself between the staff outside and the van door so that no one could see what was inside. He quickly slammed the rear door shut but still seemed agitated, and so different to the calm, cool individual of before. The hotel owner was taken aback by the sudden change of his manner.

The following day, two forestry workers were busily felling trees on the edge of the Tōpuni State Forest. They were working right next to the main road that runs between Whangerei and Auckland, further south, and were very close to a lay-by where trucks often dropped off deliveries. Around 2.30 p.m. a camper van suddenly appeared, swerving quite fast off the road and into the lay-by. Then, instead of stopping, it went round in a circle and shot back onto the road again before disappearing out of view. The workmen immediately sensed that something was wrong and became even more suspicious when, about ten minutes later, an estate car also arrived. The driver seemed to want to stay out of view and moved to the far side of the lay-by, as far as he could from where the foresters were working.

Wondering if a criminal gang might be at work, the two labourers walked cautiously towards the car. Inside, they saw two large motors, some large blue bags and several canisters of petrol. They asked the driver if there was anything they could do to help him but he replied

that he was simply waiting for a camper van to arrive, which was
due any minute. The foresters told him that a similar vehicle had
arrived just a very short while before and then headed off northwards,
towards Whangerei. The driver seemed to be startled by the news
and within moments had roared off in the same direction.

The amateur photographer, the hotel manageress and the two foresters had all felt sure that something was not quite right on those
two successive days in July 1985. Visitors, incidents and encounters like
that were simply not part of everyday life and routine. None of them
had enough reason to go to the police but all of them took a mental
note of those they encountered or, in the case of the two labourers,
of the car's registration number.

At the time, however, none of them could possibly have known
that they were witnessing the preparatory work of one of the most
infamous, and bungled, espionage operations that any Western
intelligence service has undertaken in recent decades. This was the
bombing of the *Rainbow Warrior*, a vessel that, at the time of the
attack, the international environmental organisation Greenpeace was
using to stage protests against French nuclear testing in the Pacific.
The attack inadvertently killed an innocent man, caused a huge political scandal in Paris, blackened France's international standing and
reputation, while also hardening anti-French sentiment in a region,
the South Pacific, where French officials badly wanted to maintain
their influence.

The *Rainbow Warrior* affair has subsequently been the subject of
exhaustive studies that have considered, above all, the complicity
of the French government, and tried to explain the extraordinary
ineptitude of those involved. But one aspect of the incident that
has merited more attention is the indirect role and influence of the
'Anglo-Saxons' on French policy. Some French officials in Paris
thought that Greenpeace was unintentionally advancing the interests

of the United States, and to a lesser extent Great Britain, by undermining what was left of the French colonial empire.

The *Warrior* had been Greenpeace's flagship ever since 1978, when the organisation had purchased it, at the then exorbitant cost of £37,000, from the British government. It was an impressive acquisition, measuring 131 feet in length and weighing more than 400 tons. Although it was in poor shape when it came into the organisation's hands, and needed several months work to reach a seaworthy state again, work that was funded by Greenpeace's generous donors, it was soon capable of moving at an impressive speed over long distances.

The directors of Greenpeace wanted to use the trawler to shadow ships that were engaged in activities that the environmental organisation disapproved of. These included illegal, dangerous or barbaric practices such as whaling, the dumping of radioactive waste and nuclear testing. The idea was that the ship's crew could, at the very least, film any wrongdoings or malpractice and then use the footage to embarrass the guilty party. Even the mere threat of such exposure, ran the argument, might sometimes be enough to intimidate a government or company. But Greenpeace also used more dangerous tactics. Sometimes its activists blockaded the path of another vessel, or shipped protestors to a controversial site. Some of its members had even sailed into the open sea in motor-driven dinghies, known as Zodiacs, and daringly positioned themselves in front of the terrifying harpoons that some sailors, mainly from Japan and Norway, used to kill whales.

It was to undertake a similarly audacious mission that, on 21 March 1985, the *Rainbow Warrior* had set sail from Jacksonville, in Florida. The *Warrior* had stayed there for several long months and in this time had been overhauled, upgraded and modernised with much more up-to-date equipment. Eventually its eleven-strong crew, drawn from all over the world, was ready to embark upon an arduous and demanding 19,000-mile journey all the way to New Zealand.

Greenpeace planned to arrive in New Zealand on, or very close to, a carefully chosen anniversary. Exactly forty years before, in August 1945, the Allies had dropped atomic bombs on the Japanese cities of Hiroshima and Nagasaki, bringing a swift end to the Second World War but killing tens of thousands of innocent civilians by doing so. The environmentalists wanted to use the anniversary to publicise the dangers of nuclear testing.

The organisation's members knew that in August the French would be testing their nuclear warheads on Moruroa, a tiny atoll in the Pacific Ocean. The French had been using it as a test site ever since 1962, when they began exploding warheads in specially built underground bunkers that they claimed were entirely safe to use. But many environmentalists were not nearly so sure and pointed out that radioactive material could easily escape and contaminate a much wider area. Their worst fears were realised in July 1979, when a nuclear accident on Moruroa not only devastated the atoll but also triggered a minor tsunami. A few years before, there had also been allegations that some of the tests carried out in Tahiti and New Caledonia, both French 'overseas territories', had been executed with poor safety standards, leading to widespread nuclear contamination.[294]

In Paris, however, Admiral Henri Fages of the French Navy was not one for compromise. As head of the Direction du Centre d'Expérimentations Nucléaires, he was most keen to carry out the test-firing of several warheads and did not take kindly to the prospect of Greenpeace or of any other environmental organisation getting in the way.

As a military man, Fages may have seen the tests, and Greenpeace's protests, through the narrow prism of national self-defence. But the experiments and the protests were about much more than just that. They were also all about his country's grandeur.

Most obviously, France's nuclear programme was integral to the country's international standing. This had been a central driving force of the programme ever since its inception in the mid-1950s. In September 1958, for example, President de Gaulle had justified France's accession to an international summit, alongside Britain and America, 'because the Western monopoly of atomic weapons would very soon cease to belong exclusively to the Association [between Britain and America], now that we were about to acquire them'. *Le Général* had added that, as a result of France's forthcoming nuclear status, NATO 'should henceforth be placed under a triple rather than a dual direction'.[295]

But the French were supremely sensitive not just about their possession of the bomb but also about their right to test the fissile material in the same way as other members of 'the nuclear club'. Again, a quarter century before, de Gaulle had pointed out how France's first nuclear test explosion, at Reggane in the Sahara Desert in 1960, 'was preceded by all manner of warnings, inspired by the Association [of existing nuclear powers], relating to the risks of atmospheric contamination to which the explosion might give rise'. He added, darkly, that 'it was with a certain degree of irony that we observed this coalition of alarm on the part of so many states which had watched without the slightest indignation while the Americans, the British and the Soviets had exploded some two hundred atomic devices'.

Greenpeace's protests threatened to do more than just disrupt France's nuclear testing. They would also violate its national sovereignty. Moruroa was part of French Polynesia, which had been a French colony since the 1880s, and in 1985 it was an 'overseas territory' that was ruled directly from Paris. In other words, any foreign protests against France's activities, nuclear or otherwise, on its own territory, were an affront to both France's national sovereignty and to its prestige.

This was one reason why opposition to French nuclear testing had become very closely linked, in the eyes of Paris officials and of many people in the South Pacific, with the cause of independence.

In 1973, for example, the leaders of the South Pacific Forum, which represented some of the political leaders of the islands in the region, pointed out that the 'liberation' of the French territories would deny Paris the right to carry out tests there.

If this was bad enough in French eyes, then even worse was the fact that there were growing demands in Moruroa, and New Caledonia, for more freedom and even independence. By the end of the 1970s, for example, several of the mainstream political parties in New Caledonia were calling for a clean constitutional break with Paris. And just a generation after the loss of its colonies in sub-Saharan Africa, Algeria and Indochina, Greenpeace's association with these growing demands for independence was always likely to touch a raw nerve in France's national mindset. Officials in Paris, notably in the ministries of defence and of overseas territories, feared that a successful attempt to stop France from carrying out nuclear tests in Moruroa would simply encourage nationalist movements on the island and beyond. It would send an unequivocal message that France no longer exerted sovereign rule.[296]

Not only did the French see a link between nuclear testing and independence in the region, but they associated independence with 'Anglo-Saxon' influence. This association was particularly clear not in Moruroa and New Caledonia but on the South Pacific island of New Hebrides.

Since the 1880s, New Hebrides had been jointly owned by both Great Britain and France. After 1945 there had been growing calls on the island for independence but these had emanated mainly from the English-speaking Protestant population, while French-speaking Catholics veered much more strongly towards staying within the French Empire but having more autonomy. Eventually, in 1974, New Hebrides broke its colonial links with France, expelling seven hundred French residents. But this seemed to be a victory for Britain because the island, now renamed as Vanuatu, had immediately joined the British Commonwealth.

At the same time, French nuclear testing was provoking a growing chorus of criticism in two Anglophone 'Anglo-Saxon' countries that were both former British colonies – Australia and New Zealand. In Australia, protestors boycotted French restaurants and even carried out some incendiary attacks on French diplomatic offices. And in 1983, the Australian government, led by Bob Hawke, imposed a ban on the sale of uranium to France, called for the establishment of a nuclear-free zone in the South Pacific, and spoke out in support of the independence movement in the region.

By the late 1970s, the remnants of the French Empire in the South Pacific, notably the two overseas territories of New Caledonia and French Polynesia, were also coming under increasing nationalist pressure. The new Vanuatu government began to voice strong support for independence movements in New Caledonia, championing their cause at the United Nations and criticising French nuclear testing in the region. But here, too, support for and opposition to independence closely mirrored the fault-line between Catholic and Protestant, reinforcing the French perception that nationalism was essentially an 'Anglo-Saxon' phenomenon. By the early 1980s, support for independence parties began to grow sharply.

Riots and gun battles increasingly broke out in the streets between security forces and pro-independence protestors, notably in January 1985, just as Greenpeace was drawing up plans to disrupt French nuclear tests in the region. Meanwhile, demands for independence were also growing in French Polynesia. In 1975, for example, activists formed a more militant pro-independence party, which called for France to hand over political power as well as to bring an immediate halt to nuclear testing.

The link between independence, opposition to nuclear testing and

'Anglo-Saxon' influence had all merged together in 1973, when Australia and New Zealand joined Fiji to bring a court case against France at the International Court of Justice. The nuclear tests caused radioactive fallout, the litigants argued, which risked contaminating the local population. The French pulled out of the judicial hearing, effectively ignoring it, but later gave ground, announcing that in future they would undertake testing only underground. At the same time, a wealthy Canadian businessman called David McTaggart had donated his own yacht, the *Vega*, to Greenpeace, and sailed with other members to Moruroa. They made two trips to the island and on the second occasion were badly beaten by French soldiers, who used Zodiac dinghies to storm their protest ship and then assault the crew with truncheons. The environmentalists used hidden cameras to film the attack and their photographs went round the world, causing the French government serious embarrassment. Relations between Paris and the 'Anglo-Saxon' Canadian government sank to a new low.

It is quite likely that, as the *Rainbow Warrior* set sail from Florida in the early hours of that March morning in 1985, neither the crew on board nor the Greenpeace leaders knew anything about the growing nationalism in the South Pacific. And it is possible that, even at this stage, they were not quite sure what their tactics at Moruroa would be. They certainly wanted to rally local supporters to the cause and then lead a flotilla of ships, with the *Warrior* at the helm, to the atoll. Such a protest would be difficult for the French to ignore, but quite what would happen after that was unclear. Perhaps their mere presence in the area would be enough to make Paris think twice about conducting further nuclear tests. The French would surely worry about incriminating photographs that would seize international headlines and damage their country's standing. Or maybe the environmentalists could be more audacious and try landing on the atoll, or even storming a French vessel.

The guiding force behind the DGSE's mission was thousands of miles away, in Paris. Early in 1985, the head of the DGSE, Admiral Pierre Lacoste, had discussed with colleagues a number of plans to deal with this apparent threat to French national interests. He spoke firstly with heads of departments and senior officers within the DGSE, and then met with Charles Hernu, the Minister of Defence. Then he approached the President, François Mitterrand, and put forward his proposals.

Similar plans had been proposed before and occasionally acted upon. 'There were a number of operations', recalled Alexandre de Marenches, a former head of the DGSE who had left the service four years before the *Rainbow Warrior* incident, 'in which the people seeking to monitor our [nuclear] experiments encountered mechanical problems ... let us just say that a few back-handers made sure that a large number of boats suffered breakdowns and damage.'[297]

Twelve years on, there were individuals within the French government who would have been spoiling for another fight with Greenpeace. This may have been because France, in the mid-1980s, was in a particularly dire economic mess, heightening sensitivities about the country's international standing. In 1983, the Mitterrand government had been forced into making a deeply humiliating economic U-turn, reverting from high-spending, high-taxing socialist policies, which failed miserably, to cost-slashing and tax-reduction. For some French men and women, the prospect of suffering a national humiliation in the Pacific Ocean at the hands of a multinational environmentalist organisation would have been unpalatable. It was just such a climb-down that France had already suffered once before, within just months of the 1973 *Vega* incident.

The foreign intelligence service also had its own ghosts to exorcise, having made some serious blunders in Lebanon after a deadly attack on French and American Army barracks in October 1983, when fifty-nine French soldiers had died. Above all, the DGSE's operatives had botched a revenge attack, positioning a car bomb outside the Iranian embassy in Beirut that failed to detonate. French jets had also attacked the suspects' base but missed their targets, an error that was attributed to poor intelligence-gathering.[298]

Attacking Greenpeace was about much more than just re-establishing a damaged reputation. In French eyes, a Greenpeace victory at Moruroa would be a victory not so much for the environmental lobby but rather for the assortment of infiltrators into the Greenpeace movement. There was speculation in the French media and security services that some of these were Communist sympathisers and Soviet agents. 'It is not unusual', remarked the head of the DGSE, 'for organisations which have the words peace or *pax* in their titles to originate from the services of the Eastern bloc.' But some people also thought the 'Anglo-Saxons' were involved: allegations were made, for example, that Greenpeace was financed by British Petroleum because it had a vested interest in disrupting the French nuclear industry.[299]

But although the French feared 'Anglo-Saxon' interference, so too was the attack on the *Rainbow Warrior* a consequence, to an important degree, of the support that they felt that Washington would give them. In other words, the instigators of the attack were, in a paradoxical way, relying upon American support to counter 'Anglo-Saxon' influence.

This attack took place during the Cold War, at a time when the Reagan presidency's rhetoric about Moscow's 'Evil Empire' and its policies, such as the arming of proxy armies in Asia, Africa and Latin America, was particularly belligerent and aggressive. So too was its nuclear policy. In such a climate, the more hawkish figures in Paris would have calculated that they would be far more likely to win American approval for any attack on Greenpeace.

This was partly because French officials knew that Greenpeace was deeply unpopular in Washington, where it was regarded as a threat to America's nuclear resources. 'Greenpeace was regarded in Washington as a misguided pest that was an ideological bedfellow of the Soviet Union,' admits a former State Department official. The United States military had also had its own disputes with Greenpeace. In 1971, for example, the American government had abandoned nuclear testing on Amchitka Island, off Alaska, after a Greenpeace flotilla set sail for the site, generating a huge amount of publicity and causing a public outcry.[300]

In particular, Washington had good reason to fear Greenpeace's presence in the South Pacific. By 1985 the Americans were using an atoll in the Marshall Islands, Kwajalein, as a site for the Strategic Defense Initiative (SDI), better known as the 'Star Wars' programme. Intended to intercept and shoot down incoming nuclear missiles, the Pentagon considered SDI as a vital part of American national security. If Greenpeace won a battle against the French in Moruroa, then it could easily lead a flotilla against Kwajalein in a bid to demilitarise the entire Pacific Ocean.

Of course this does not mean that anyone in Washington is likely to have had any foreknowledge of the DGSE operation against Greenpeace. But some of the operation's sponsors might have felt confident about the level of sympathy that any such strike would win from the United States. If, on the other hand, Washington worked against them, then the New Zealand authorities would have had a much greater chance of detecting the DGSE's undercover operation.

Washington was unlikely to harbour much sympathy for the New Zealand government. Exactly one year before, in July 1984, a strongly anti-nuclear candidate, David Lange, had won New Zealand's elections and become Prime Minister. 'Nuclear weapons are morally indefensible', he argued before an audience of British students at Oxford, shortly after his election. Almost as soon as he took up office, his government barred any nuclear-armed foreign ship from entering New Zealand's waters, even if they were American ships.[301]

It is no coincidence that in early February 1985, just as French officials were weighing up options to strike back at Greenpeace, relations between Washington and Wellington reached a nadir. On 5 February, within hours of Lange formally refusing a request from Washington to allow the nuclear-armed USS *Buchanan* into New Zealand waters, an infuriated American government retaliated by downgrading New Zealand from the status of 'ally' to 'friend'. Members of the New Zealand armed forces were no longer allowed to visit and train alongside their American counterparts. Restrictions were placed on contact between diplomats and government representatives, and on New Zealand's membership of the security alliance with Australia and the United States. In particular, the CIA stopped sharing intelligence with its sister organisation in Wellington.

Without American counter-intelligence information to contend with, the French had far more scope to employ hard-hitting tactics against Greenpeace. The New Zealanders had much less advanced intelligence-gathering than their American counterparts and would, on their own, be much less likely to pick up on the movement of French undercover personnel as they moved in and around New Zealand, and then made their subsequent escape.

Even if, in its worst-case scenario, the French involvement in the sabotage operation was exposed, Paris calculated that Washington would not want to penalise an operation against Greenpeace, given its anti-nuclear stance. And French officials would also have felt confident that the Americans would veto any diplomatic move against them that the Soviets, or New Zealand, might subsequently make at the United Nations.

The possibility of more active American collusion with the operation cannot readily be discounted, so it is conceivable that the French acted 'with a nod and a wink' from the American government, which had a vested interest in striking a blow to the morale and resources of Greenpeace. In his memoirs, de Marenches described how 'I have often staged operations abroad and have been to see our traditional friends and allies about them. I told them, "France has a particular problem. This is how I think it can be resolved. Will you help me?"' The second question, he added, was 'would you mind turning a blind eye on such-and-such a day or at such-and-such a time?'[302]

In other words, the officials who sponsored the attack on Greenpeace in the summer of 1985 needed American support to carry out an attack that was pitched, in their eyes, against 'the same Soviet–British–American link-up that was seeking to banish the French from the Pacific'.[303]

Any such American fears would have been realised as the *Rainbow Warrior* continued its journey across the Pacific en route to Auckland in the weeks preceding the attack. The vessel had by now reached the Marshall Islands, where its crew made a spontaneous protest against the American presence on Kwajalein. And as the ship made its way thought Kwajalein's harbour, sailing past myriad radar dishes, giant telescopes and antennae, several crew members jumped into Zodiac dinghies and landed on shore. They ran towards a high protective fence and along it unfolded a huge banner that read '*We Can't Relocate the World – Stop Star Wars*'. Lots of photographs were taken, all ready to be distributed to the world's press, before the protestors were escorted, in a quite civil manner, off the island.

Meanwhile, thousands of miles away in the Pacific Ocean, four Frenchmen were sailing an impressive yacht, the *Ouvea*, from New Caledonia towards the New Zealand coast. One of them had chartered the 25-foot sloop from an office in Paris several weeks before and had then joined his fellow crew members before flying into New Caledonia to start their journey. Another member of the team had also acquired a Zodiac dingy in London, knowing that after the operation this would lead a false trail back to *la perfide Albion*.

They were well-prepared for the voyage, loaded with considerable supplies of food on board as well as boasting a highly sophisticated navigation system that drew its information from a satellite. They also had a direct radio link with Paris, using a very powerful transmitter to send and receive messages over thousands of miles.

Each of these four men, all DGSE agents who were using false identities, had been tasked with laying the foundations of the attack on the *Warrior*. 'Eric Audrenc' was really Petty Officer Gerald Andries, who had been serving with the DGSE's Service Action branch, responsible for specialist, covert operations, for the past six years. The real name of 'Jean-Michel Berthelo' was Jean-Michel Barcelo, while 'Raymond Velche' was in fact Chief Petty Officer Roland Verge. Prior to the mission, all three men had been based at a highly secretive base run by the French Navy at Aspretto in Corsica. It would have been here that each of them would have been given specialist training in underwater diving. The role and identity of the other crew member – 'Xavier Maniguet', which was perhaps his real name as well as the one he used on the mission – is not clear. But he is known to have been a qualified doctor, and he may have had long-standing links with the French military and intelligence services.

On the afternoon of 22 June, after several days at sea, the *Ouvea* slipped quietly, and almost entirely unnoticed, into New Zealand waters. To begin with, it made its way into a creek called Parengarenga, located along a particularly remote stretch of coast, and then journeyed through a very dangerous stretch of water that daunted even the most experienced sailors. Finally, in the later afternoon, it reached a tiny village called Te Hapua where the crew members dropped anchor and stepped on shore. The venue was isolated, barren and inhospitable.

The *Ouvea* team worked fast to find places where they could hide the Zodiac dinghy, its outboard motor and the explosives. Then, before they aroused suspicion, they travelled a short distance up the coast to contact local customs officials.

At almost exactly the same time, a young Swiss couple, Alain and Sophie Turenges, were stepping off an Air New Zealand flight that had just touched down at Auckland international airport. Both were charming, friendly and relaxed, and both spoke some English, although Alain's language skills were very much better than Sophie's. The customs staff looked carefully at their passports and papers but saw nothing unusual – he was a businessman while she was an academic who lectured on sociology – and quickly allowed them on their way. After passing through the control points, they cashed a large sum of money before heading off to a nearby hotel.

The customs officers would have had to look very closely indeed to have noticed some very minor imperfections in the passports, which were in fact forged. For the Turenges, like their counterparts who were sailing into the country further north, were also DGSE agents. Their real names were Captain Dominique Prieur, thirty-six, who was a commando, while Major Alain Mafart, thirty-four, was in fact a senior-ranking officer. And far from being a married couple, they had a strictly professional relationship and were doing their utmost to resemble a couple in love.

The two agents would now work hard to make contact with the *Ouvea* crew. First they would need to find out where the dinghy, motor and explosives had been concealed and then they could collect them. They also wanted to hire a van to pick them up before transferring their deadly cargo into the hands of the other agents who had been briefed with the dirty task of carrying out the bombings.

At the same time, the members of the *Ouvea* crew were doing all they could to attract attention, drinking, socialising and

womanising with as much vigour as they could, and with great success. This meant that, when the New Zealand police started looking
for culprits, as they soon would, they would be pointed towards
the crew but chase only a red herring: once they had dropped
off and hidden the explosives, dingy and motor, the four *Ouvea*
sailors would have virtually no further involvement in the operation
other than to distract attention from the other members of the team,
giving them a chance to escape.

It was upon the complex manoeuvres of some of these secret agents
that several New Zealanders accidentally stumbled in late June and
early July. In Auckland harbour, the amateur photographer saw
Dominique Prieur on the deck of the *Ouvea*, while her 'husband' was
talking with the crew members, briefing them on the whereabouts of
the hidden items and arranging a rendezvous. The two foresters witnessed Maniguet and Velche waiting to meet the Turenges in order
to move the dinghy and motor into their van. And the hotel owner
nearly saw something else, perhaps fuel tanks, perhaps a back-up
motor, or maybe even the explosives, which might have exposed the
operation. All of these New Zealanders knew that something was
out of order. But no one could guess what was about to happen.[304]

In the early evening of 10 July, at around 7 p.m., two men walked
down a path that led into the icy cold seas off at Stanley Point,
a peninsula that lies north of Auckland's harbour. They carried a
dinghy up as far as the water's edge and then slipped away into
the mist and dark. Whoever they were, the two men certainly had
specialist training in both underwater swimming and the use of
explosives. They made their way a short distance southwards, landing
unnoticed at Teal Park, just off Mechanics Bay on the south coast.
They were now just a mile and a half away from Marsden Wharf,
where the *Rainbow Warrior* was moored. They could finally plant
their bombs on the ship's hull and escape before it was blown.

The frogmen reached out and felt the ship's hull, covered with seaweed and shells, and moved downwards towards the rudder. This was where the first bomb would go off, unleashing a limited blast that would scare the crew off the vessel before the second, more powerful blast, would erupt. They used straps to fix a limpet mine to the propeller shaft, while the other was placed in a carefully located spot, right next to the engine. The divers then set the fuses and headed back.

That night, the eleven crew members planned on sleeping in the ship. After their meeting, a few of them were staying up late and sharing a few bottles of wine and beer, although others, including the captain, Pete Wilcox, had already headed off to bed.

Shortly before midnight, the crew members heard a loud thud. Some woke up, startled, wondering if another ship had collided with the *Warrior*. They knew it was time to get out, before the ship sank or before there was another explosion, or whatever it was. Wilcox shouted out, telling everyone to go.

Within minutes ten members of the eleven-strong crew were all standing on the quayside when they saw and heard another, similar explosion. The ship rocked on its side uneasily, but could not last long. The bombs had blasted two enormous holes in its stern – one of them measured six feet by eight – and within minutes it started to disappear into the water.

The emergency services had worked desperately hard throughout the night to find anyone who had been caught in the blast. In all the confusion they simply lacked any clear idea about who may have been inside the ship when the blast took place. During the night, specially trained Navy divers had arrived on the scene and they now led the way in working through the smoke, debris and darkness. Before long they had found the body of 35-year-old Fernando Pereira, a Portuguese photographer who had been chatting with colleagues when the bombs exploded. Everyone else had rushed off board but he had raced to his cabin to retrieve his cameras and drowned when a sudden torrent of water had poured into the ship and overwhelmed him.

Stunned and confused, many Greenpeace crew members wondered if there had been a major engine malfunction. One of the explosions, after all, had come from the engine room. But sabotage was the only explanation because, as the police had immediately discovered, the hull had been blow inwards by something on the outside, and that more or less ruled out any accident.

The police felt sure it was the French who were responsible. Who else, they asked, would have had a motive to carry out such an operation at that particular moment? They combed through a number of incident reports that had emerged over the past few hours, and quickly joined the dots.

The French had never intended or expected to kill anyone who was on board the *Rainbow Warrior*, and they were mortified when the news broke that Pereira had died in the blast. They did not expect the New Zealand authorities to immediately suspect their complicity and then catch two of the agents, the 'Turenges', and sentence them to prison, although both were eventually released.

Amidst a flurry of accusations and sanctions, Paris eventually paid millions of dollars in compensation to the New Zealand government. In Polynesia and New Caledonia, nationalist feelings and antipathy towards France hardened. In Paris, the bombing caused a political explosion of outrage as accusatory fingers were pointed at a succession of chiefs in the intelligence services and in government ministries before finally turning towards the President himself. 'It seems likely that Mitterrand and his senior ministers had drastically misjudged the reaction of the French media,' recalled a former Western diplomat, who was based in Paris at the time. 'He probably calculated that the French press, given its long-standing dependence on the government for subsidies and advertising, would be compliant and play down the complicity of France in the attack.' Instead the French media joined an international chorus of excoriation that blasted and embarrassed the Mitterrand presidency.[305]

But five years after the *Warrior* affair, Mitterrand was to become embroiled in another scandal. This time, once again, French rivalry and competition with the 'Anglo-Saxons' lay at the heart of his policy.

The French Navy confronts Greenpeace, October 1985.

CHAPTER 13

RWANDA AND THE AGE OF *HYPERPUISSANCE*

On the evening of 3 October 1990, as he rested on board a French naval frigate that was anchored off the coast of Abu Dhabi, President François Mitterrand received some startling and dramatic news.

Far away, in Africa's Great Lakes region, a powerful, well-armed force of several thousand militiamen had crossed the border from Uganda into the tiny neighbouring state of Rwanda. They were members of the armed wing of the Rwandan Patriotic Front (RPF), and so many government troops had dropped their arms and fled that it was perhaps only a matter of time before they would seize the capital, Kigali.[306]

Meanwhile, in Paris, the President's son, Jean-Christophe, had already heard the news from the Rwandan leader, President Juvénal Habyarimana. The Rwandan was ordinarily a quiet and softly spoken man, but he pulled no punches when he phoned the head of the Élysée's 'Africa Cell' to inform him of the dramatic news.

Mitterrand 'the younger' had the authority to make a quick

decision if he deemed it necessary to do so and he ordered an immediate troop deployment to bolster the Kigali regime. 'We are going
to bail him out,' Jean-Christophe told an African analyst who witnessed events in Paris on that day. 'In any case the whole thing will
be over in two or three months.' Meanwhile his father, still in the
Middle East, asked his chief military adviser to make an urgent trip
to Kigali to support the embattled government. The French government had a long-standing agreement to support the Rwandan
government, the President pointed out, and now the moment had
come for it to do its duty.[307]

The highly secretive deployment of several hundred French soldiers to Kigali, codenamed Operation Noroît, was to prove one of
France's most controversial post-war foreign interventions. The
Mitterrand government was now strongly supporting a regime that,
in the months and years ahead, was to deliberately perpetrate the
mass killings of hundreds of thousands of ordinary Rwandans, all
drawn from the Tutsi tribes. Estimates of the number of deaths,
most of which were perpetrated during a few savage months in the
summer of 1994, vary wildly. Perhaps a million died, although most
'guestimates' put the figure at around 800,000, nearly all of whom
were victims not of automatic fire but of the *panga* (machetes) and
rugu (clubs) that were wielded by squads of young men, all members
of rival Hutu clans and tribes, who roamed city streets, setting up
roadblocks and executing anyone they identified as a Tutsi.

Some high-ranking individuals in Paris knew about the extent
of the persecution and could have done more to prevent it. Long
before it won independence from Belgium in 1962, Rwanda had been
afflicted by intense ethnic mistrust and sporadic outbreaks of violence. It was therefore susceptible to similar outbursts in the future.
But clear warning signs had also become apparent after the French
intervention began in 1990. There were, for example, indications of a

bloodbath as early as 1991, after the RPF invasion stirred a powerful anti-Tutsi reaction, yet French diplomats and officials who were on the ground either downplayed or ignored these. Towards the end of 1993, not long before *Interahamwe* ('paramilitary') militia and presidential guards began to kill in earnest, these warnings were even harder to ignore. Propaganda against the 'cockroach' Tutsi became yet more virulent and the threats against them, sometimes uttered even by the high-ranking and powerful, ever more ominous. But still the French continued to strongly support the Kigali regime, even after it had unleashed the full fury of its genocidal campaign, which began in April 1994.[308]

The story of the Rwandan genocide and of French complicity in those atrocities has been extensively documented. Over the five years that followed the opening salvos of Operation Noroît, individuals within the French government authorised or organised the deployment of contingents of soldiers, observers and high-level advisers, who were very closely knit with Rwandan government leaders and generals, and orchestrated the delivery of huge quantities of arms and equipment. Some of the individuals were acting in an official capacity, like Colonel Gilbert Canovas, the deputy defence attaché, who was tasked with providing 'appraisal and advice' to the Rwandan government soon after Noroît began. Others acted without any such official sanction, but their activities were quietly encouraged, or overlooked, by the French government. This was true, for example, of the maverick 'security expert' Paul Barril, who worked in Rwanda in an independent capacity, but in practice had close links with the Élysée.

Of course, not all high-ranking officials in the French capital shared these sympathies. In particular, there were moderate figures within the Foreign Ministry who always pushed for a negotiated settlement and who sponsored peace talks between the warring parties, even if that might have meant compromising Habyarimana's regime.

Yet any such efforts were vastly outweighed by the overwhelming drive of Habyarimana's allies who wanted keep the RPF at bay.

This was a secret war. The President and his ministers made very few public references to the deployment of French troops into Rwanda and did everything they could to downplay media interest in the story. French troops were on the ground, ran the official version, only to protect the lives of their fellow nationals, expatriates who faced a real threat of violence. Media reports, written by the most determined journalists working for the most independent newspapers in France, surfaced only sporadically. The French government continued to manipulate the media in the same way as it always had, threatening to pull funding from any papers or media outlets if the wrong stories appeared: as the minister of culture, Alain Carignon, admitted to the British ambassador, both the left-leaning daily *Le Monde* and the Communist *L'Humanité* were dependent on government subsidies. It was only in the summer of 1994, after an outburst of ferocious violence had seized international interest and caused deep alarm, that the civil war in Rwanda, and the nature and scope of France's role there, suddenly became a big talking point in Paris and beyond. The Foreign Minister, Alain Juppé, emerged to make a series of public pronouncements to the world media. The French government was jolted out of its denials and suddenly put onto the defensive.[309]

It is not immediately apparent why the French government gave such strong support to the Kigali regime and why it was prepared to overlook the blood-soaked atrocities its protégés were responsible for. In obvious contrast to the former French colonies of west Africa, Rwanda is a diminutive, land-locked state that has very few natural resources of any real value. On the eve of the civil war that erupted on that October day in 1990, it was best known for its output of tea and coffee. Those who knew the country were also painfully familiar with the shocking poverty endured by its eight million inhabitants, who fought a daily battle to subsist. Densely populated and rife with ethnic tension, it was a place that a foreign power would be much more likely to avoid rather than fight for. Nor had Rwanda ever been a French colony. After the Berlin Conference of 1884–85, when the leaders of Europe had met to decide the fate of the African continent, it had fallen into German hands before being wrestled away by Belgian soldiers at the height of the First World War in 1916.

Underlying France's interest in this unappealing land, and its support for such a brutal and unsavoury regime, was its rivalry with the United States and Britain. Habyarimana's supporters in Paris viewed the RPF as a 'Trojan Horse' from which Anglophone influence could spring and undermine France's importance in Central Africa, notably the Congo, and beyond.

This fixation with 'Anglo-Saxon' influence in the region emerges from the pages of confidential correspondence between high-level politicians. For example, one of the President's senior advisers, Bruno Delaye, noted in a secret memorandum the 'complicity of the Anglo-Saxon world' in supporting the advance of the RPF, which 'has been steadily scoring points on the military and political map'. And in a meeting on the Rwanda crisis, which was held at the Élysée with senior ministers, advisers and generals, the President argued that France 'cannot limit [its] presence. We stand [in Rwanda] on the very edge of an English-speaking region.' One of his former ministers later testified that President Mitterand

> felt that the Americans, who were openly helping both Ugandans and the RPF, were harbouring hegemonic intentions over this region and perhaps over Africa, and he was not wrong either. Subsequently the role of the Americans has become increasingly clear. We should not forget that they are the ones who have trained the

Ugandan Army and RPF Army. It is probably also true that they gave them arms.[310]

And speaking on 2 June 1998 to a French parliamentary committee that was tasked with investigating the links between Rwanda and France, the former Minister of Cooperation, Bernard Debré, claimed that 'President Mitterrand judged that the Americans had designs to establish a hegemony over the region, and perhaps even over Africa as a whole. And I didn't disagree with him.'[311]

This obsession was also clear to insiders such as Gérard Prunier, an expert on Africa who had access to decision-makers at the highest level and who noticed how 'the equation thus suggested was "Uganda equals Anglo-Saxon equals RPF … equals Tutsi". This of course implied something else: "Rwanda equals France equals common front equals Hutu"'. And it becomes evident, too, from publications reputed to have been authored and published by the French government, which emphasised the vital strategic importance of the Great Lakes region. In a similar vein, one pamphlet argued that 'the region cannot be left in the hands of an Anglophone strongman who is completely aligned to American views and interests. This is why, since 1990, France has supported … Juvénal Habyarimana in order to fight the RPF.'

The same attitudes were harboured by senior officers in the French military, one of whom was heard to agonise that 'The worst is yet to come. These bastards will go all the way to Kinshasa now. And how in God's name am I going to explain to our friends [allies in former colonies] that we have let down one of our own?'

A researcher on French involvement in the region also came across an anonymous but revealing pamphlet that was 'reputed to be from French government circles'. It argued that 'considerable political and geostrategic interests are hidden behind the Rwandan heap of corpses', and claimed that the region could not be 'lost' to Anglophone influences, such as Uganda and 'the Great Satan' of America.[312]

In particular, French suspicions were focused on two specific individuals.

One was the Ugandan leader, Yoweri Museveni, who had allowed the RPF to form and then thrive in his country from the mid- to late 1980s, when increasing numbers of Tutsi refugees had fled persecution in their native Rwanda. Uganda was a former British colony and English was its official language but Museveni added to French fears because, almost as soon as he had come to power in 1986, he had found admirers in Washington. At a time of real tension and rivalry between the superpowers, he seemed to be a man with whom President Ronald Reagan and other Cold Warriors could do business. He abandoned his Marxist rhetoric and turned instead to Western lenders to rebuild the national economy. Several visits to Washington followed and soon afterwards the White House established military links between the two capitals and set up a programme of civilian aid. In French eyes, it was no coincidence that when the RPF launched its attack on the Rwandan capital in 1990, Museveni was not in Uganda but in the United States, where he had been attending the annual session of the UN General Assembly.[313]

The other individual was Paul Kagame, a tall, wiry Rwandan officer with a bird-like face. In the summer of 1990, the Kigali regime and its French allies would have known that Museveni had selected Kagame, at that time the head of the RPF's intelligence services, to attend a training course at Fort Leavenworth in Kansas. Although a Rwandan, Kagame, alongside a few other top RPF leaders, had become very closely integrated into the Ugandan government and its army.

In his parliamentary testimony, Bernard Debré reaffirmed his suspicion not just of both men but of Uganda in general: 'American military bases actually existed in Uganda, one of them being called

Camp Genesis. The American military was training Ugandan soldiers so that they could take up the fight against Sudanese extremists.'

The truth, however, was somewhat more complex. While the United States armed forces did train Ugandan personnel at some of its bases on American soil, this fell a very long way short of a formal alliance between the two countries. Membership of the training programme in question, known as 'IMET' (International Military Education and Training), was more symbolic than real, not least because Washington could only afford to subsidise the training of just a handful of foreign soldiers from respective countries. 'We focused on vehicle mechanics, medical technicians, and logistical management plus a few basic infantry officers' courses,' recalled one career diplomat. In any event, Kagame was at Fort Leavenworth for just a few months – much less than the year-long term he had signed up for – and the Americans had also given similar such support to Habyarimana after he seized power in 1973. They did this by starting a military assistance programme that offered a small number of army officers the chance to study in the United States, and by providing his armed forces with a variety of 'non-lethal' items.[314]

While Museveni had been in New York at the same time as many other leaders and representatives from across the globe, to attend the UN General Assembly, there is no evidence that he had any high-level talks with any Washington officials. Habyarimana was in New York at the same time and for the same reason, and when the RPF attacked Rwanda, on 1 October, American officials did offer him political asylum in the United States. But this was probably a knee-jerk sympathy rather than a deliberate conspiracy to replace him with a more compliant protégé.

It is not certain that the Ugandans were in fact sponsoring the RPF invasion, as the French feared. Museveni denied any involvement and his claims were plausible since he did not have enough troops at his disposal to stop so many Rwandan exiles crossing the border back into their homeland. The rebels had made their way into Rwanda from a remote, uninhabited region of scrubland between the border posts of Kagitumba and Gatuna where there was barely even a token Ugandan Army presence. The invasion had its own dynamic, and the role of any foreign actors was at best peripheral and passive.

But what may at the time have heightened tension, and misunderstanding, was American interest not in Uganda but in its neighbour, Sudan.

In the summer of 1989, an army officer called Omar Hassan al-Bashir had carried out a *coup d'état* in Sudan and seized power. Within weeks he had struck up an alliance with an Islamist party led by a charismatic firebrand, Hassan al-Turabi, who immediately ordered the implementation of strict Muslim Sharia law.

Towards the end of 1989, long before the 'al Qaeda' franchise of militant Islam had even been conceived, the advent of a new Islamist regime in Khartoum would not have been viewed with any particular alarm in Washington, and this perception probably did not change for several more years. What did matter, however, was Turabi's stance on the Gulf War.

On 2 August 1990, Mitterrand woke at his country home in southwest France to hear the dramatic news that the Iraqi Army had invaded Kuwait. The Middle East was in turmoil and President Bush immediately dispatched American troops to defend Saudi Arabia from any possible encroachment. A massive military American build-up in the Middle East was under way. By the following January, when Operation Desert Storm began and the Iraqis were driven out of Kuwait, there were half a million American troops on Saudi soil.

Saddam did not have many foreign friends in the wake of his invasion on that August day. But one of the few leaders who voiced their support was Hassan al-Turabi, who professed his outrage that 'infidel'

Western soldiers should be based in Saudi Arabia, Islam's most revered land.

In the weeks that followed the invasion of Kuwait, the Americans covertly increased their surveillance of developments in Sudan, using Uganda as a listening post to gather more information. They did this partly to please their Saudi allies, who viewed Turadi as a troublemaker. In Saudi eyes, Turadi was capable of inciting disturbances within the Saudi kingdom as a potential ringleader of regional criticism against Riyadh and perhaps even an instigator of low-level attacks on the Saudi coast from bases across the Red Sea. After the arrival of Osama bin Laden in Sudan in December 1991, the Americans would have come under even stronger pressure from the Saudis, who viewed bin Laden as one of their most determined enemies, to keep a close eye on the country.[315]

Another reason for Western interest in Sudan was the large number of expatriates who lived and worked there. It seemed quite possible that, after Saddam's defeat, Turadi and his followers could take vengeance on Western civilians, just as more than two years before, in May 1988, seven Westerners had been killed in a terrorist attack on the Acropole Hotel in Khartoum, which was a favourite venue for expatriates and foreign visitors. Fearing similar atrocities in the event of a US-led invasion of Kuwait, and perhaps even of Iraq, Western governments stepped up their surveillance of Sudan in late 1990.

It is very likely that, in the weeks between the Kuwaiti invasion and Mitterrand's decision to support the Kigali regime, French intelligence detected the presence of American undercover operatives in Uganda. What the French were unaware of, however, was that the Americans were monitoring Sudan rather than planning to carve out a sphere of influence in Africa at French expense. However, misreading American motives, Mitterrand decided to take counter-measures.[316]

When, in October 1990, President Mitterrand stepped in to support the Kigali government, he was not motivated by any deep, long-running antipathy towards the United States. On the contrary, his views of American power were as complex as those he held on almost every other issue. In the wartime years he was a supporter of the Vichy government but also a member of the Resistance. As a student, he briefly joined the Volontaires Nationaux, an organisation with links to the extreme right, but then gravitated to the left. When his political career got under way in the 1950s, he found support from both left and right, and when he won the Presidential election in 1981, he chose Communist ministers as well as right-wingers. Although himself left-leaning, he also rejected ideological constraints, notably by performing economic U-turns, and despite his egalitarian sympathies, no Western head of state in recent memory has had a more regal touch. He was, in the words of one biographer, 'a study in ambiguity'. Fittingly, he recognised how France and the United States needed each other but also had different and sometimes conflicting interests. 'We are members of the Atlantic Alliance ... we are friends,' he told the Syrian President, Hafez al-Assad, in 1984, 'but we are a bit like cat and dog in the same house.'[317]

Nonetheless, tensions between Paris and Washington had started to surface almost as soon as Mitterrand became President in 1981. Despite the warnings of his right-wing critics that within days Russian tanks would be rolling through the streets of Paris, the French nation had suddenly leaned towards socialism, making a switch that became known as the *alternance* ('turning-point'). In the elections to the National Assembly in June, American officials were alarmed to watch the French Communist Party winning forty-four seats and four of its representatives then joining the Cabinet. Mitterrand quickly phoned President Reagan to assure him that the transatlantic alliance was safe in his hands but his promises hardly alleviated American fears. And when a State Department communiqué, expressing concern about the presence of Communist ministers in Mitterrand's Cabinet, was leaked to the press, it caused a storm of protest in France, uniting left and right in collective outrage. 'Ronald Reagan is mistaken if he thinks France is El Salvador,' fumed *Le Figaro*.

Then, not long after he came to office, Mitterrand vindicated his critics in Washington by making a speech that seemed to propose redrawing the geopolitical map of western Europe, breaking France away from American influence and taking it closer to Moscow instead. 'I don't want a Europe which is the auxiliary of a United States that is on the offensive,' he argued. 'If new possibilities for a modus vivendi with the USSR emerge, it would be a good thing.' His suspicions of American motives and policies were also shared and put forward by a number of senior ministers, notably Claude Cheysson, the minister for external relations. Cheysson pointed out how Franco-American relations 'can give the impression of remarkable contradictions: perfect agreement on East–West relations, reciprocal annoyance and incomprehension over a whole series of sectors, and divergences on economics which could lead to a serious crisis'. Cheysson also added that the Mitterrand government was highly critical of the American 'obsession' with the Soviet Union.[318]

The President openly disapproved of American support for repressive dictatorships in Latin America and publicly voiced his dissatisfaction with America's economic 'hegemony' and its tendency to 'summon its allies with a whistle when in fact it is serving its own national interest'. One particularly bitter row erupted in the mid-1980s over a joint west-European plan to help the Soviets build a pipeline from Siberia to Western markets. And when, in 1984, Mitterrand brokered an improvement in relations between Paris and Moscow, the CIA launched a covert campaign to disrupt them.

Tension then became particularly acute when Washington pushed ahead with its 'Star Wars' defence programme. Mitterrand, aware that 'Star Wars' would make France highly dependent on an American defence shield and render France's own independent deterrent obsolete, infuriated the White House with his criticisms of the programme and his proposals for a European alternative that would challenge the American one. Another particularly bitter row erupted in May 1986, when Paris denied American warplanes permission to fly through French airspace as they made their way from their British bases to attack Libya.[319]

But equally there were also occasions when he infuriated the Russians and delighted the Americans. So in January 1983 he took an uncompromising line on one of the hottest political questions of the day – the deployment of American missiles on West German soil. 'Anyone who gambles on "decoupling" the European and American continents', propounded Mitterrand as he reiterated his strong support for the deployment, 'would be calling into question ... the maintenance of peace.' Former Secretary of State Henry Kissinger phoned him to convey his personal appreciation, while Reagan commented that the President's remarks were 'of inestimable value'. Above all, Mitterrand was aware that France needed America's military support in Europe: 'I don't want to give the Americans a pretext to reduce their commitment,' he commented darkly.[320]

It was in this spirit that Franco-American relations ebbed and flowed, sometimes with vitriol, during the Mitterrand years. But if the President's views of the United States, like those of so many of his contemporaries, had been mixed and unpredictable, what pushed him yet further away was the sequence of events that began in November 1989, with the fall of the Berlin Wall. French support for the Kigali regime, in other words, was not just a consequence of any American interest and presence, real or imaginary, in Uganda. The underlying pressures that were driving French foreign policy, and fuelling such mistrust between the capitals, went much deeper.

In late 1989 Moscow had lost its empire in eastern Europe, as vast numbers of protestors forced the Communist regimes to surrender to democratic reforms, and within another two years the Soviet Union itself had also imploded. But since the Second World War, the Soviet Union had openly challenged the United States and checked its otherwise unrestrained power and influence in the world. Now that the Soviet counterweight had suddenly disintegrated, the United States was from this moment a 'hyperpower', as Foreign Minister Hubert Védrine later called it.[321]

Viewed through French eyes, there was now a real danger that America would become more bullying and controlling than ever before, making France and the rest of Europe subservient to its wishes. When plans for a new European defence structure were discussed in 1991, Mitterrand warned his German counterpart, Chancellor Helmut Kohl, that 'the American presence is going to ... enclose Europe in a structure that is totally dependent on Washington'. The proposals also seemed to create a risk that Washington would get involved in overly ambitious foreign policy ventures, notably the disastrous American 'nation-building' operation in Somalia in 1992–93. The rhetoric that emanated from Washington, and from other international capitals, was often saturated with such hubristic terminology.[322]

In France, as elsewhere, there were fears that the United States was exploiting the Kuwaiti crisis in order to establish a presence in parts of the world where it did not belong. Some conspiratorially minded people claimed that Washington had even encouraged Saddam to attack his neighbour in order to find an excuse to step into the Middle East. Such a huge American presence in the region hardly alleviated the fears of those who felt that the United States was becoming simply too powerful for its own good.[323]

In his conversations with the Russian leader, Mikhail Gorbachev, Mitterrand expressed concerns about how the Americans had become 'the masters of war [who] from their point of view [can] use force independently without turning to the UN Security Council'. Equally, the President worked hard to negotiate with Middle Eastern leaders, pursuing a diplomatic course that was independent, although supportive, of Washington, and which later allowed him to claim that France had 'maintained its role and rank' during the crisis rather than being steamrolled by America.[324]

Such fears of untrammelled American power were voiced in his Cabinet by Defence Minister, Jean-Paul Chevènement, who was deeply concerned about France becoming too subservient to America and who resigned on these, and other, grounds, in January 1991. And in the National Assembly, a spokesman for the neo-Gaullist 'Rally for the Republic' (RPR) party, Philippe Séguin, argued that Mitterrand's support for the US-led coalition would only help Washington: 'This war is a form of stupidity,' he claimed, 'and we are giving the United States tremendous power and leeway, without knowing where this will lead us.' On the left, Communist politicians voiced similar sentiments. André Lajoine, for example, argued that

> the US doesn't want a peaceful settlement ... how can anyone believe that US radar, satellites and other eavesdropping equipment had failed to see the Iraqi army getting ready to attack Kuwait ... it is the pretext for the sending of the US army into the Gulf ... the first consequence has been to block every diplomatic initiative ... we need to block American aspirations to be world policeman.[325]

Others were deeply conscious that the post-war international order was in a state of flux and that France could easily be the loser. There were no longer any 'certainties' in the world, mused the future Prime

Minister Édouard Balladur, because 'everything could change in quite a number of ways'. It was not 'appropriate' to harbour any optimism. And for the politician Pierre Méhaignerie, the crisis in the Middle East was 'a revelation of our weaknesses, and we must face up to them and draw lessons for the future'. These sentiments mirrored the consensus that a new world order had been born, with dramatic speed and profound consequences.[326]

America's critics in Paris, and elsewhere, failed to see the other side of the argument: that so many of its resources, and its attention, were diverted to the Middle East that the United States was hardly in a position to pose any threat to French influence in Africa. And when Washington was under such pressure in the Middle East, it needed France's cooperation more than ever before. This was equally true before the Iraqi invasion of Kuwait. In 1989, Herman J. Cohen, the Assistant Secretary of State for African affairs, had remarked that the United States was allocating less money to sub-Saharan Africa than before because Washington was prioritising Egypt, Israel, Turkey and Greece and 'after you give money to all of those there is very little left'. Two years later, President Bush was more preoccupied with helping to reconstruct eastern Europe and the former Soviet Union, as well as paying for the Iraq War.[327]

But for Mitterrand and his ministers, one of the most alarming consequences of such profound, revolutionary events in eastern Europe during 1989–91 would be the challenge they posed, or seemed to pose, to French dominance and influence in Africa and elsewhere. On the one hand, if the people of eastern Europe now had new democratic freedoms, then, in all likelihood, their counterparts in Africa would also feel entitled to demand them. 'The winds of change are sweeping through *le cocotier* (land of coconuts),' remarked Jacques Pelletier, the Minister of Cooperation. So too might the United States demand such changes from a former colonial power that was interested not in promoting such freedoms but in retaining its post-colonial grip, *la Françafrique*, even if that meant supporting sympathetic dictatorships. Washington no longer needed anti-Soviet allies in Africa, or elsewhere. Its spokesmen and representatives spoke openly of finding new markets 'on a level playing field' in which its companies could compete and probably outbid its European competitors. Given their size and assets, American companies seemed certain to win big stakes. 'The African market is open to everyone,' argued a senior American official, and should offer 'free and fair competition ... and equality for all actors'.[328]

France's ties to its former colonies were under pressure. At La Baule, near Nantes, on 19 June 1990, Mitterrand hosted a conference with leaders of the former French colonies. It was the sixteenth Franco-African summit – they had been held annually since 1974 – but this was the first time that democracy had been on the agenda. Mitterrand seemed to acknowledge that times were changing. 'French aid will be lukewarm towards authoritarian regimes', he asserted, 'and more enthusiastic for those initiating a democratic transition.'[329]

But these ties were also under pressure from 'Anglo-Saxon' influence. Although French officials may have exaggerated and misjudged Washington's interest in Uganda in late 1990, there were other places, notably Zaire, where American interest was growing. And within four years, there were convincing reports of a covert American military presence in the Great Lakes region. French fears were not, in other words, without foundation.[330]

CHAPTER 14

WAR BY PROXY IN CENTRAL AFRICA

In the months that preceded the RPF's attack on Rwanda in 1990, and Mitterrand's subsequent decision to send troops and bolster Habyarimana's regime, the American presence in Africa seemed to be looming ever larger. In Uganda, the French oil giant Total fought hard with its American rival Exxon to win drilling rights. American companies also showed a strong interest in the Ivory Coast's cocoa trade, and when the giant US food company Cargill made a bid there to buy a subsidiary of Jean Abile Gal, which was the leading *chargeur* (supplier), it was not long before an alarmed French government created its own consortium that could challenge this American 'aggression'. And news that Pascal Lissouba's government in Congo-Brazzaville had reached out to the American oil firm Occidental and bestowed exclusive drilling rights caused dismay in Paris. 'How can we defend our interests against the Americans?' sighed the Minister of Cooperation, Michel Roussin. There was, he remarked, an '*offensive commerciale américaine géneralisée*'.[331]

In the early 1990s there were several developments, in Africa and beyond, that seemed to render the threat from America all the more challenging. One was a drastic change in US policy towards Zaire, a country that had been the setting for Franco-American rivalry thirty years before.[332]

Although a former Belgian colony, Zaire was still nonetheless a major component, geographically vast and asset-rich, of *la zone francophone*. In the early 1960s, Mobutu had fought his civil war with American backing, but successive French governments had nonetheless subsequently worked hard to win influence in and support from Kinshasa. President Giscard visited the Zairean capital in 1975 and established a close rapport with his counterpart, even dispatching French troops to fight off a series of invasions launched from neighbouring states in the late 1970s.

Washington had been happy to watch this growing accord between France and Zaire because it helped to steer Mobutu away from the Soviet Union. Despite his dictatorial and often brutal rule, and the personal fortune of $2.5 billion he was reputed to have stashed away during his long tenure in power, much of which was siphoned from American aid, Mobutu was fêted in Washington. In June 1989, just months before the fall of the Berlin Wall, the Zairean leader was invited to meet President George H. W. Bush at the White House, where he was personally congratulated for his prominent role, as one of 'America's oldest friends … and Africa's most experienced statesmen', in ending the civil war in neighbouring Angola.

But times were changing and Mobutu had soon outlived his Cold War usefulness. In the early months of 1990 a congressional chorus of criticism grew louder. As he gave testimony to the House Appropriations Subcommittee on Foreign Relations on 5 April 1990, for example, Congressman Stephen J. Solarz compared Mobutu to the toppled leaders of eastern Europe and urged an immediate cessation of American foreign aid. 'Sooner or later, Mobutu will go. When the time comes, it will not be in our interest to have been perceived as propping up this discredited dictator.'[333]

A few weeks later, Solarz's warnings seemed to be vindicated. Confronted by growing demands for democracy, Mobutu ordered a security crackdown. On the night of 11 May, Zairean security men brutally attacked students at the University of Lubumbashi, which they suspected of being a hotbed of unrest and dissent. Mobutu's men, who were carrying clubs and meat cleavers, went berserk and killed an unknown number of students before trying to hide the carnage by spiriting the bloodied corpses away. Huge street protests followed.

Mobutu's congressional critics seized on the Lubumbashi massacre to demand an immediate reduction in American overseas aid. Over the summer the Bush administration made an official request for $4 million in military aid and claimed that a $40 million package for economic assistance could bypass the Zairean government if it was channelled through humanitarian agencies. But anti-Mobutu sentiment was running high and on 3 November, just as the Rwanda civil war was getting under way, Congress cut all funding to the Kinshasa regime.

In Paris, the RPF's attack on Rwanda was seen as inseparable from the threat to Mobutu's rule in Zaire. If one fell to 'Anglo-Saxon' influence, then so would the other. If the Americans had a presence in Kinshasa, they would easily establish one in Kigali and vice versa. This was not just because Mobutu had close links with President Habyarimana. It was also because eastern Zaire, in particular, has very close cultural and economic links with the surrounding regions of east Africa. Equally, President Museveni of Uganda had also once had links with the sworn enemies of Mobutu.[334]

There seemed to be a real chance, in other words, of a 'domino effect': the loss of French influence in one place would be followed inexorably by a loss in others. It was not just Zaire or Rwanda or

Uganda that was at risk of falling into America's sphere of influence. In French eyes, they were all likely to fall together.[335]

There was another reason why, during and after the Gulf War of 1990–91, the French came to fear growing American interest in their African *pré carré* ('fiefdom'). After the Iraq War the United States became more conscious than before of its 'energy security'. For decades its economy had been dependent on huge quantities of oil imports but, after Saddam's invasion of Kuwait, it seemed more important than ever to find alternative sources of supply, outside the Middle East, that could sustain burgeoning domestic demand.

Senior French officials now wondered if the United States might exploit its post-Cold War hegemony in the African continent. For example, nearly a decade before the Gulf War, in the early 1980s, a Greek businessman, an imaginative and flamboyant former arms dealer called Basil Tsakos, had found interest and support on Capitol Hill for a wildly ambitious scheme to build a Trans-Africa Pipeline that would move Saudi oil to the United States. Under his plan, oil would be shipped across the Red Sea to the Sudanese coast and then piped all the way through the Central African Republic and Cameroon, terminating at the port of Douala. From there, the crude could be moved onto tankers and shipped to America. Senior French officials were well aware of the plan, and Colonel Maurice Robert of the SDECE even met with representatives from several African countries to discuss the details. But, despite the support of several senior senators, the proposal became mired in political scandal and fell apart.[336]

If such plans were resurrected then, in French eyes, they would not only give the United States an excuse to meddle in France's *domaine réservé* but, more specifically, would bring its former colonies under the geopolitical orbit of Saudi Arabia and, by extension, of its close strategic ally, the United States. For example, the Central African Republic was landlocked and would become economically dependent on the flow of Saudi oil, while Cameroon would want the transit fees that a pipeline would offer.

By 1990 it also seemed possible that Rwanda and Zaire might suffer from a comparable dependency on the 'Anglo-Saxons'. In the mid-1980s, plans had been floated for a 'Northern Corridor' that would link these two countries by road and rail to the huge Kenyan sea port at Mombasa. In 1986 these countries signed a treaty of cooperation that was intended to take these ambitious plans further forward. Four years later, more plans were drawn up to extend the Mombasa–Nairobi oil pipeline to Uganda and Rwanda. Since Kenya and Uganda were former British colonies, it seemed that 'Anglo-Saxon' influence was resurgent and that Zaire and Rwanda would become drawn into the influence of the Anglophone states. In the French capital, the British ambassador was sometimes directly asked if London was planning to supplant French influence in the African continent.[337]

Besides the 'unipolarity' of American power, there were other profound changes in the world order that were heightening French feelings of insecurity. In particular, the fall of the Berlin Wall in 1989 immediately raised the prospect of a united Germany, formed by a merger of the union of democratic West Germany and Communist East Germany. If this happened, then France would be overshadowed. Within days of the collapse of the East German regime, Mitterrand had publicly warned against reunification, arguing that 'we must avoid at all costs anything that could poison what is already a very complex situation'. Such a prospect deepened what one leading commentator called the 'bad mood' of a country that was 'unsure of its place and status in a new world'. After 1945, the alliance with West Germany had been at the forefront of France's efforts to punch above its diplomatic weight. But now the prospect of German reunification threatened the very foundations of that alliance. In Paris, some officials also wondered if France's seat on the United Nations Security

Council was under threat, perhaps from a resurgent Germany, and argued that the French would have to reassert their country's influence in Africa in order to justify its seat or in a worst-case scenario to compensate for its loss.[338]

But in the course of 1994, French policy-makers had more reason than before to be concerned about American and British intervention in Central Africa. By this time, the American government appears to have taken a conscious decision to expand its influence in the region. Without congressional approval, it authorised a large-scale, covert operation to support the RPF and to topple the Rwandan government. There are credible eyewitness accounts of American Special Forces and CIA operatives, conceivably with British undercover support, now arriving in Uganda and Rwanda to back Kagame's forces. A war by proxy with France had begun.[339]

Exactly why Washington took this decision remains unclear. When the scale of the operation later emerged, Pentagon officials naturally claimed to have had an altruistic motive, pointing out that 'if Rwanda is unstable, that's going to lead to instability throughout Central Africa'. But such claims were hardly convincing. If they wanted to bring stability to the region and end the slaughter of Tutsi civilians, then they could have pushed for a ceasefire and brokered an interim coalition government rather than a drive for regime change. This suggests that the most likely motive was that Washington regarded Kagame as a sympathiser and ally who could help establish American influence in the wider region. In particular, the RPF would help the CIA to topple Mobutu, who was now seen as a liability and a discredited force in the mineral-rich Congo. Rwanda, admitted one Washington insider, was a 'target of opportunity' and the key to a wider 'zone of influence' in east Africa.[340]

This is exactly what now unfolded. Towards the end of 1994, Kagame's RPF militia stormed into the Rwandan capital and by doing so brought the civil war to a swift and dramatic end. But the bloodshed continued. Huge numbers of innocent Hutus, perhaps as many as half a million or more, died from vengeance killings carried out by the Kigali regime, and from starvation and disease. Violence also spilled over into neighbouring Zaire, where whole regions had become a place of refuge for Rwandan civilians who were fleeing the violence in their homeland.

Kagame, who was now the Vice President and Minister of Defence in Kigali, accused President Mobutu of allowing Hutu rebels to operate from Zairean territory and to launch attacks against Rwanda. Either out of mistrust and suspicion, or because Kagame was looking for an excuse to attack, events quickly started to spiral out of control. In the course of 1995 and 1996, Kagame's forces started to establish close links with Congolese rebels, led by Laurent Kabila, who were opposed to Mobutu's rule. Then, in early October 1996, Kagame secretly sent his soldiers across the border to topple Mobutu and support a rebellion that had just broken out south of the city of Goma. Rwandan forces were also on the ground to help the rebels capture several key towns and cities, including the key copper-producing town of Lubumbashi, Kenge, Kisangani and the capital, Kinshasa.

The Rwandan leader denied having any American support but applauded Washington for 'taking the right decisions to let it [his attack] proceed'. However, the ties between them went much further than he was prepared to admit. Kagame certainly had a good rapport with senior figures in Washington, such as General George Joulwan, who had described him as a 'visionary'. More importantly, shortly before the attack on Zaire began, Kagame had completed a trip to the United States, where he had met senior officials in the State Department and 'other people', even if he later stated that they had been unable to strike any agreement about what course of action to take. Washington insiders had noted the RPF's strong presence in the

American capital: its representatives were often present at high-level meetings and were even allowed to occupy the Rwandan embassy, authorising visa requests, before they had even captured Kigali.[341]

By this time the American government was also strongly backing Kabila. US Special Forces conducted psychological operations and tactical exercises in support of Kabila's forces, helping to train them and accompanying them into battle. Kathi Austin, at that time a young investigator into the arms trade, visited the region regularly, and had 'observed full-dress [US] military personnel in western Rwanda since early 1995 ... it was very clearly military exercises taking place on the ground in western Rwanda in the border regions as early as the beginning of 1996.'[342]

At first sight, it was difficult to see a clear American motive in backing Kabila. In Paris and other capitals, there were whispers that the rebel leader would be a compliant leader who would give American companies preferential rights in Zaire's vastly lucrative mining sector. But US companies had already won exclusive rights under the Mobutu regime. The American-owned Barrick Gold Corporation, for example, had close links with General Kpama Baramoto, one of the most powerful people in the land, and in 1996 the company formed a joint venture to mine the mineral-rich area, which included the vast gold reserves at Kilo Moto, around Bunia. There was no guarantee that Kabila, once settled into power, would remain sympathetic towards the United States. The Americans were, in any case, still wary of any involvement in Africa, so soon after their debacle in Somalia in 1992–93, and a 1995 Pentagon briefing declared that the United States had 'very little traditional strategic interest in Africa'.[343]

These considerations may explain why, after Kabila's men launched their offensive in late 1996, the State Department threw its voice behind Mobutu, urging Zaire's neighbours to keep out of the conflict and acknowledging that Mobutu was the victim of foreign 'aggression'. The United States, pronounced Secretary of State Warren Christopher, has 'strongly recommended their withdrawal, in order to avoid an escalation of the conflict'. And in Kinshasa, Ambassador Daniel Simpson also condemned how 'Zaire has been attacked by Rwanda and Uganda' and 'the political and humanitarian problem' this had caused. Similar statements followed over the weeks ahead, as American diplomats pressed for an immediate ceasefire, a withdrawal of troops and a lasting settlement.[344]

America's covert support for Kabila was not, therefore, a policy that commanded universal support in Washington, and foreign policy was multifarious, as different departments, and perhaps different case officers within them, pursued agendas that were quite at odds with others. It seems likely that the State Department's position was sidelined by the Pentagon and the National Security Council, and there were many reports that drew a convincing picture of a secret agenda harboured by Kabila's sympathisers in Washington. These were reports of American demining units in Rwanda helping the rebels cross the border into Zaire; American armoured vehicles in Kisangani and direct contacts between Kagame and Washington; mysterious transport planes, flown by anonymous Americans, which moved arms and other supplies directly to the rebels; an American non-governmental organisation helping the rebels to install anti-aircraft artillery and supplying them with reconnaissance information; and up-to-date communications equipment being installed in the surrounding region to monitor events in Zaire and to coordinate the rebels' movements. A respected campaigner on human rights also met and spoke with a number of former Zairean soldiers, who gave 'compelling testimony' of an American presence in Kabila's lines. 'The influence of powers external to Africa', stated the Burundian leader, President Pierre Buyoya, 'is obvious.' There was, he continued, 'a struggle between Western powers in Africa', adding that 'no African power helps Kabila as much as certain exterior powers', which he did not specify.[345]

America's growing but secret interest in the region alarmed French officials. For example, Bernard Debré, the Minister of Cooperation at this time, publicly expressed alarm that the United States was now supporting Kabila's men in just the same way that it had allegedly assisted Museveni's army since 1990. The French intelligence services, which had agents on the ground, felt sure that at least one hundred American 'advisors', all of whom were Special Forces from Fort Bragg, were inside Zaire and Rwanda to support Kagame's army. These reports of American personnel on the ground were vindicated by a number of independent and plausible eyewitnesses, including a Rwandan priest who claimed to have met a captured American soldier. The French security services also claimed, perhaps out of vindictiveness after such an international furore about links between Paris and Kigali during the genocide, that Washington was well aware of the mass killings of Hutu civilians but did nothing to stop them.[346]

The most likely explanation is that, during his trips to the United States from 1990 onwards, Kagame had convinced a number of senior officials in Washington that he was a loyal and reliable leader who would help to guard and pursue American interests in Zaire if his protégé, Laurent Kabila, came to power. Others in Washington may have felt that the fall of Mobutu, who was already in his mid-sixties and suffering from serious illness, was imminent in any case and that a Kabila–Kagame alliance presented the best long-term bet of imposing peace and finding an ally. Given Zaire's immense natural resources and the huge material rewards that regime change might bring, elements within the CIA or the Pentagon decided to actively but covertly assist Kagame and Kabila. This was a course wholly at odds with the policy of the State Department.[347]

By this time, relations between Paris and Washington had reached a new low. Tempers flashed towards the end of 1996, when the French government led an international effort to protect the huge numbers of Hutu refugees in Zaire and proposed extending the mission's remit to protect Mobutu. But Washington vetoed the French proposals and allowed Kabila's men to continue their advance, prompting a furious response from Paris, where the politician Hervé de Charette publicly accused the Americans of behaving irresponsibly and of being wholly disinterested in the plight of ordinary Africans.[348]

Other issues, besides the future of Central Africa, made a bad situation worse. In particular, the French Foreign Ministry angered the Americans by making a number of diplomatic initiatives in the Middle East and by supporting Boutros Boutros-Ghali's re-election as Secretary-General of the United Nations. There were sharp disagreements, too, about NATO's inner politics. In 1995 the French government had agreed to rejoin the military alliance on the condition that NATO's southern command was reorganised but, towards the end of 1996, Washington started to resist making those changes.[349]

Africa was one of the few places where France could hope to maintain a unique degree of influence that would counterbalance America's apparent ascendancy. But fears were rife that this influence was still under real pressure. In Paris, ministers held a series of meetings to determine how to defend French economic interests against a growing American challenge, while President Jacques Chirac publicly condemned 'the Anglo-Saxons [who] dream of pushing France out of its position in Africa without paying a price'.[350]

In an atmosphere of such intense mistrust, French hardliners advocated stepping in to support an embattled Mobutu against his Rwandan-backed enemies. On 31 October 1996, at the request of President Jacques Chirac, Mobutu met in secret with the former French Interior Minister, Charles Pasqua, and requested the active support of the French government, including its assistance in

recruiting mercenaries. How much the Élysée knew about this mercenary operation, and how much was the outcome of an independent
effort by Pasqua's own private network, remains unclear.[351]

The man who now orchestrated the formation of a mercenary force
was a former police commissioner called Jean-Charles Marchiani.
After leaving the police force some years earlier he had begun a new
career as a political adviser and deal-maker, and while working as an
aide to Pasqua he had become involved in efforts to build links with,
and find information about, insurgent groups that were operating
in parts of Africa and the Middle East. He found sympathisers in
other departments, notably amongst members of the French internal
security service, the Direction de la Surveillance du Territoire. By
this time Jacques Foccart was dead, but the mercenary venture nonetheless attracted strong interest and support from a veteran French
diplomat by the name of Fernand Wibaux, a protégé of Foccart who
had subsequently taken up an ambassadorship in Kinshasa.[352]

Another of Marchiani's key contacts was a mysterious Serb officer,
'Colonel Dominic Yugo'. The two men had met in the course of the
Bosnian War of the mid-1990s, when Yugo had helped to secure
the release of two French pilots who had been shot down and captured in Bosnia. Now, two years later, Marchiani and Yugo worked
together to organise the formation of an international mercenary
army, using a telecommunications company, with offices in Paris,
Belgrade and Kinshasa, as a front organisation.[353]

The 'White Legion' was put under the command of a veteran
Belgian by the name of Christian Tavernier. A long-term confidant
of President Mobutu and an old soldier who had served alongside
Bob Denard and Mike Hoare in battles fought three decades before,
Tavernier worked hard to find more supporters at the highest level of
the French government. However, only around sixteen members
of Tavernier's force, which totalled less than three hundred, were

Frenchmen. The majority were drawn from eastern Europe and were veterans of the Balkan wars.[354]

But the mercenary group made little impact on the ground, arriving at the end of 1996 and pulling out just weeks later, in the middle of February. Their efforts could not prevent Kabila's army from advancing and capturing Kinshasa, where Kabila pronounced himself President on 17 May. Tavernier's army had already started to disintegrate by this time, its soldiers disillusioned by poor pay and the non-existent fighting spirit of Mobutu's men.

The mercenary force does not appear to have had much active support in Paris other than from a limited circle of nationalists, of which Marchiani was an active member. And this was a clear indication that times were changing. 'A process of normalisation' was under way.[355]

La Françafrique was no longer quite the force it was. In the thirty-five years that followed the independence of many of its African colonies, France's armed forces had regularly intervened in their affairs, averaging one such operation every year. But from the mid-1990s, such military interventions became less common. And although the political links between Paris and its former colonies remained strong, and continued to ebb and flow in the years ahead, French policy-makers were generally much less preoccupied with maintaining them. France's aid budget to African countries started to fall sharply, and the Ministry of Cooperation, which once enjoyed such freedom of operation, and whose activities were so hidden from the public gaze, was put firmly under the watchful eye of the Foreign Affairs Ministry. There were still official and unofficial *réseaux* ('networks') between France and its former colonies – networks that in some regions remained powerful and influential – but they were now increasingly sidelined. They had become, as two analysts have put it, 'privatised … lobbies that pursue their own objectives, whether or not these objectives implicate the state'.[356]

This was partly because a whole generation of post-colonial leaders was passing away and memories of empire were fading. In particular, Félix Houphouët-Boigny, the staunchly Francophile President of Côte d'Ivoire and a one-time French Cabinet minister, died in 1993. The new generation of leaders would not have the same ties with France as its predecessors, and some African leaders, such as Nicéphore Soglo of Benin and Alassane Ouattara of Côte d'Ivoire, had lived and been educated in the United States. Such individuals regarded the prospect of uninvited French intervention in their affairs as an imperialistic and insulting anachronism.

Similarly transformational changes were already taking place in Paris. François Mitterrand died in 1996 and Jacques Foccart passed away the following year. But for the reformers of the mid-1990s – men like Pierre Joxe, the Minister for Defence, Jean-Pierre Cot, the Minister of Cooperation, and Édouard Balladur, who became Prime Minister in April 1993 – *la Françafrique* was not much more than an inconvenient burden on France's overstretched national resources.

By the mid-1990s, the covert links between Paris and African capitals were also coming under much stronger media scrutiny within France than ever before. A number of determined and brave investigative reporters, such as Stephen Smith for *Libération* and Patrick de Saint-Exupéry for *Le Figaro*, as well as a succession of formal enquiries, exposed a massive scale of corruption that scandalised France and led to the formal investigation, extradition and even imprisonment of former ministers and a President. Huge amounts of France's public money was being wasted in former colonies, it emerged, to subsidise corrupt and sometimes tyrannical regimes that in return bought overpriced French exports and hired inefficient French companies. The truth about France's intervention in Rwanda inflamed public anger even more, sending political shockwaves throughout France and outraging many ordinary French citizens. France's international image and reputation had been badly dented by the tragedy, and it could ill-afford to incur any more condemnation.[357]

But none of this meant that, by the mid-late 1990s, 'la Françafrique' was dead. It had, instead, merely changed form. France continued to play a special role in much of sub-Saharan Africa. This was partly because of its historic connections and influence in a region that, in the early twenty-first century, was still home to around a quarter of a million French nationals, and which remained a vital marketplace for French goods.

In 1995, under President Jacques Chirac, the French armed forces developed a more multilateral approach to intervening in African affairs, one that involved working alongside the members of the African Union and the United Nations. Seventeen years later, one of his successors, President Nicolas Sarkozy, adopted the same approach in Mali, lobbying hard for United Nations approval to send French troops alongside those of an African body, the Economic Community of west African States. When, in January 2013, the security situation in Mali suddenly deteriorated and President François Hollande saw the urgent deployment of thousands of French troops as the only response that would save the Malian regime from insurgent attack, he still waited for a formal invitation from its government and consulted closely with other African leaders, such as South Africa's Jacob Zuma and Algeria's Abdelaziz Bouteflika. French intervention in the continent had also become more formal and open, as well as more multilateral: dialogue between Paris and African capitals was now conducted through official diplomatic channels rather than by the more shadowy advisers of before.

There was another reason why la Françafrique, far from disappearing, was instead only evolving. This was French grandeur. By maintaining a presence and influence in Africa, French leaders and their electorates could still convince themselves of their national greatness. In particular, they could raise the status of their nation before *les anglo-saxons*.

Like *la Françafrique*, France's traditional rivalry with the 'Anglo-Saxons' looked, at first sight, to have lapsed, or even disappeared. In Paris, leaders openly acknowledged that France needed the economic and material support of Britain and America if they were to retain any influence in their former colonies. France was hit hard by global recession in the early 1990s: in 1994, for example, 12 per cent of the French workforce was unemployed, while national output had taken a plunge. As a result it could not easily afford to undertake adventurous policies in former colonies without the support of its allies. In September 1993, Prime Minister Balladur proclaimed an 'Abidjan Doctrine', which made France's economic support for its former colonies conditional upon their cooperation with two international institutions – the International Monetary Fund and the World Bank – that Paris had previously condemned as American-controlled 'Anglo-Saxon' bodies. Four months later, Paris devalued the 'African franc', which fifteen former colonies used as a common currency. Strongly opposed by eighty-year-old Jacques Foccart, the devaluation was an unmistakable sign of change in Paris: the French government was no longer prepared to spend vast sums of between $2 and $3 billion every year subsidising the standards of living in the developing world. Not only was France less able to challenge foreign lenders at a time of economic recession, but it also needed to brace itself for economic and monetary union with other member states of the European Union that wanted to create a common currency. This involved keeping a tight grip on the budget deficit.[358]

New initiatives were also undertaken to integrate any future French military interventions in Africa with the armed forces of other member states of the European Union, including Britain, and with the United States, while also allowing the Africans more scope to look after themselves. At the Saint-Malo summit in December 1998, for example, French and British leaders made a joint declaration of their willingness to cooperate more closely on the African continent and to promote 'human rights, democratic principles, the rule of law and good governance while tackling the debt problem and maintaining a significant level of developmental assistance' there.[359]

France, in other words, was working closely with the 'Anglo-Saxons', just as it always had. But the old feelings of rivalry were still there. They were too deeply ingrained over long centuries just to disappear within the space of a few years. France was still playing a Great Game of competition and rivalry with Britain and America, even if its manoeuvres were not always easy to see.

CHAPTER 15

FRANCE'S LIBYAN VENTURE

On Thursday 15 September 2011, the French President, Nicolas Sarkozy, and the British Prime Minister, David Cameron, flew together to the Libyan city of Benghazi. They were greeted by large crowds that gave them a rapturous welcome. 'Merci Sarkozy ... thank you Britain!' some of them shouted out jubilantly at their two visitors. Not surprisingly, neither could conceal their glee. 'You wanted peace, you wanted liberty, you want economic progress! France, Great Britain and Europe will be on the side of the Libyan people!' proclaimed an exultant Sarkozy as he addressed a large gathering. His counterpart spoke in similarly glowing terms. 'It is great to be here in free Benghazi, and free Libya,' exulted Cameron. 'Your city was an inspiration to the world as you threw off the dictator and chose freedom. People in Britain salute your courage.'

It was a triumph for France and the two 'Anglo-Saxon' powers, Britain and America. All three countries had worked closely together to carry out a joint attack on Libya and to topple its leader, Colonel Muammar Gaddafi. On 19 March, French warplanes had struck Gaddafi's armed forces, and hours later the British and Americans had joined the fray, launching salvos of missiles from submarines and warships that had been lying in wait off the Libyan coast. Gaddafi's regime had held out for several long months but, towards the end of August, rebel militia had swept into the capital and a temporary government, the 'National Transitional Council', proclaimed victory. The operation bore testimony to the success of the doctrine of 'liberal intervention' in the affairs of foreign countries as well as to the spirit of cooperation between France and the 'Anglo-Saxons'. The old 'Great Game' for influence and prestige was ever more of a fading memory.

Such, at any rate, were the sound bites and such was the posturing. Soon, however, the Cameron–Sarkozy rhetoric sounded hollow and the media images looked superficial. Libya quickly began to disintegrate into a state of anarchy ruled only by criminals, Islamist extremists, refugees and their traffickers. Some time later, Libya's tragic fate even caused a transatlantic dispute when President Barack Obama ventured blistering criticisms of the operation with an openness that was unprecedented for a serving American President.

Equally superficial was the image of French cooperation with the two English-speaking nations. The story of the Libyan intervention was in fact much more complex than it at first appeared, and there were really strong undercurrents of rivalry beneath the veneer of cooperation. In days gone by, France had sometimes pursued its own agenda, one that was quite independent of Britain and America or even quite adversarial. But in 2011 Sarkozy had worked closely with those two countries in order to give his country the upper hand. France was still playing the Great Game, in other words, but in a way that was not as easy to see as it had been on the playing fields of earlier ages.[360]

The Libyan crisis had begun in early 2011, when it seemed that Libya was just starting to feel the rising temperatures of what later became known as 'the Arab Spring'. Over the preceding few weeks, a series of popular protests and demonstrations had started to gather pace in north Africa and the Middle East. On 14 January, Tunisian President Zine El Abidine Ben Ali had resigned from office as protestors engulfed the streets, while mass protests also broke out in Cairo and other Egyptian cities on 'the Day of Revolution', 25 January. And when, on 15 February, the Libyan authorities arrested a human rights activist in the city of Benghazi, sparking violent protests, many observers wondered if Gaddafi's regime would be swept away and a new, more liberal and democratic era would begin.

Heavy fighting broke out in Benghazi between government troops and rebel militia. Reports also emerged that Gaddafi had started to use warplanes to attack and bomb protestors in Benghazi, Tripoli, and a number of other cities where riots had erupted. When two Libyan warplanes landed in Malta, their pilots stating that they had preferred to desert rather than carry out such orders, it seemed that Gaddafi would stop at nothing to cling to power. Pointing out that Gaddafi was already unleashing 'genocide' against his own people, Libya's representative to the United Nations then broke ranks and called for the outside world to intervene.

It was into this bloody fray that the French President, Nicolas Sarkozy, stepped. He now advocated the imposition by NATO warplanes of a no-fly zone over Libya, where no Libyan planes would be allowed to operate, 'to prevent the use of that country's warplanes against its population'. His Western allies were much more cautious, and the British Prime Minister judged that 'we are not at that stage yet', while Washington at that point had no interest in military intervention. But Sarkozy continued to lobby hard for the use of force and wanted to back up such measures with a package of harsh economic sanctions against Tripoli. Sidelining the European Union's 'Foreign Minister', Catherine Ashton, Sarkozy adopted the cause of the Benghazi rebels as his personal humanitarian crusade, claiming that France had a 'role before history' in stopping Gaddafi's 'killing spree' against people whose only crime was to seek to 'liberate themselves from servitude'.

It soon became clear that Sarkozy was in fact looking for an excuse to carry out regime change in Tripoli, and that the events in Benghazi, or rather the allegations about what was happening there, provided him with the fig leaf of respectability that he needed to disguise his belligerence. The most convincing explanation is that he wanted to establish France's influence in a region that he regarded as its natural sphere of influence and stop other countries, above all the Americans, from doing so. Libya was never a French colony, having been ruled for long centuries by the rulers of the Ottoman Empire before the Italians seized it in 1911. But it does lie adjacent to seas and territories that France regards as its *domaine réservé*.

Sarkozy's determination to use force against Libya became clear almost as soon as the crisis began, when he worked hard to make the Libyan intervention his war, France's war, while relegating his two partners into a secondary position. In February, as the crisis in Libya grew, he had enlisted the support of David Cameron to confront Colonel Gaddafi, and despite his initial hesitancy, Cameron eventually threw his voice behind Sarkozy and declared his support for a no-fly zone over Libya. Meanwhile, at the United Nations, French and British diplomats busily drafted a resolution that would sanction the use of force.

But while other foreign powers struggled to keep pace, Sarkozy pressed ahead with yet more ambitious plans to intervene in Libyan affairs. Again, he was keen to enlist British support. On 11 March, as European leaders gathered at a high-level meeting in Brussels to discuss the Middle East crisis, the President was 'increasingly emotional' about the issue and became so angry with the failure of other leaders to support his own tough line against Gaddafi that he stormed out of a formal dinner. By this time, the French leader had also recruited the United States into his ranks, even though Obama had initially been reluctant to join him. The Americans felt they were being 'bounced into action', as one biographer has written.[361]

At around the same time, Sarkozy had met two members of the self-declared 'Libyan opposition' at the Élysée Palace. This meeting, which had been brokered and arranged by a left-wing philosopher and media star called Bernard-Henri Lévy, lasted several hours, and, when they left, the two Libyans held a press conference in which they made a dramatic revelation. 'France', they announced, 'recognises the Libyan Transitional National Council as the legitimate representative of the Libyan people.' As a result, they continued, President Sarkozy would shortly be dispatching an ambassador to their stronghold of Benghazi. Sarkozy's drive for war had taken a big step forward, without the support of Britain or indeed any other country.

But while London, for the moment, refused to echo this revolutionary call, French diplomats continued to lobby hard for a United Nations resolution that had enough teeth to threaten the Libyan leader. They wanted much more than the imposition of economic sanctions that an earlier resolution, adopted on 26 February, had imposed, and instead advocated a far more drastic approach. On 17 March, the UN Security Council adopted Resolution 1973, which imposed the no-fly zone and, short of actually occupying the country, allowed 'all necessary measures' to protect the Libyan people from the wrath of its leader. The reference to 'all necessary measures' meant that foreign countries could, if they chose, effectively declare war.

Sarkozy proudly proclaimed this new resolution as a triumph for his own diplomacy and for the Libyan people. In Paris, he denounced Gaddafi's 'murderous madness' and argued that 'in Libya, the civilian population, which is demanding nothing more than the right to choose its own destiny, is in mortal danger'. It was 'our duty', he added, 'to respond to their anguished appeal'. Such sentiments were echoed in London by David Cameron, who pointed out that Gaddafi had already killed 'more than one thousand' of his own people, and had 'begun airstrikes in anticipation of what we expect to be a brutal attack using air, land and sea forces' that would show 'no mercy and no pity'. And if any of his allies had doubts about what might lie ahead, then Sarkozy was quick to try to dispel them, inviting Hillary Clinton, the American Secretary of State, over to Paris on 18 March and assuring her that he and David Cameron were not repeating the mistakes made by the Americans after their invasion of Iraq eight years before.

But some commentators and observers were puzzled. Why was the French President taking such a harsh line against a regime with which his country had strong commercial ties? Since 2004, when the European Union had lifted its economic sanctions against Tripoli, French companies had sold huge quantities of arms, worth around half a billion dollars, to Colonel Gaddafi. The French national oil giant, Total, also had a strong presence in Libya, although its Italian and Spanish competitors had more exposure there. Successive French governments had worked hard to secure these contracts with a leader whose humanitarian record was far from clean, even if Gaddafi was not as brutal and ruthless as many other Middle Eastern and African regimes, past and present, that France and other Western countries regularly did business with.

Two days later, as it patrolled the no-fly zone, a French plane attacked and destroyed a Libyan Army jeep as it made its way through the desert that surrounded Benghazi. The French, it seemed, were very keen to initiate hostilities, striking Libya before its air defences had even been neutralised and making no effort to coordinate their own attacks with the British. This sent an obvious signal – that this was France's war. Meanwhile, Sarkozy chaired a 'dramatic meeting' in Paris and took the credit for getting battle under way. 'We are not schoolboys in short trousers,' he told his British counterpart. 'We are men.'[362]

The French then took another big step forward. An official in the Defence Ministry in Paris told reporters that soon afterwards several French jets had 'destroyed a number of tanks and armoured vehicles', while others had made reconnaissance flights over 'all Libyan territory', rather than in the much more restricted no-fly zone. Hours later, Royal Air Force jets roared away from their bases and headed for Libyan airspace. The Americans, in the meantime, were still not fully engaged, having announced only that they would use their 'unique capabilities' to ensure the Libyans respected the no-fly zone.

But as Allied jets streaked over the Libyan skies, some people began to question Sarkozy's ostensible motives. In Washington, American officials were aware that Sarkozy had established links with the Libyan rebels – the 'Council' led by Mustafa Abdul Jalil – far earlier than he had admitted. At the end of February, three weeks before the United Nations had passed Resolution 1973, the President had even ordered his foreign intelligence service, the DGSE, to actively support Jalil's organisation and to offer it 'money and guidance' as well as diplomatic support and recognition if it seized power. Once they had established close links with the rebels, the French spies soon started to supply them with arms. An American newspaper reported that the first supplies from France, as well as Qatar and Egypt, had arrived in Libya around the end of February, amounting to a clear breach of the arms embargo imposed by UN Resolution 1970. By June, French military support to the rebels was an open secret: France had airdropped 'light arms such as assault rifles', said one spokesman, for civilian communities 'to protect themselves against Colonel Gaddafi'.[363]

The findings of several independent human rights watchdogs also raised doubts about what the Élysée was really doing. Some reported that, on the eve of France's armed intervention, Gaddafi's men had in fact killed far fewer protestors than the watching world had been led to believe. The real figure was a few hundred, which was of course bad enough but only around one third of the supposed casualties. Most of these had in any case been killed in street battles between government troops and armed militia. Even if Gaddafi's army had stormed Benghazi, there had never been any reason to suppose that they would carry out the ferocious, almost genocidal violence that Western audiences were told would happen. Gaddafi had faced other uprisings before and he had always executed only the ringleaders, not innocent civilians. The story about Libyan warplanes bombing and strafing protestors was also fabricated. It had been concocted by Libyan rebels, 'vindicated' by pilots who wanted political asylum and then aired by an Arab news network but never seriously questioned. Claims of such atrocities are usually backed up by footage and photographs that go viral on the web, but they were conspicuously absent on this occasion.[364]

Most glaringly, the French-led intervention expressly violated the terms of the UN resolution that Paris and London had sponsored. This resolution called for 'the immediate establishment of a ceasefire and a complete end to violence … with the aim of facilitating dialogue … [to] find a peaceful and sustainable solution'. In other words, the use of force was merely a last resort that could be used only if, in a worst-case scenario, dialogue had failed. Sarkozy could have pursued this peaceful alternative without even resorting to the United Nations: by early March, several governments, notably those of the African Union, Turkey and Germany, were supporting a detailed proposal drawn up by a non-governmental organisation. This called for an immediate ceasefire followed by negotiations 'aimed at replacing the current regime with a more accountable, representative and law-abiding government'.[365]

The French President, in other words, had been trying to find an excuse to go to war. Gaddafi immediately complied with the United Nations resolution by calling for a ceasefire and by offering to open negotiations, but his offer was quickly rejected by the Libyan rebels and ignored by Paris, although a scathing David Cameron did concede that 'we will judge him by his actions not his words'. And as tension mounted over the days that followed, Gaddafi reiterated his conciliatory words but was once again sidelined, while efforts by both Turkey and the African Union to mediate were brushed aside. A ceasefire was not enough, the Libyan rebels now insisted as they raised the bar even higher, because Gaddafi had to stand down first. Still Tripoli extended a hand of peace, venturing more offers of a ceasefire on 30 April, 26 May and 9 June, but still these were rejected by the rebels and by the British, American and French governments.

By the third week of March it was already too late for Gaddafi to save himself and his regime. British and French warplanes had by this stage already struck Libya very hard, flying thousands of missions to give strong and close support to the rebels as they marched from their strongholds towards the capital. By the end of August they had Tripoli in their grip, and Colonel Gaddafi was captured and killed on 20 October, allegedly at the instigation of the French intelligence services.[366]

It was obvious that Sarkozy, as the orchestrator and ringleader of the Libyan intervention, had wanted an excuse to intervene and topple Gaddafi. But it was less easy to see why. Analysts and commentators ventured a number of possible reasons but none of them were convincing.

In particular, some wondered if the Libyan crisis had simply offered Sarkozy an opportunity to steal the political limelight both within France and beyond. The conflict, pondered the British general Sir David Richards, was about French *gloire*. Perhaps Sarkozy calculated that leading an international charge to war would provide a huge boost to his own personal popularity and to France's national prestige, which was under growing pressure from an assertive Germany. For as she worked to reform the institutions of the European Union and to support lagging EU members, the German Chancellor, Angela Merkel, seemed to be overshadowing her French counterpart.[367]

Sarkozy had previously reached for the trigger to hit a political target at home and boost his flagging popularity. In February 2008 he had appealed to the traditional French spirit of *activisme* by sending troops into Chad to bolster the embattled regime of President Idriss Déby and to evacuate Western expatriates. As a result, his popularity had soared. But three years on, his poll ratings were once again going into freefall. So perhaps Sarkozy wanted to repeat the tactic and spearhead a successful intervention that would distract the nation from its woes and rally popular sentiment behind him. Little more than a year before the next Presidential election, he badly needed a boost.

But this suggestion holds little weight. If he had wanted to win a ratings war against his political adversaries at home, then Sarkozy had nothing more to gain by removing the existing regime in Tripoli than by enforcing a no-fly zone in Libyan skies. He did, however, have much more to lose, since regime change was a complex task that risked going badly wrong. It is true that at first the Élysée basked in the adulation of victory, but the longer the war continued, the greater the chance of tragedy and disaster. When, on 19 June, a French missile smashed into a block of flats in Tripoli, killing nine innocent civilians and injuring many more, Sarkozy had to rely on the reverential and deferential French press to keep the incident quiet.

Instead of waging war against Gaddafi, Sarkozy could simply have taken a lead role as a peacemaker in the same way he had done in August 2008, when he intervened in the armed clash between

Russian and Georgian forces in South Ossetia and helped to broker a ceasefire. He often performed well at these kinds of diplomatic and political initiatives: for example, he had fostered his image as 'Super Sarko' by calling for an entirely new system of monetary regulation that would alleviate the financial crash and prevent another from occurring. And if he had wanted to use military force, then he could have done so in parts of Africa where limited strikes against relatively ineffectual Islamist militias would have been a much safer bet.

Others wondered if the French President was making a desperate and far-sighted bid to resolve a growing migration crisis. In the summer of 2010, an increasing number of migrants had started to sail from Libya's coast on the Mediterranean Sea for European shores. Desperate to escape poverty, they were prepared to endure extreme hardships and run a very real risk of drowning in their bid to start new lives. In late 2009, Colonel Gaddafi struck a deal with Italy, which was bearing the brunt of the refugee flow, to curb the exodus, and soon Libyan patrol boats had sharply reduced the numbers.

But patrolling Libya's vast, 1,000-mile coast was a costly and time-consuming business that diverted Gaddafi's resources away from other tasks. He was subsidising, in other words, a European problem. In August 2010, during a trip to Italy, he had made a bid to win concessions: unless European money helped to meet his cost, he seemed to threaten, then the migrant flow would continue unabated. Europe would become 'another Africa' as a result of the 'advance of millions of immigrants. Tomorrow Europe might no longer be European and even turn black as there are millions who want to come in,' he said. 'We don't know if Europe will remain an advanced and united continent or if it will be destroyed, as happened with the barbarian invasions.'[368]

Perhaps Sarkozy was afraid that Gaddafi would allow migrants to cross from the Libyan coast into western Europe, further fuelling his determined opponents on the political far right in France:

on 8 March, just as Sarkozy was leading the charge against Libya, a new opinion poll gave the National Front enough votes to win the Presidential election. It is possible that he calculated that a new, more compliant regime in Tripoli would not dare to turn against the Western powers that had backed it.

However, this does not quite explain the President's interest in toppling Gaddafi. There was no guarantee that any new regime in Tripoli would be any more able or willing than its predecessor to curb the flow of migrants from Libya's coast. Even in a best-case scenario, stemming the refugee exodus from one country merely pushed the same people to move and try their luck elsewhere. There were lots of different routes, notably through Turkey and Greece, that migrants were increasingly using to head westwards. And if this issue had really been his chief concern, then the French President could simply have negotiated with Gaddafi and offered to send French patrol boats into the Mediterranean to work alongside their Libyan counterparts.

In Paris, rumours also abounded that Sarkozy wanted to keep Gaddafi quiet for the same reason that, decades before, President Giscard had allegedly wanted to silence Emperor Bokassa. In 2011, Gaddafi's son claimed that Libya had helped to finance Sarkozy's 2007 election campaign and had been toppled because he wanted to the money returned. And the following year, researchers for a French investigative website, Mediapart, also claimed to have seen a confidential note suggesting that Gaddafi had contributed as much as $50 million.

But even if these allegations were true, then they would seem to have given Sarkozy at least as much reason to support Gaddafi as to seek his removal. By backing the rebels, the French President risked immediate exposure by a vindictive leader. But by supporting Tripoli, or at least keeping out of the rebellion in the spring of 2011, Sarkozy would at least have had a chance of keeping any such matter quiet.

Long before the onset of hostilities, many people had also wondered what France and Britain could gain from oil, Libya's great asset. Rumours and stories swirled that Sarkozy wanted a new regime in Tripoli that would return the favour and give French companies preferential treatment. In particular, the state-owned oil giant Total would win huge new contracts, chiefly at the expense of its Italian rival, Eni.

American spy agencies detected the hand of the French oil lobby in Sarkozy's intervention. 'In return for their assistance,' ran an internal email to Secretary of State Clinton on 22 March, 'the DGSE officers indicated that they expected the new government of Libya to favour French firms and national interests, particularly regarding the oil industry in Libya.' Another leaked American government document also disclosed that representatives of leading French companies, notably in the oil and defence sectors, regularly boarded humanitarian flights from Paris to Tripoli, where they were met and escorted by armed French undercover officers to meetings.[369]

It is true that Libya's oil sector potentially has much to offer foreign companies. 'Its high quality "sweet" crude can be cheaply and easily piped to the markets of Western Europe,' as one oil analyst explains. 'Large areas of its coasts remain unexplored while its existing fields have barely been touched by the latest, most up-to-date methods of "enhanced recovery" that are designed to squeeze every last barrel.' Gaddafi's regime had also imposed harsh conditions on foreign operators. When Washington started to lift its sanctions on Libya, from 2004 onwards, and Tripoli auctioned some of its fields, the Libyan National Oil Corporation demanded extortionate up-front payments in return for licences and then took a large chunk of the proceeds of extracted oil. In particular, the Libyan authorities infuriated foreign oil companies by imposing new taxes and conditions after their contracts had been signed: in 2009, for example, Tripoli put forward a new law that obliged foreign oil companies to make 'charitable' contributions.[370]

Perhaps Sarkozy also gambled that a new, more compliant Libyan government would not only offer more generous contract terms but also show a favouritism to Total at the expense, above all, of its Italian rivals. Italian oil companies had long-standing links with Libya, dating back to the 1950s, and after 2004 Gaddafi had offered them lucrative contracts to explore and develop his oil and gas fields. By early 2011, Tripoli was also negotiating a number of arms contracts, collectively worth over a billion dollars, with Italian defence firms.

There was another reason why allegations about Sarkozy's links with the oil industry seemed to be convincing. The Élysée's close ties with Total and other state-owned oil companies had long been an open secret in France, although only the most extreme cases became the stuff of scandal. The most notorious case had surrounded Elf, an exploration company that had been founded in 1965 during Charles de Gaulle's presidency. It had immediately become an effective instrument of French foreign policy, sometimes paying vast sums of money to keep sympathetic leaders in power, mainly in Gabon and other west African states, and to ensure that they awarded contracts to French companies, not British, American or other foreign rivals. Its revenues flooded the coffers of Gaullist political parties and its facilities were used and abused by senior politicians, such as the Gaullist politician and interior minister Charles Pasqua, who made numerous personal trips on its corporate jets. Elf was eventually immersed by a torrent of allegations, rumours and court cases, which even engulfed France's former Foreign Minister, Roland Dumas, who was jailed in 2001 for receiving illicit but vast payments from its funds. Two years later, France was rocked by a huge corruption scandal and a gripping trial that led to the imprisonment of Elf's former chairman and other company officials who had siphoned off €350 million from the company's accounts in order to buy political favours. However, by this time Elf had merged with another state-owned company to form Total, which continued to maintain very close links with the presidential office.

But the very close links between governing elites and Total also undermine the argument that, in 2011, Sarkozy took France to war with Libya over oil or any other business interests. For it was at the instigation, or with the tacit approval, of French policy-makers that Elf and Total had typically used bribes to win contracts. And if bribery had worked, or so nearly worked, in other countries, then there was no reason why it could not be used in Libya, a country in which corruption is not just endemic but routine. Such an approach would have been much cheaper than waging war against Gaddafi's regime: by the end of September 2011, France had exceeded its allocated budget for foreign military operations by around €300–350 million. A much cheaper alternative, and a much more targeted approach, would have been for French officials to simply bribe their way into the Libyan market.[371]

Sarkozy would also have known that, even if he had toppled Gaddafi, then Eni and other foreign oil companies would have stayed in Libya to fulfil their contracts. Most oil and gas companies sign long-term agreements that commit them to spending perhaps twenty or more years in that country so that they can claw back the millions of dollars they spend on setting up rigs and other vital infrastructure. Although the new regime in Tripoli might have renegotiated the terms of its existing contracts, just as Gaddafi had done when he came to power, it had nothing to gain by forcing those companies out of the country altogether. This would have caused massive disruption to Libya's oil production and scared off other companies from doing business there.

A clue to what really lay behind Sarkozy's determination to topple the Tripoli regime comes from the volte-face that he made in the space of just four years.

In July 2007, just weeks after coming to office, Nicolas Sarkozy had visited Libya, greeting Colonel Gaddafi warmly before signing major deals for the sale of French arms and to cooperate on nuclear matters. In December the following year, the colonel then made his own return visit to the French capital, his first trip there since 1973. Gaddafi's lavish five-day trip infuriated human rights protestors but amused onlookers who watched his followers pitch an enormous tent outside his official guesthouse and who saw his large entourage of four hundred servants and forty female bodyguards follow him around.

What, then, had changed in such a relatively short space of time? One difference was that the 'Anglo-Saxons' suddenly seemed to be making serious inroads into a country that, in the eyes of Sarkozy and other French officials, lay within their own natural sphere of influence.

Libya's relations with both Britain and America had started to warm after 2003, when Gaddafi had renounced his ambitions to build weapons of mass destruction and accepted his responsibility for the bombing of an American airliner, Pan Am Flight 103, in 1988. Washington had lifted economic sanctions but relations between the two countries were not properly restored until 2008, when Libya offered Washington a 'final settlement' that compensated American victims of Libyan acts of violence. This agreement was signed on 14 August 2008.

It was at this point that America reached out to Libya in a bid to establish 'military to military' ties. In late February 2010, several American military officers visited Tripoli to hold talks about 'inviting Libyan officers to visit Army schools in the United States, holding discussion on border security, conducting medical exchanges and sharing helicopter procedures', as Major Philip Archer, US Army Africa's North African Regional Desk Officer, explained. Then, in May 2010, a senior American general, William B. Garrett III, visited Tripoli to meet several Libyan leaders to discuss building closer links and enhancing regional cooperation. 'We are gradually opening a dialogue that has not existed between our land forces in a long time,' Garrett told the press. 'Times have changed and relationships must change too.' Washington was keen to integrate Libya into Africom, its military command for Africa, and to establish bases on Libyan soil that its personnel could use.[372]

In fact, it was always most unlikely that Gaddafi would join Africom, let alone NATO. 'Gaddafi was capable of taking the world by surprise,' one former ambassador to Tripoli has pointed out, 'but there was never any chance of him signing a formal defensive alliance with Washington.' There was too much mistrust between the two capitals: Gaddafi would have viewed an American military presence on his territory as an outright threat.[373]

Instead, the posturing and rhetoric by American visitors to Libya mattered because it was an unmistakable sign of the influence that Washington wanted to exert in Libya, and had wanted ever since it entered the Second World War. The region had enormous geostrategic significance, not just because of its oil but also as a vantage point overlooking the entire Mediterranean Sea.

Sarkozy would have viewed any such alliance between Gaddafi's Tripoli and Washington, hypothetical though it was always likely to be, with mixed feelings. On the one hand, before he was even elected as President, 'American Sarko' had adopted an openly pro-Washington line that was far removed from the scepticism and even outright hostility of traditional Gaullism. When France refused to join Washington's attack on Iraq in 2003, he had disapprovingly remarked that 'the Americans felt that they were abandoned by a nation with which they had felt close historical ties and shared values'. His strong feelings for the United States, which some friends and acquaintances described as a 'fascination', were perhaps engendered by stories he had heard of the liberation of France in 1944–45, or by the influence of his father, who had once wanted to emigrate there.

But whatever its origins, relations between the two countries soon began to improve drastically after his election. This was not just a difference of style but also of substance: in June 2008, as he stood alongside President George W. Bush, Sarkozy announced that the following year France would rejoin NATO's command structure, forty-three years after de Gaulle had pulled French forces out.[374]

But this was not quite the full picture. Sarkozy's opinions of the 'Anglo-Saxons' were really as complex as those of many of his fellow nationals. In the true style of a Frenchman, he often criticised the 'Anglo-Saxon model' of economics, arguing that it explained why Britain was 'in a far worse economic situation than France', and he fought hard for tighter regulation of European markets, claiming that his proposals 'turned the page' on a dominant 'Anglo-Saxon capitalism'. And in November 2010, after signing a new defence relationship with David Cameron's government, he raised eyebrows by ducking a journalist's searching question, refusing to specify if he would send a French aircraft carrier to the Falklands in the event of confrontation with Argentina. It was significant that, during a trip to Buenos Aires several years later, he volunteered to 'help bring sides together regarding the Argentine claim over the Falklands'.[375]

At the same time, Sarkozy the patriot had quietly clung to what was left of la Françafrique, clinging to the 'rotting corpse' of a policy that allowed him and his compatriots to convince themselves that their country was still a global power to be reckoned with. Despite publicly proclaiming his commitment to a post-colonial retreat, one that would allow 'no more nodding and winking, secrets and ambiguities', he continued along the same neo-colonial paths as his predecessors, perpetuating, as one journalist has written, 'France's time-honoured tradition of parallel diplomacy in Africa' and giving les réseaux 'a new lease of life'. The only explanation was that 'francophone Africa is still an echo chamber for France's international pretensions'.[376]

The French leader would have felt indignation at being pushed out of a region that he regarded as lying within France's own sphere of influence. Libya was a former Italian colony but the Mediterranean Sea was France's traditional *domaine réservé* and had been for centuries. The security of France's southern borders clearly depended on it. In the early twentieth century, French commanders had feared British control of Tangiers or the establishment of a German base in Morocco just as, centuries before, they had fought the Barbary pirates who used the north African coast as a base from which to attack Europe. It was also a key maritime route to the outside world – one that had linked the French mainland to its empire in Asia as well as to the Maghreb. As a French general had put it, 'the Mediterranean runs through France as the Seine runs through Paris'. Other strategists argued that France's connection with its colonies and former colonies in Africa existed along a geostrategic axis that ran from Paris through north Africa to Brazzaville.[377]

It was significant that, long after the independence of Tunisia, Morocco and Algeria, the French government still did not welcome official visits by American representatives in those countries and feared Chinese economic expansion there. For the same reason, from 2007 Sarkozy had championed the establishment of *L'Union pour la Méditerranée*, the 'Club Med', that he envisaged as a more modest version of the European Union. He wanted France to shape and lead this union, allowing it to play a leading role in the region and restore something of its lost imperial grandeur, not least to compensate for Germany's growing influence in central and eastern Europe. But by the end of 2010, any dreams of establishing a Mediterranean Union had been rapidly dispelled by the Arab revolutions that began in Tunisia. The future of the region had simply become too uncertain to entertain such grandiose ideas.[378]

Yet, just briefly, in the spring of 2011, it seemed quite possible that

France was going to lose its influence in the wider Maghreb region – and that the United States would gain its own influence there at its expense.

In the course of January, the Tunisian government, led by President Zine El Abidine Ben Ali, had been shaken by violent street protests. As talk and speculation of an 'Arab Spring' grew, Ben Ali's security forces cracked down hard on the protestors, opening fire with live ammunition and making mass arrests. But, as they did so, Paris openly supported his regime. The French Foreign Minister, Michèle Alliot-Marie, decreed that the French police would provide its 'know-how' to help Ben Ali's forces maintain order: the gendarmes, she claimed, could train their Tunisian counterparts because the 'skills, recognised around the world, of our security forces allow us to resolve security situations of this type'. At the same time, the Culture Minister, Frédéric Mitterrand, sprang to Ben Ali's defence and stated in public that Tunisia was not an 'unequivocal dictatorship'. And as the violence worsened and more protestors were shot dead, Paris still refused to condemn Ben Ali. The links between Paris and Tunis caused more embarrassment when it emerged that Alliot-Marie had visited the country after the rioting had started and used a private jet that belonged to a businessman who had very close links to Ben Ali.[379]

As news of these links broke, the Tunisian rebels denounced Sarkozy for his 'complicity' with Ben Ali's government. And in Paris, Sarkozy's rivals denounced his government and argued that France would pay a heavy political price for its apparent sympathy with Ben Ali. Martine Aubry, the Socialist Party leader, said that the government should 'draw the consequences from such a serious error which makes us lose credibility, and not only in Tunisia'. By this time it had also become clear that the government's support for the Tunisian regime had been in vain, for Ben Ali's nerve broke and he fled the country on 14 January.

Sarkozy (centre) with his wife, Carla Bruni, and Ben Ali, April 2008. Sarkozy's support for Ben Ali was instrumental in explaining his intervention in Libya in 2011.

The United States, by contrast, had sided with the demonstrators. On 7 January, spokesmen in Washington had declared their support for the protestors' right to assemble and demonstrate, while on 25 January, in his State of the Union address, President Obama had decreed that, in Tunisia, 'the will of the people proved more powerful than the writ of a dictator'. He went further. 'Let us be clear: the United States of America stands with the people of Tunisia, and supports the democratic aspirations of all people.' At the same time, the American government had also shown a cautious sympathy towards demonstrators in Egypt who were protesting against the rule of President Hosni Mubarak. While the French government said nothing, Robert Gibbs, a spokesman for Obama, had publicly urged Mubarak to 'demonstrate [his] responsiveness to the people of Egypt' by recognising their 'universal rights'.

French support for Ben Ali threatened to provoke an angry reaction from other repressed Arabs who identified with the Tunisian rebels. In early February, it looked as though no regime in the Middle East was safe. On 11 February, as massive street protests rocked his country, President Mubarak resigned from office. And when trouble broke out in Libya just a few days later, it seemed quite possible that France would reap a whirlwind of popular anger: Gaddafi's enemies could seize power in Tripoli and turn away from France, looking for support elsewhere. They, and other rebels in the region, were much more likely to be well disposed to the United States than to France.

As news broke of an insurrection in Benghazi on 16 February, Sarkozy saw his chance to redeem himself and stop France from losing out. If he could help topple a vulnerable-looking Libyan leader, then he would win the sympathy and loyalty of the rebels in Libya, who would feel a strong debt of gratitude to Paris, and of other protestors whose anger was threatening to sweep away existing regimes elsewhere in the Middle East and Maghreb. Perhaps he could even redeem himself before the Tunisian rebels who had toppled Ben Ali. So Sarkozy saw no need to question the claims about mass slaughter and bloodshed but instead had every reason to hype them up, knowing that they gave him the perfect excuse to launch an attack on Gaddafi and carry out regime change in Tripoli. Thinking that Gaddafi's days were numbered, he followed Talleyrand's maxim that 'the art of statesmanship is to foresee the inevitable and to expedite its occurrence'.

There was another reason why toppling Gaddafi helped Sarkozy redeem his government from its apparent complicity with Ben Ali: the Libyan leader had for some while been a close ally of the Tunisian dictator. Gaddafi had even ordered his security officials to guard Ben Ali as he stood down from power and flew into exile. As the rebels seized power in Tunis, Gaddafi also appeared on Libyan national television to condemn the revolution and urge Tunisian people to recall their deposed leader. If Sarkozy had been seen to support or sympathise with the Tripoli regime, in other words, then he would have risked being seen as complicit with the old order in Tunisia.

Toppling Gaddafi was not a task he could have done on his own and he knew that he depended upon the diplomatic and military support of the British and Americans. But he could at least lead the charge and take as much credit for the outcome as possible. He had little difficulty in recruiting the British leader, who was anxious not to be outdone and left behind by Sarkozy's determined actions and lofty rhetoric about 'protecting' the Libyan people and preventing a repetition of the massacre at Srebrenica in the Balkans in 1995, which Western governments had failed to prevent.[380]

David Cameron was in a position to influence and temper Sarkozy's *excès de zèle*, but failed to do so. If he had withheld British military support, then Sarkozy would have had to abandon his

David Cameron (right), Nicolas Sarkozy and Carla Bruni meet during the Libya crisis, May 2011.

crusade before a shot had even been fired. Even the combined might of the British and French air forces soon ran short of precision-guided bombs and ammunition. Libya 'has not been a very big war', as John Pike, the director of a defence think tank, told an American newspaper. 'If [the Europeans] would run out of these munitions this early in such a small operation, you have to wonder what kind of war they were planning on fighting. Maybe they were just planning on using their air force for air shows.' Without British support, France would have lacked the resources to fight: its navy has just one aircraft carrier, the *Charles de Gaulle*, which was based in the Mediterranean for the first four months of the conflict until it was forced to return to dock for essential maintenance. 'The French were especially weak in terms of logistics and capability,' emphasises a retired British general, and could only operate, for an extended period, in the least demanding of operations.[381]

Sarkozy's show of unity with Britain and America in the triumphant days and weeks that followed Gaddafi's demise was therefore a superficial one, for rivalry and competition with the 'Anglo-Saxons' had never been far beneath the surface. But this was true not just of Libya but also of another conflict that had started to rage at the same time.

CHAPTER 16

SYRIA, FRANCE AND THE GREAT GAME

While Gaddafi's security forces were fighting bitter street battles with the people of Benghazi, trouble had also broken out in the Syrian city of Daraa, in the south-west of the country. It had been triggered by the arrest of several young boys who had been scrawling graffiti that was critical of the government regime led by President Bashar al-Assad. News of their arrest and subsequent mistreatment immediately sparked a local protest, and within hours the demonstrations had spread to the capital, Damascus, where thousands of people swarmed into the streets to vent their anger at Assad's eleven-year rule. As in Libya, the security forces opened fire, furiously trying to suppress the rebellion, but instead succeeding in stoking the fires of popular anger, killing hundreds of protestors and creating martyrs by doing so. A national rebellion now got under way. The Syrian civil war had ignited.

France, Britain and America watched the growing violence with real concern, aware that it could easily become contagious and engulf the wider region, triggering an exodus of refugees. All three countries urged Assad to 'respect the people's right to peaceful protest' and to introduce 'the timely implementation of reforms' and 'freedoms', but on 18 August, after mass protests and a savage government response, they took a harder line by openly calling on him to 'step aside'. As reports grew of mass shootings and torture by government troops, the Quai d'Orsay publicly condemned Assad's 'abysmal record', while the Foreign Minister, Alain Juppé, worked hard with his British counterparts to push a hardline resolution through the United Nations Security Council, although his efforts were vetoed by the Russians and Chinese.

In the first few months of the uprising, the three Western countries stood steadfastly together, but in the ensuing months, Paris began to take a more aggressive line and continued to rigidly insist on Assad's removal from office. But such rigidity made little sense because it had by this time become clear that Assad had not suffered, and was not likely to suffer, the same swift end as the leaders of Egypt and Tunisia, who had been toppled, in the early weeks of 2011, by overwhelming street power. The war in Syria was instead looking likely to be a protracted one. In Western capitals, there was widespread revulsion at Assad's regime, which was undoubtedly guilty of heinous crimes against civilians, but it was not obvious why his resignation from office needed to be an article of faith for the French, British and American governments. Such a rigid approach simply reduced any room for diplomatic manoeuvre and made it harder to find a compromise.[382]

But Paris remained hawkish. In November 2012, some of the rebels set up a self-proclaimed 'National Coalition for Syrian Revolutionary and Opposition Forces' (also known as the Syrian National Coalition or SNC) and President François Hollande became the first Western leader to formally recognise this new body as a legitimate opposition to the existing regime. 'I announce today that France recognises the Syrian National Coalition as the sole representative of the Syrian people, and as the future government of a democratic Syria, bringing an end to Assad's regime,' the President told a packed press conference on 14 November, just three days after the group's formation. But Britain, America and other Western governments were much more cautious, pointing out that it was too early to formally recognise a self-declared 'opposition movement' that they knew little about. President Obama waited another month to recognise the SNC, and it was only on 12 December that he took the 'big step' of describing it as a 'legitimate representative of the Syrian people in opposition to the Assad regime'.

But Hollande went further than just formally recognising the SNC. It was only a matter of time, he continued, before its followers established their own independent zones of control, similar to those that the anti-Gaddafi rebels were setting up in Libya. And when that happened, he continued, then 'everywhere free zones are established under the authority of the [provisional] government, they must be protected' by foreign powers that were willing to intervene. He also argued that the rebels should be given 'defensive weapons' to use against the government regime.

These proposals were not just aggressive but also misleading. There had been unconfirmed press reports in the French media about undercover DGSE operations to train the Syrian rebels, loyal to an embryonic 'Free Syrian Army' (FSA), as early as November 2011. A year later, reporters discovered that French government proxies were giving strong financial support to Assad's enemies, delivering large quantities of cash that were smuggled across the Turkish–Syrian border into the hands of rebel leaders who used these resources to purchase arms on the local black market. And in an interview with a French author, Hollande admitted secretly delivering weapons – including cannons, machine guns, rocket-launchers and anti-tank missiles – to the rebels in the course of 2012. But at this time the

European Union had embargoed arms exports to Syria. This was only eased, at the instigation of the French and British governments, the following May.[383]

The French government was so determined to remove Assad that it was even prepared to overlook the increasingly extreme nature of his opponents. By the summer of 2012, the armed struggle against Assad was no longer dominated by the supposedly 'moderate' FSA. Instead, a number of openly Islamist militias, such as Jabhat al-Nusra, whose members declared their loyalty to al Qaeda, were gaining ground. In Washington, Assad's enemies and critics advocated support only for more 'moderate' elements, but the French government seemed unconcerned. In early May, François Hollande declared that it was French policy to aim for a transition in Syria 'that excludes President Bashar al-Assad, but comprises all opposition groups as well as some individual components of the regime'. Six months later, in December 2012, Foreign Minister Laurent Fabius decreed that Jabhat al-Nusrah was 'doing a good job on the ground' against Assad's forces.[384]

At the same time, France's visceral opposition to Assad undermined diplomatic initiatives that were launched to end the war. On 30 June 2012, the United Nations joint envoy Kofi Annan put forward a peace plan, 'Geneva I', that allowed for some members of the Syrian government to stay in power on a 'transitional' basis in an administration that 'could include members of the present government'. The resolution was deliberately phrased in vague terms but left open the possibility of allowing Assad to stay in power. Yet, within hours of Annan's announcement, French diplomats had reiterated their earlier demand that Assad should stand down. Laurent Fabius told a television programme:

> Even if they say the opposite, the fact that the text says specifically
> that there will be a transitional government with all powers means

> it won't be Bashar al-Assad ... because it will be people that are
> agreed to by mutual consent. The opposition will never agree to him,
> so it signals implicitly that Assad must go and that he is finished.[385]

Paris also took a distinctively hard line in August 2013, when reports emerged that the Syrian regime had deployed chemical weapons in the suburbs of Damascus, killing hundreds. Quoting unnamed 'intelligence sources', but unable to prove that Assad was responsible for the 'massive and coordinated' attack, the French government led the charge for Western intervention against the Syrian government. Paris soon became isolated, however, after Britain and the United States backed away from military action against the regime and instead accepted a Russian initiative to eliminate Syrian stockpiles of chemical weapons. Meanwhile, French officials were also pushing hard for stronger diplomatic measures against Assad's government, launching an investigation into its alleged war crimes and proposing a UN resolution to protect civilians from its deadly barrel bombs.

These differences of approach also resurfaced later on in the conflict: in September 2014, France joined the British–American coalition against the radical and fanatically anti-Western Islamic State movement (IS), whose militias were rapidly overrunning vast areas of Syria and Iraq. But François Hollande initially refused to strike its positions, because to do so would bolster Bashar al-Assad's power.

French hawkishness towards Syria became even more glaring towards the end of 2015, when Britain and the United States moderated their opposition to Assad, preferring instead to at least consider a compromise with his regime, while France remained implacably opposed. This led to France's exclusion from international talks that were held in October, prompting French diplomats to make a desperate last-minute bid to gather the main protagonists in the French capital for negotiations. 'Clearly, the train has left without us and we're trying to catch up with it,' one former diplomat admitted to the press.[386]

But while Hollande and Fabius were openly critical of the Syrian leader, publicly imploring Britain and America to 'punish Assad' and use military force to destroy his regime, they were less open about their reasons for their position. Their public pronouncements were of course inevitably full of references to the atrocities that Assad's regime was responsible for: the Syrian leader, as Hollande pronounced in a speech in August 2012, was guilty of perpetrating 'unbelievable violence … to massacre the people, destroy cities and kill women and children'. Such terminology certainly made media-friendly sound bites, but hardly explained why Hollande had consistently taken such an inflexible approach and had not instead pressed for a ceasefire and an interim deal that would have allowed Assad to stay in power until a lasting, longer-term solution was found.[387]

Some commentators wondered if the French viewed Assad as an unwelcome influence in neighbouring Lebanon, which both Syria and France regarded as their own rightful zone of influence. This clash of interests had emerged in 2004, for example, when President Jacques Chirac had worked with the American administration of George W. Bush to put diplomatic pressure on Assad to curtail his influence in Lebanon. The two Western countries had then drawn up United Nations Resolution 1559, which called for the withdrawal of 15,000 Syrian troops from Lebanon and demanded an end to Syrian interference there.

But Syria's influence had already been drastically curtailed after the assassination of Lebanon's former Prime Minister, Rafic Hariri, in February 2005, which was widely blamed on Damascus. In the wake of the killing, vast numbers of ordinary Lebanese had come into the streets to demand an end to Syrian influence in their country. This 'Cedar Revolution' ceded results, forcing Assad to respect Resolution 1559 and pull his troops out of Lebanon. Although he subsequently managed to regain a foothold there, this was only after the onset of the Syrian civil war in March 2011, and after France had already taken sides. And there was no guarantee that a post-Assad regime would be any more compliant towards French interests in Lebanon, or indeed anywhere else.[388]

A clue to French motives towards Syria comes from the change of position that took place in the years that preceded the outbreak of the rebellion in 2011. This was a reversal that was as striking as the one that took place over Libya at around the same time.

When he first took office, in May 2007, Nicolas Sarkozy had worked hard to establish a close rapport with Damascus. He wanted Syria to join his Mediterranean Union, the 'Club Med' (see Chapter 15), claiming that it was better to engage Assad than to isolate and ostracise his regime, as President Chirac had tried to do. Then, in July 2008, Sarkozy invited the Syrian President to attend a major international summit in Paris and watch the Bastille Day parade as a guest of honour. The Élysée also released an upbeat statement, welcoming Assad's 'determination' to establish better relations with Lebanon and Israel. Two months later, Sarkozy made a return trip to Syria, while in February 2010 the French Prime Minister, François Fillon, made a brief visit to Damascus that was intended to improve relations between the two countries and to finalise several trade deals. Although there was disagreement between the two men over human rights in Syria, which were discussed in a 'frank and direct' way, Syria was now closer to France than any other Western country.

The Élysée's subsequent change of position towards Syria, in other words, was striking and dramatic. For as soon as the Syrian civil war gathered pace and Bashar al-Assad looked to be in danger, Paris took an aggressive position and demanded his removal from power. But it was never necessary for France to take such an inflexible course of action. Even if French officials had wanted Assad to step aside, they did not need to make this a formal policy. 'The decision to do so led to a rupture of all diplomatic ties between Damascus and Western capitals, making a negotiated settlement even harder to achieve,' one former Western diplomat has explained. 'And in 2011 there was not even any organised opposition that was in a position to step into Bashar's shoes.' This suggests that a more viable alternative for France, and other Western governments, would have been to simply press for a ceasefire followed by negotiations.[389]

It was no coincidence that French policies closely resembled those of several Middle Eastern states. Amongst them was Qatar, which helped to form the Syrian National Coalition in November 2012 and then recognised it as 'the legitimate representative' of the Syrian people, while another was Saudi Arabia. Soon after the Syrian rebellion broke out, the Saudis and Qataris reportedly supplied the rebels with arms and money to fight back, resolutely opposing proposals to talk with Assad's regime and insisting that he should stand aside before any peace negotiations began.[390]

This was because they saw Assad as a threat. Over the preceding thirty years, Damascus had built a closer alliance with Iran and with the Lebanese organisation Hezbollah, both of which were led by Shia Muslims. The two Gulf states, however, are Sunni regimes that both have sizeable, disadvantaged and sometimes rebellious Shia populations. And both are kingdoms ruled by monarchs whose claim to have a hereditary right to rule has been implacably opposed by Tehran ever since the Islamic revolution, which championed divine rather than hereditary rule, in 1979. Bashar al-Assad, in other words, was seen as a key link in an 'Iran–Damascus–Hezbollah' axis that posed a clear existential threat to the two Middle Eastern principalities.

And because Iran's power and influence grew dramatically after the American-led invasion of Iraq in 2003, it seemed to pose an ever greater menace to the two Gulf States.[391]

In the course of 2009 and 2010, Saudi Arabia and Qatar had reached out to Assad, wanting to end his diplomatic isolation. It was more sensible, ran the thinking in Riyadh and Doha, to engage Damascus and lure it away from its Iranian and Lebanese allies. In October 2009, Assad even visited Riyadh and held meetings with King Abdullah, while Saudi diplomats told their American counterparts that 'Syria had been isolated for too long'. But as soon as rebellion broke out in March 2011, they saw their chance to oust Assad and, at some point in 2012 or even 2011, started to actively arm the rebels.[392]

Either French policies were mirroring those of Saudi Arabia and Qatar, or those two kingdoms were following the lead of France. But it seems much more likely that the two Gulf principalities were forming the policy. They had a stronger vested interest in ousting Bashar al-Assad, whose rule did not pose any clear threat to French interests. Most obviously, the two Middle Eastern states also possess vast resources of oil and natural gas, and huge quantities of 'petrodollars', which they have earned from their exports, and they represent major markets for foreign suppliers.

Soon after he became President, Nicolas Sarkozy had tried to reach out to Qatar. Although Qatar is a geographically tiny kingdom with a population of little over two million, Sarkozy recognised how valuable its market could be to French exporters and how much Qatar had to offer France. As major exporters of natural gas, the Qataris benefited from the sharp increase in the price of energy that took place around 2008–09, and earned vast quantities of foreign exchange to invest abroad. France soon caught the eyes of Qatari investors, who bought up large shares of big French companies in many different sectors.

By October 2012, the ties between the two states had become so close that the International Organisation of La Francophonie (IOF) even invited Qatar to become a member, claiming spuriously that it was eligible because of its 'inclusion of the French language into its official school curriculum at the beginning of this year, in addition to launching a French-speaking radio station'. Three years later, the Qataris signed a huge contract, worth over $7 billion, with France's arms giant, Dassault Aviation, for a large consignment of its state-of-the-art Rafale warplanes and missiles. 'This confirms the closeness of diplomatic and economic relations between France and Qatar,' proclaimed a triumphant Laurent Fabius.

At the same time, the French government was working hard to draw closer to the Saudis. Paris had not only adopted the Qatari–Saudi agenda in Syria, demanding the removal of Bashar al-Assad, but also closely echoed the Saudi line towards Iran. It opposed Iran's representation at the Geneva II peace talks that were held in early 2014, even though the Iranians were major players in the Syrian civil war. And it harshly criticised an interim deal on Iran's nuclear pro-gramme that Washington and Tehran had struck in November 2013. By this time, France had become the most aggressive of the Western powers that were involved in negotiating with the Iranian govern-ment, representing a sharp contrast with the much more moderate stance it had taken a decade before. In November 2013, for example, Fabius refused to endorse a draft American–Iranian nuclear agree-ment, claiming that it did not impose sufficiently harsh measures on Tehran, and his uncompromising position reputedly led to heated exchanges between American and French officials. During a high-profile trip to the Saudi kingdom in May 2015, when he spoke at the first-ever summit between France and the Gulf states, President Hollande played up the 'Iranian threat', referring to the 'dangers emanating from countries' designs and interference in [the Gulf's] internal affairs'. At almost the same time, Fabius visited Riyadh and reiterated French 'support, especially political', for the Saudi involvement in Yemen's civil war. The Foreign Minister also wanted to reassure Riyadh about France's hostility towards the nuclear deal that Washington had now finalised.[393]

Of course not everything that France has done in the course of the Syrian civil war has pleased its Gulf allies. In November 2015, Hollande ordered a massive aerial bombardment of the so-called Islamic State (IS) militia in Syria and Iraq, even though IS has reputedly had strong backing from Saudi donors. But Hollande had little choice but to do so, since Islamic State was responsible for a series of brutal attacks on the French mainland on 13 November.

French interest in Saudi Arabia, like Qatar, was partly commercial. This became clear in 2013, when President Hollande led a large delegation of thirty French business leaders to Riyadh to meet King Abdullah, as well as the former Lebanese Prime Minister,

The leaders of Britain, France and the US meet in London to discuss Syria, May 2014. Laurent Fabius (second from left) stands next to John Kerry, who is facing William Hague.

Saad Hariri, and leaders of the Syrian opposition. And in June 2015, Saudi's deputy leader, Mohammed bin Salman, undertook an official visit to France to sign deals worth $12 billion and to discuss the feasibility of building two nuclear reactors in the kingdom.

But there was, and remains, a wider dimension to the relationship between Riyadh, Doha and Paris. France was not moving closer to the two Middle Eastern principalities just because of any commercial interest. More broadly, it was filling a political void that another country, for many long years a very close ally of both states and an active player in Middle Eastern affairs, is creating. That country is the United States.

America's involvement in Saudi Arabia is a long-standing one, which dates back to the discovery of oil in the kingdom in 1933. In 1943, President Franklin D. Roosevelt had declared that 'the defence of Saudi Arabia is vital to the defence of the United States', and eight years later the two countries had signed a deal that established a strategic alliance between them. Their closeness became plain to see in 1990–91 after Saddam Hussein's invasion of neighbouring Kuwait, which posed a clear threat to the security of Saudi Arabia. The American government immediately began a massive deployment of troops into Saudi Arabia to guard its ally as well as to liberate Kuwait (see Chapter 15).[394]

In recent years, Washington and Riyadh have remained close, but their relationship has come under strain. One major reason has been the thaw in American–Iranian relations that followed, but also made possible, the signing of a nuclear agreement in 2013. At the same time, there have been claims and revelations that the 9/11 hijackers, responsible for the deaths of thousands of innocent Americans, had much closer links with the Saudi regime than was previously realised. Washington's condemnation of the human rights record of the kingdom, as well as other Gulf states, made matters worse:

for example, the fate of the Saudi blogger Raif Badawi, who was sentenced to 1,000 lashes in 2014, and the beheading of a Burmese woman in January 2015, provoked strong criticism from Washington and an even harsher one from American lobby groups.

Oil has been another cause of tension between Washington and Riyadh. The advent of the shale industry since around 2009 has meant that the United States is no longer so dependent on Saudi oil. But relations worsened from late 2014, as the Saudis ramped up their own output of crude oil in a bid to drive down prices and bankrupt the American shale industry, which depends on a higher price to survive, and to scupper ambitious and hugely expensive plans to extract Arctic oil. The Saudis wanted to maintain their grip on world oil production, even if that meant falling out with Washington in the process. Fearful that America could no longer be trusted to guard their interests against Iran, the Saudis had in 2015 undertaken a bloody intervention against Iranian-backed rebels in Yemen, leading a coalition of several Arab states.

In fact, America seemed to be pulling back from the wider region, not just Saudi Arabia in particular. In a major speech in Cairo in 2009, President Obama promised that America would make a 'new beginning' with the Arabs, and two years later had raised eyebrows once again when he decreed that the Asia-Pacific region was now a 'top priority' for Washington and that the United States would play a 'larger and long-term role in shaping this region'. As a result of this 'pivot to Asia', some of America's allies in the Gulf region wondered if Washington was no longer trustworthy, and these suspicions seemed to be confirmed in 2011, when America's former long-term ally, President Hosni Mubarak of Egypt, was toppled by popular protests that Washington seemed to just stand back and watch. 'It's the lowest ebb since World War II for U.S. influence and engagement in the region,' a former senior diplomat told one newspaper.[395]

It is of course true that since the onset of the Syrian civil war, the United States has stood alongside France and Britain to push for Assad's removal from office, echoing the Gulf line. But it has probably had different reasons for doing so. Some Washington insiders believe that President Obama was 'captive to Cold War thinking about Russia and China', and regarded Assad as President Putin's closest ally in the Middle East.[396]

The Syrian civil war, in other words, coincided with a growing rift between America and Saudi Arabia that other countries could exploit. The Saudis were amenable to advances by competitor countries, which were in a position to fill the political void that Washington had created. China, which has had close relations with Iran in recent years, was not a candidate. Germany and Italy, although major exporters, have very limited military capabilities of their own. France and Britain, on the other hand, had the exports, particularly the military hardware, that the Saudis and Qataris needed. And both also had highly trained and capable military personnel who they were willing to send abroad to support the Gulf states, for example, by helping the Syrian rebels or the Saudi forces in Yemen, if the need arose.

Paris was jockeying to fill this geopolitical void, knowing that a closer alliance of its own with Riyadh and Doha would bring huge contracts for French exporters, and perhaps even some semblance, or pretence, of an empire that would raise French national prestige. 'France was and will always be your friend,' President Hollande solemnly pronounced in Riyadh in May 2015. 'It is determined to remain a strong, credible and reliable ally and partner ... We are faithful to our friends and to our commitments. France never hesitates to do the right thing, even if it is military action.' He continued by reiterating that 'I want to work with all my force to deepen this relationship and strategic partnership, with your member states and with your organisation, at all levels: political, security, economic, energy, and cultural'. The French leader was for this reason prepared to openly support the intervention of the Gulf States in Yemen. 'France supports you in what you have done to restore stability in Yemen, from Operation Decisive Storm to Restoration of Hope,' he told the Gulf Cooperation Council. And he continued to advocate an uncompromising stance over both Iran's nuclear programme and the removal from office of the Syrian President. By this time, there were numerous unconfirmed reports of French Special Forces actively supporting the Saudis' covert war in Yemen.[397]

François Hollande with Crown Prince Salman Bin Abdulaziz Al Saud of Saudi Arabia, Paris, September 2014. The relationship between France and Saudi Arabia is crucial to understanding France's hawkish position towards the Syrian government.

By taking this position, Hollande hoped to outbid the British effort to lure the Saudis into their own orbit: Britain is Saudi Arabia's largest supplier of arms and, like their French counterparts, officials in London also immediately supported the Saudi intervention in Yemen. The British worked hard to stake out their own sphere of

influence in the Middle East: in December 2014, the British government announced a landmark deal to build and operate a new
base in Bahrain, its first permanent base in the Middle East since
it formally withdrew from the region in 1971. During the five-year
period between 2010 and 2015, Whitehall had exported around
£2.8 billion worth of arms to Riyadh, even though Saudi bombing
in Yemen had reportedly killed thousands of civilians. And in June
2016, it even emerged that members of the British police force were
training their Saudi counterparts to use high-tech detection skills,
despite accepting that they could 'identify individuals who later go
on to be tortured'. Such deals, for the most part, meant pushing out
other competitors, such as France.[398]

As the Syrian civil war continued, it seemed unclear if France
would succeed in its aim and extend its influence, at British and
American expense, in the Gulf. Washington was still making sporadic
attempts to rebuild its lost rapport with the Saudis, for example, by
sending an exceptionally impressive American delegation, headed
by the President himself, to King Abdullah's funeral in Riyadh in
January 2015. At the same time, French exporters were increasingly
eyeing the Iranian market, which was just opening up to foreign
businesses as the American government lifted its sanctions. But
whatever the eventual outcome, over the preceding few years France
had continued to vie with Britain and America for influence abroad.
Underneath the cooperation with Britain and America over Syria
lay traits of the old rivalry.

CONCLUSION

In the years ahead, will France continue to play its Great Game with Britain and America? Or, in an age of 'globalisation' and pan-European cooperation, are such sentiments of rivalry and competition set to become a fading anachronism?

For the most part, France will of course continue to work very closely with its two Anglophone partners, confronting shared challenges. Recent attacks on mainland France by Islamist insurgents, such as the tragic events of November 2015, are an unmistakable reminder that now, at least as much as at any previous time, France needs the support of both Britain and America against a mutual foe. Each of these Western countries is confronted by the same enemy. Despite all the differences between them, they are non-Islamic powers that have at one time or another intervened in the Middle East. Through the eyes of violent, Islamist extremists, they all represent a single 'Western' entity. As a result, France will continue to work with both countries to counter the threat posed by radical Islamist militias. Paris will need to share intelligence information with both countries, as well as all of its neighbours. The three countries will need to work together on foreign battlefields, as they have done in Afghanistan and Libya, and at the time of writing are doing so in Syria, in order to confront this shared threat.

There are also other influences that seem to be pushing the 'Great Game' ever more into obscurity. One is the rise of China. Although it offers enormous commercial opportunities and benefits for the rest of the world, most notably for the people of Africa, Beijing has also become a rival to the United States and, in recent years, there has been much speculation about the military threat that China might pose in the years ahead. Clashes between the two countries, as they vie for influence and resources, seems a possibility. Such fears have been voiced in France as well as Britain and other countries. But in any such scenario of tension, or outright conflict, between China and America, France's influence and alliances abroad would acquire particular importance. This is true, for example, of Djibouti, off the east African coast, which has had a close relationship with Paris since it won independence from France in 1977. It would be hugely important because it overlooks the sea lanes along which Arab oil is shipped to China, which has no indigenous petroleum sources of its own. A presence in Djibouti, in other words, bestows considerable prestige upon France and confirms its role as a key regional player.

There is another influence that pushes France and 'the Anglo-Saxons' closer together. Neither France nor Britain can afford to intervene in Africa, or anywhere else in the world, in the way they once did. Since the mid-1990s, the French have for this reason been imploring the outside world to do more to help Africa, and these financial pressures have been even more acute since the onset of a global economic crisis in the late 2000s. The crippling costs of military intervention became particularly clear during the Libyan intervention.

French cooperation with Britain and America became clear in the summer of 2007, when fighting flared up in Mali between Islamist militias and the government. President Nicolas Sarkozy decided to intervene, arguing that the fall of Mali to the Islamists would desta-bilise the entire region and significantly elevate the terrorist threat to

France itself as well as the surrounding region. As a later government report argued, 'the establishment of a terrorist base at the gates of Europe would have been disastrous not only for Westerners and Europeans ... but also for the Saharan region and western Africa, which would have been seriously destabilised: Mali is a continental country that has seven borders'. Several years before, Sarkozy had publicly repudiated *la Françafrique*, but any such pronouncements did not stop him from now ordering a large-scale deployment in its true spirit.[399]

Sarkozy had done this with the full support and cooperation of the Americans. On the one hand, the French were willing to put boots on the ground and had the spare soldiers to do so: there were at this time around 12,000 French soldiers based on the African continent, more than double the American military presence. French officials and soldiers prided themselves on their local knowledge, of Africa's climate, people and politics, that the Americans lacked. Washington, however, had the technology, and the financial and political power, to support any French action. Since the economic collapse of 2007–08, the French economy had been in a highly troubled state, and in 2008 a defence White Paper had prompted a series of drastic cost-cutting measures, which included the closure of several west African bases and the scaling-down of others. Six years later, the French economy remained in a perilous condition, not least because a wider crisis within the Eurozone, perhaps triggered by a Greek default, could erupt at any time.[400]

Franco-American cooperation had moved a step closer in early 2013, when Paris had dispatched several thousand soldiers to Mali to help fend off a determined Islamist offensive. Defence Minister Jean-Yves le Drian argued that France had no choice but to fight back: 'There is a major risk', he told the media, 'that jihadists will thrive in the area that runs from the Horn of Africa to Guinea-Bissau.' Operation Serval quickly proved to be a success, and a number of key towns and cities were defended or quickly recaptured. The speed and accuracy of their response suggested that the French commanders were strongly supported by surveillance drones, which the Americans had in abundance.[401]

The following summer, the French launched Operation Barkhane, a major counter-terrorist drive that involved the deployment of a 3,000-strong force across Chad, Burkina Faso, Mali, Mauritania and Niger. It was no coincidence that this began just three days before African leaders were due to meet their American counterparts in Washington. These initiatives also had wider support across the European Union.[402]

Washington continued to back France's assertive foreign policy in the African continent. On 11 August, in a memorandum to Defense Secretary Chuck Hagel and Secretary of State John Kerry, President Obama authorised a grant of $10 million 'to assist France in its efforts to secure Mali, Niger and Chad from terrorists and violent extremism'. The decision opened, in the words of one commentator, 'a new chapter in French–American relations. There is an unprecedented level of cooperation going on.'[403]

At the same time, France had also moved close to Britain. In November 2010, Sarkozy and the British Prime Minister David Cameron had signed a new agreement that was intended to 'develop cooperation' by building a 'Combined Joint Expeditionary Force'. Critics cynically dubbed it the *entente frugale*, since it was designed to pool resources and to save both sides money, but no one could deny that it was a sign of closer relations. It was in the same spirit of cooperation that, just three months later, Sarkozy enlisted the support of David Cameron to confront the Libyan leader Colonel Gaddafi. Despite his initial hesitancy, Cameron eventually threw his voice behind Sarkozy and declared his support for the military action in Libya, initially to impose a no-fly zone over Libya but then to carry out regime change.

However, underneath this framework of cooperation, something of the old spirit of national rivalry and competition will continue to lurk. This is partly because, over the coming decades, the United States is likely to remain the world's most powerful nation, even if it is increasingly challenged by an ascendant China. Some French men and women are therefore likely to resent the power and influence of the United States for the simple reason that it is the most powerful nation on earth.

But something else will also be at work in the French psyche. Its national suspicion of *les anglo-saxons* has been historically so deep-rooted and powerful, so integral to the formation of France, that it is unlikely to completely fade as long as the French nation exists. No matter how much future French governments cooperate with their British and American counterparts, and how close and cordial their relations, something of the old 'Fashoda complex' will always remain.

SOURCES AND ENDNOTES

AMAE   Archives du Ministère des Affaires Étrangères, La Courneuve, Paris

FRUS   Foreign Relations of the United States

SHD   Le Service historique de la Défense

PRO   Public Records Office, Kew. These have been designated as PREM (Prime Minister's Office), CAB (Cabinet Office), ADM (Admiralty), WO (War Office), FO (Foreign Office) and FCO (Foreign and Commonwealth Office).

1. FRUS 1947, vol. VI, pp. 110–11
2. See below, Chapter 9
3. *The Sun*, 3 October 1968. See below, p. 79
4. *The Rwanda Crisis: History of a Genocide* (London: Hurst & Co, 1998), pp. 104–5
5. J. Michelet, *Tableau de la France, Géographie, Physique, Politique et Morale* (Paris: Hachette, 1947), p. 82
6. Fashoda: C. de Gaulle, *Mémoires de Guerre*, vol. I, *L'Appel* (Paris: Plon, 1954), p. 10
7. Resistance: R. Gildea, *Fighters in the Shadows: A New History of the French Resistance* (London: Faber, 2015). French mistrust: J. Fenby, *The General: Charles de Gaulle and the France He Saved* (London: Simon & Schuster, 2010), p. 132. Jamet: C. Glass, 'Melancholy Actions', *London Review of Books*, 17 December 2009
8. On France's affinity with Descartes and rationalism, see S. Hazareesingh, *How the French Think: An Affectionate Portrait of an Intellectual People* (London: Penguin, 2015)
9. Palmerston: K. Bourne, *Britain and the Balance of Power in North America, 1815–1908* (University of California Press, 2008), p. 255. Disraeli: B. Disraeli, J. A. Wilson Gunn & M. G. Wiebe, *Benjamin Disraeli Letters: 1857–1859* (Toronto: University of Toronto Press, 2009), p. 523
10. American diplomat: Wall, op. cit., p. 61

11. J. F. V. Keiger, *France and the World Since 1870* (London: Hodder, 2011) pp. 17–18

12. Keiger, op. cit., p. 201

13. Eyewitness: *Chicago Tribune*, 31 May 1945

14. 'Personal from His Majesty's Minister Damascus for Secretary of State', 30 May 1945, FO/954/15D PRO

15. Eden: Hansard, House of Commons Debates, 30 May 1945, vol. 411 cc314–32. Churchill: FO/954/15D PRO

16. K. Fedorowich & M. Thomas, *International Diplomacy and Colonial Retreat* (London: Routledge, 2000), p. 81

17. Quoted in J. Fenby, *The General*, p. 288

18. Stumbling block: Duff Cooper to London, 5 October 1944, FO 660/313 PRO

19. Fedorowich & Thomas, op. cit., p. 82

20. Lieutenant: Foreign Office meeting of 13 May 1943, ADM 1/13540 PRO. North Africa: Telegram of 5 April 1943, FO 371, 36177 PRO. Darlan: under Article 4 of the Clark–Darlan agreement, the Allies had control of naval bases while Article 9, which was less clear, gave the Allies further rights. 'This agreement does give the Allies rights analogous to those of an occupying power, and even now the French are attempting to have it amended', in the words of a Foreign Office official, WO 106/5416A PRO.

21. Monnet: H. Macmillan, *The Blast of War 1939–45* (London: Macmillan, 1968), pp. 326–33. Catroux: This letter was known to British and American intelligence, see PREM 3/121/4 PRO

22. Letter of 8 March 1942 to Admiral William D. Leahy, President Roosevelt's Secretary's File, Diplomatic Correspondence, 1933–42

23. *Washington Star*, 29 August 1941; *New York Times*, 1 September 1941; see British Embassy telegram to Foreign Office, 5 September 1941, WO 106/5416A PRO

24. Commander-in-Chief Middle East, memo to the War Office, 5 August 1941, WO 106/5416A PRO

25. FO memo to Washington, 16 June 1942, WO 106/5416A PRO

26. J. Crémieux-Brilhac, *La France Libre* (Paris: Gallimard, 1990), pp. 278–86

27. Russia: A. Crawley, *De Gaulle* (London: The Literary Guild, 1969), p. 169. Boisson: M. Michel, 'The decolonization of French Africa and the United States and Great Britain 1945–58', in R. Bridges (ed.) *Imperialism, Decolonization and Africa*, 1999 (Basingstoke: Macmillan, 2000), p. 155

28. West Africa: 30 January 1943, based on a meeting with President Vargas at Natal, Brazil. See State Department *Bulletin* of 20 January 1943, p. 95 and FRUS, 1943, vol. V, p. 653. New Caledonia: C. Weeks, 'Hour of temptation: American interests in New Caledonia 1935–45', *Australian Journal of Politics and History*, vol. 5, no. 2, 185–200, August 1989, p. 191

29. See J. Fenby, *The General*, op. cit., pp. 196–7. De Gaulle determined: *Mémoires* (Paris: Gallimard, 2000), p. 507

30. Anti-American feeling: Telegram from Douala to Foreign Office, 13 April 1943, WO 106/5416A PRO. Dangerously affected: Eden, op. cit., p. 387. French suspect: Eden to Churchill, 22 September 1942, PREM 3/120/6 PRO

31. *Lettres, Notes et Carnets 1943–5*, pp. 274 and 293–5, 12 volumes (Paris: Plon, 1970–71). J. Fenby, op. cit., p. 250

32. Memorandum of conversation by Adolf A. Berle, 21 October 1943, Department of State, FRUS, 1943, China, Washington, DC, 1957, pp. 883–4. See G. R. Hess, 'Franklin Roosevelt and Indochina', *The Journal of American History*, vol. 59, no. 2, September 1972, pp. 357–8

33. 'Roosevelt and Stalin Discuss the Future of French Rule in Indochina', Teheran Conference, 28 November 1943, from T. G. Paterson & D. Merrill (eds.), *Major Problems in American Foreign Policy, Volume II: Since 1914*, 4th edition (Lexington, MA: D. C. Heath and Company, 1995), p. 189. 'Franklin Roosevelt on French Rule in Indochina', Press Conference, 23 February 1945, from Paterson & Merrill, op. cit., p. 190

34. Document: 'United States Policy with Regard to French North Africa', Memorandum by the Policy Planning Staff, 22 March 1948, FRUS, Western Europe, vol. III, p. 684

35. C. de Gaulle, 'Discours prononcé par le général de Gaulle à l'ouverture de la Conférence de Brazzaville, le 30 Janvier 1944', see *Mémoires de Guerre: L'Unité, 1942–1944* (Paris: Plon, 1956), pp. 555–7

36. Bretton Woods: E. Conway, *The Summit: The Biggest Battle of the Second World War* (London: Little, Brown, 2014), p. 228

37. C. de Gaulle, *Mémoires de Guerre: Le Salut* (Paris: Plon, 1959), p. 338. In his memoirs, Cordell Hull seemed to verify this, saying that Roosevelt 'wanted a Four-Power organization to be the world policeman, using the forces of the United States, Great Britain, Russia and China. All the other nations including France were to be disarmed'. C. Hull, *Memoirs*, vol. 2 (London: Hodder & Stoughton, 1948), pp. 1642–3

38. Eden: 12–13 July 1943, *The Eden Memoirs: The Reckoning* (London: Cassell, 1965), pp. 372, 397–8

39. De Gaulle, *Le Salut*, pp. 181–3; Churchill, *Finest Hour*, vol. VI (London: Houghton Mifflin Company, 1983), pp. 403–4

40. Greatness: C. de Gaulle, *Mémoires de Guerre: L'Appel 1940–42* (Paris: Plon, 1954). De Gaulle, 'Appel du général de Gaulle aux Français, le 18 Juin 1940', speech reprinted in *Mémoires de Guerre: L'Appel*, 2

41. Polls: J. Rioux, *La France de la Quatrième République*, vol. 1 (Seuil, 1981), p. 20; J. Fenby, op. cit., p. 283

42. A. Horne, *A Savage War of Peace: Algeria 1954–62* (New York: NYRB), p. 27. De Gaulle, *Le Salut*, op. cit., p. 223

43. Fedorowich & Thomas, op. cit., p. 83

44. Chesneau: Tananarive, 27 February 1947, Doc. 85, 8.H.114 SHD. World War veterans: Activité du Mouvement Democratique de Renovation Malgache à Fianarantsoa. Memo of Commander Gautier, Tananarive, 23 December 1946, 8.H.114 SHD, Paris. (Tananarive is now Antananarivo.)

45. Memo from Cdr Gautier, Tananarive, 8 Jan 1947, no.13/2-S/420-D, 8.H.176, d.3, SHD

46. Memo from Cdr Gautier, Tananarive, 8 Jan 1947, no.42/2-S-420/A, 8.H.177, d.6, SHD

47. Cargo ship: Au Sujet d'activité du MDRM, Memo of Cdr. Chesneau, Tananarive, 26 February 1947, 8.H.114 SHD. Rahenja quote: Renseignement Sur L'activité du MDRM à Fianarantsoa, no.134/2-3/420A, 8.H.114 SHD. Raseta meeting: Renseignements 170/0, 15 April 1947, 8.H.176 SHD. British meetings: Memo from the Foreign Affairs Ministry, Paris, to the French ambassador in London, 22 March 1946, 57Q02 AMAE

48. Renseignements 251/BDOC, 12 June 1946, SHD Paris

49. 'Note Préliminaire: Les activités Britanniques à Madagascar', Troisième Partie, K.60.7, 57QO7 SHD

50. Mitchell visit: 'Les activités Britanniques à Madagascar', Annexe I, le 'Major' Morris. K.60.7, 57QO7 SHD. Raherivelo: 'Les anglais et la rébellion Malgache', Annexe III Troisième Partie, K.60.7, 57QO7 SHD

51. Memo from the 3rd Bureau, Direction des Affaires Politiques, Min. for For. Affairs, 19 March 1947, 57QO7 SHD

52. Memo of Administrateur-Adjoint Y. Durand to le Chéf de Batallion Perrier, Moramanga, 28 March 1947, 8.H.177 SHD; Memo of Administrateur Conty to Governor General of Madagascar, Moramanga, 4 April 1947, 8.H.177 SHD
53. 'Les opérations dans la subdivision centre', 8.H.114 SHD
54. Letter of Commander Joubert, Tananarive, 18 April 1947, 8.H.197 SHD
55. Fernald: See D. Little, 'Cold War and Colonialism in Africa: The United States, France and the Madagascar Revolt of 1947', *Pacific Historical Review*, 1990, p. 540. Franciscan order and death toll: *Tronchon L'insurrection Malgache* (Paris: Karthala, 1986), pp. 712–14. Quoted in P. Leymarie, 'Deafening Silence on a Horrifying Repression', *Le Monde Diplomatique*, March 1997
56. Rapport confidential à M. le commissaire à titre personnel, 8.H.114 SHD
57. Shot on capture: Compte-Rendu d'Opérations, Lieutenant Sadoul, Ambositra, 15 June 1947, 8.H.182 SHD Memo of Administrateur Conty to Governor General of Madagascar, Moramanga, 4 April 1947, 8.H.177 SHD
58. Conty, letter from Tananarive, 19 April 1947, 8.H.114 SHD
59. Shops: Memo from Chief Administrator Bordier to the high commissioner, Tananarive, 12 and 15 April 1947, 8.H.114 SHD. Barbed wire: Memo of Captain Loyer, Tananarive, 24 May 1947, 8.H.176 SHD. US witness: Memo from Ambassador Bonnet to Foreign Minister Bidault, 11 February 1947, 91QO127 AMAE. The allegations surfaced just a few weeks before the rebellion began, prompting the French ambassador to Washington to warn Paris that 'at the moment it is particularly important not to let rumours and allegations, about how we treat indigenous people in our colonies, blacken our reputation before the American opinion'. Looting: Rapport confidential à M. le commissaire à titre personnel, 8.H.114 SHD. Execution: Letter of Lt Sadou, 'Compte-Rendu D'Opérations', Ambositra, 16 June 1947, 8.H.114 SHD
60. Debate in the National Assembly, 8 May 1947, p. 1510
61. Memorandum from Tananarive, 19 April 1947, 8.H.114 SHD
62. Tribes: Report of Col. Missonier, Paris, 7 May 1947, 8.H.177 SHD. Crazy zeal: 'Les opérations dans la subdivision centre', p. 23, 8.H.114 SHD. 'Burnt out': 'une certain lassitude', Bulletin de Renseignements, Tananarive, 7 May 1947, 8.H.114 SHD. April 1947: Rapport sur L'Insurrection à Madagascar, 14 April 1947, 8.H.176 SHD
63. North sector: Report of Colonel Missonier, Paris, 7 May 1947, 8.H.177 SHD. Railways: 'La situation à Madagascar', Report of Colonel Missonier, Paris, 21 May 1947, 8.H.177 SHD. September: La Rébellion et Les Opérations dans La Subdivision Sud, March–September 1947, 8.H.114 SHD
64. French media: P. Albert, *La Presse Française*, Paris, La Documentation Française, 1990, p. 72. R. Kuhn, *The Media in France* (London: Routledge, 1994), p. 41
65. Extract from a report of the French high commissioner to Tananarive, 2 August 1947, p. 12, 8.H.177 SHD
66. René Malbrant, Debate in the National Assembly, 8 May 1947, p. 1510
67. V. Auriol, *Journal de Septennat 1947–54*, vol. I (Paris: Armand Colin, 1970), pp. 155–5, 480–86, 606–7
68. Padmore: Consul de France a Accra a Paris, 22 October 1947, K149.5, 57QO7 AMAE. Parliamentarian: René Malbrant, Debate in the National Assembly, 8 May 1947, p. 1511. 'Evolution politique des Hindous de Madagascar', government memo, 9 November 1948, K.60.7, 57QO7 AMAE
69. Malbrant: René Malbrant, Debate in the National Assembly, 8 May 1947, p. 1511. British agents: Les recherché des services de renseignement Britanniques, Annexe II Troisième Partie, K.60.7, 57QO7 AMAE. British espionage: 'Note Préliminaire:

Les activités Britanniques à Madagascar', Troisième Partie, K.60.7, 57QO7 AMAE

70. Memo to the French ambassador, London, 23 April 1948, 57QO7 AMAE

71. Memo from Tananarive to Paris, 1 May 1948, 57QO7 AMAE

72. Long Live: Déclarations Faites le 9 April par un malgache nommé Rasolo, Deuxième Bureau report, April 1947, 8.H.176 SHD. Manakara: Rapports de la rébellion avec les étrangers, 8 April 1947, 8.H.176 SHD. MDRM letter to US: 'Renseignment de Contre-Ingerence Politique', July 1947, K.60.2, 57QO7 AMAE. America: Memo from Paris to Amb. Bonnet in New York, 22 August 1947, 57Qo2 AMAE

73. Raseta: Little, op. cit., p. 538. MDRM: Little, op. cit., p. 537. US report: Paul Alling to the State Department 30 January 1947, FRUS, 1947, vol. V, pp. 673–4

74. Caffery to the Secretary of State, Paris, 14 January 1948, FRUS, 1948, vol. III, pp. 594–5

75. Gilbert de Chambrun: 'Y a-t-il une alternative à la politique étrangère de la France?' *Politique Étrangère*, 1947, p. 356. Marshall: quoted in M. A. Lawrence & F. Logevall, *The First Vietnam War: Colonial Conflict and Cold War Crisis* (Harvard: Harvard University Press, 2007), p. 202

76. US arms: The State Department replied that this would be 'difficult' because the 'sensitivity of American opinion on this matter was so great that the State Department would expose itself to the risk of misunderstanding'. It added the US would remain aware of the importance of 'sweeping away false rumours about US support and assistance to the trouble-makers', Memo from Bonnet to Bidault, 17 October 1947, 91QO127 AMAE. French officials: Memo from Paris to Bonnet in New York, 22 August 1947, 57Qo2 AMAE

77. Mauritius: Rapports de la rébellion avec les étrangers, 8 April 1947, 8.H.176 SHD

78. Rapports de la rébellion avec les étrangers, 8 April 1947, 8.H.176 SHD

79. W. Churchill, *The Hinge of Fate* (London: Penguin Classics, 2005), pp. 107 and 201. Churchill: Letter to Roosevelt, 7 February 1942, quoted in Kimball (ed.), *Churchill & Roosevelt: The Complete Correspondence*, vol. II (Princeton: Princeton University Press, 1987), pp. 334–5, 350

80. Leahy: 20 February 1942, FRUS, 1942, vol. II, p. 139. Allied alarm: WO 208/ 928, 5 March 1942 PRO

81. P. de Lagarde, 'Über die nächsten Pflichten deutscher Politik', reprinted in *Schriften für Deutschland* (Stuttgart: Kröner, 1933)

82. Roosevelt: see letter from Roosevelt to Churchill, 8 July 1943, in Kimball (ed.), *Churchill & Roosevelt*, vol. II, pp. 315–16. Palestine: On French support for Jewish terrorism, see J. Barr, *A Line in the Sand: Britain, France and the Struggle that Shaped the Middle East* (London: Simon & Schuster, 2012)

83. See for example reports by the Joint Strategic Survey Committee such as JSSC 9/1, 15 March 1943; JSSC 570/2, 2 November 1942; reports by the Joint War Plans Committee, JWPC 361/4, 25 August 1943 and JWPC 361/5, 13 September 1945

84. Clipperton: Memorandum of conversation by the ambassador to Mexico, 19 December 1944, FRUS, vol. IV, 1945, pp. 783–4. Bidault: Memo from Amb. Caffrey to the Secretary of State, 22 January 1945, FRUS, vol. IV, 1945, pp. 788–9. Hickerson: SWNCC (State-War-Navy Coordinating Committee) 106/1

85. Aurand to Patterson, 7 February 1946, HS Aurand Papers box 28. Top secret: 'United States Policy with Regard to French North Africa', Memo by the Policy Planning Staff, 22 March 1948, FRUS, Western Europe 1948, p. 684. French chiefs: Gen. J. Marchant, 'Stratégie Américaine et Stratégie Soviétique en Extrême-Orient, *Politique Étrangère*, no. 4–5, 1951

86. J. Fenby, op. cit., pp. 306–7

87. 'Lend-lease' was a wartime programme of American aid to liberated France and Great Britain. See SWNCC 106, 'Exchange of Ownership of Clipperton Island in Part Settlement of French Lend-Lease Obligations to the United States', 13 April 1945 and US State-War-Navy Coordinating Committee (SWNCC) 106/1, file CCS 093, Clipperton Island (4-13-45), RG 218, US National Archives

88. 'United States Policy with Regard to French North Africa', Memorandum by the Policy Planning Staff, 22 March 1948, FRUS, Western Europe, 1948, pp. 686–7

89. G. de Chambrun, 'Y a-t-il une alternative à la politique étrangère de la France?', Politique Étrangère, 1947, p. 357

90. Memo from Robert Barques, Tananarive, to the Ministry for Overseas Affairs, 8 June 1950, 57QO01 AMAE

91. Memo from the Ministry for Overseas Affairs to the French ambassador, Washington DC, 29 August 1950, 57QO01 AMAE

92. Propaganda: internal government memo, 19 October 1951, 57QO01 AMAE. Brockway: Letter to Joseph Raseta, 26 April 1950, copy in 57QO01 AMAE

93. Exposé de Général de Lattre au Comité de Défense Nationale du 17 March 1951, 10.H.173 SHD

94. See Marilyn B. Young, 'The Same Struggle for Liberty', in Lawrence & Logevall (eds.), op. cit., pp. 200–201

95. K. Chen, Vietnam and China (Princeton: Princeton University Press, 1969), pp. 90–93, 102–12

96. G. Moorhouse, 'He Knew Ho as OSS agent 19', in Providence Journal, 26 June 1968

97. W. Lafeber, 'Roosevelt, Churchill and Indochina: 1942–45', American Historical Review, December 1975

98. V. N. Duong, The Tragedy of the Vietnam War: A South Vietnamese Officer's Analysis (Jefferson: McFarland Books, 2008), p. 17

99. O'Sullivan to the Secretary of State, Hanoi, 24 September 1947, FRUS, vol. VI, 1947, pp. 140; Saigon consul Clayton Reed to the Secretary of State, Saigon, 26 September 1947, FRUS, vol. VI, 1947, p. 142

100. Acting Secretary of State to the Saigon consul Clayton Reed, 4 September 1946, FRUS, vol. VII, 1946. French media: Reed to the Secretary of State, Saigon, 11 July 1947, FRUS, vol. VI, 1947, pp. 111–114. Single-handedly: Vincent to Acheson, 8 January 1947, FRUS, vol. VI, 1947, pp. 58–59. French public: Reed to the Secretary of State, Saigon, 11 July 1947, FRUS, vol. VI, 1947, pp. 110 and 116. Meyer: R. Faligot & P. Krop, La Piscine: The French Secret Service since 1944 (Oxford: Blackwell, 1989), op. cit., p. 85

101. French memo: M. Attwood, 'Transnational Coalition-Building and the Making of the Cold War in Indochina 1947–9', Diplomatic History, Summer 2002, pp. 453–80

102. L'Aide Américain à l'Indochine', 25 January 1951, Schuman archive, 7Q090 AMAE

103. Vosjoli: Memo of 5 September 1951, 10.H.266 SHD. Note de Service, Colonel Brébisson, 22 June 1950, 10.H.174 SHD

104. French calls to UK: Reuters report, Saigon, 7 April 1950, 10.H.174 SHD. Malaya: Telegram from General Carpentier, 21 August 1950, 10.H.174 SHD. The British commanders were Major-General J. H. N. Poett, Commodore G. F. Burghard, Group Captain R. T. Gething, Colonel P. Gieadell, Lt-Col. J. R. H. Platt and Major R. G. J. Burrows. The meeting was also attended by the US military attaché to Saigon, Colonel Lee V. Harris. Esler-Dening: Memo, Saigon, 23 January 1951, 10.H.173 SHD

105. Rapport Militaire, June–July 1951, 10.H.138 SHD

106. See for example memos of M. Henri Bonnet, French ambassador to the US to Foreign Minister Robert Schuman, 27 July, and 12 and 17 October 1950, série B-E.U. 91QO72 AMAE

107. De Lattre: Dispatch to Robert Schuman, 28 September 1951 Schuman archive, 7Q090 AMAE

108. Discours du General de Lattre à son Retour de Washington, 21 October 1951, 10.H.173 SHD

109. French observers: Foreign Ministry memo, 14 February 1952, Schuman archive, 7Q090 AMAE. French officials: Foreign Ministry memo, 22 April 1952, Schuman archive, 7Q090 AMAE

110. Fuses: On American military support in general see M. Windrow, *The Last Valley: Dien Bien Phu and the French Defeat in Vietnam* (London: Cassell, 2005), p. 180. Shiploads: By the end of 1952, the US had sent French forces in Indochina 777 armoured fighting vehicles, 13,000 transport vehicles, 228 aircraft and 253 naval vessels as well as thousands of other items. Contribution: NSC Policy Review, 19 January 1953

111. Invading nature: General Paul quoted in *The Pentagon Papers*, vol. I, pp. 458–9. Twenty-five times: Young, op. cit., p. 202

112. US influence: FRUS, 1951, vol. VI, part I, 14 June 1951, pp. 425–8

113. Interview with the author, 11 November 2015

114. US visitor: Reed to the Secretary of State, Saigon, 11 July 1947, FRUS, vol. VI, 1947, p. 111. Torture: H. R. Simpson, *Tiger in the Barbed Wire: An American in Vietnam* (Washington, DC: Brassey's Books, 1998), p. 79. 1940: *New York Times*, 26 August 1951

115. French opinion: *Le Monde*, 20 November 1953

116. Eisenhower: Telephone conversation with Dulles, 5 April 1954, Dwight D. Eisenhower Papers, 1953–61

117. Lansdale: E. G. Lansdale, *In the Midst of Wars: An American's Mission to Southeast Asia* (New York: Harper & Row, 1972), p. 316. French memo: Faligot & Krop, op. cit., pp. 103–4

118. De Gaulle to Edmond Michelet in 1954, see J. R. Tournoux, *La Tragédie du Général*, Paris, 1967, p. 188

119. Mendès France: Quoted in Horne, op. cit., pp. 98–9

120. Intelligence reports: These claims were made by Bourgès-Maunoury in a speech to the National Assembly in November 1955. Nasser: FO 371/80-0/734, 11 March 1956, PRO

121. See Horne, op. cit., p. 129. Abdul Qadir Chanderli, one of the FLN's leaders who had been head of its arms procurement in Yugoslavia, later said that Nasser's involvement with Algeria had been 'negligible (but) because of the need for solidarity we could not say so'

122. Bargaining chip: this possibility was aired, for example, in the *Journal Officiel*, 18 December 1956, p. 6117

123. Ben-Gurion: M. Golani, *Shimon Peres* (Worthing: Littlehampton Books, 1982), p. 50

124. Couve de Murville: cited by Maurice Vaisse in Wm. R. Louis & R. Owen, *Suez 1956: The Crisis and Its Consequences*, 1956, p. 139. Robert Murphy: PREM 11/1098 346-7, 29 July 1956, PRO. Menace: Pineau is said to have told Eden that, if Britain would not join in, France was willing to attack Egypt alongside Israel. See M. Brecher, *Decisions in Israel's Foreign Policy* (Oxford: Oxford University Press, 1974), pp. 265–6. This was also the message of Admiral Nomy, Chief of the French Naval Staff, to Eden. See J. Chauvel *Commentaire Vol. III 1952–62: De Berne Paris* (Paris: Fayard, 1973), pp. 182–5

125. Thomas: J. Newhouse, *De Gaulle and the Anglo-Saxons* (London: André Deutsch, 1970), pp. 15–17. P. Marcus, *Maurice Bourgès-Maunoury: Un Républicain Indivisible* (Paris: Atlantica, 1997), p. 331

126. J. Selwyn Lloyd, *Suez 1956: A Personal Account* (London: Jonathan Cape, 1978), p. 80

127. Peres: *La Force de Vaincre* (Paris: Centurion, 1981), p. 61

128. Sharett: Bar-Zohar, *Bridge Over the Mediterranean* (Hebrew), (Tel Aviv: Am-Hassefer, 1964), p. 25

129. Oil: See letter from the British embassy in Paris 16 August 1956. Ramadier was preparing a plan 'which could be put into operation in the event of supplies of oil becoming difficult'. See Fascicule de Statistiques Petrolières. On 14 September 1956, French press reports claimed that Ramadier had asked Washington to 'lend some of the T2 tankers lying unused in American ports'

130. Depreux: Ben-Dor to Ambassador Yacov Tsur, 11 March 1956, Israeli State Archives, Jerusalem (ISA) 193/1. See in general Bar-On, *Gates of Gaza: Israel's Road to Suez and Back 1955–57* (New York: Macmillan, 1994). Ambassador: Tsur in 22 May 1956 to Abba Eban, Israeli State Archives, Jerusalem (ISA) 194/3. See Bar-On, *Gates of Gaza*

131. The vast majority of the indigenous population was disenfranchised

132. French defence officials argued that there was an 'axis' that ran between these regions. See Wall, op. cit., p. 18

133. Grossin: Interviewed by S. K. Crosbie, Paris, 1969. See *A Tacit Alliance: France and Israel from Suez to the Six Day War* (Princeton University Press, 1974), pp. 46–7

134. FO 371/115565, 18 and 25 July 1955, PRO

135. FO 371/115565, 25 July 1955, PRO

136. FO 371/115873, 27 July–22 August 1955, PRO

137. FO 371/115873, 27 July–22 August 1955, PRO

138. FO 371/121697 PRO

139. See S. W. Smith (ed.), *Reassessing Suez: New Perspectives on the Crisis and its Aftermath* (London: Ashgate, 2008), p. 96

140. Amman embassy to Foreign Office, 11 October 1955, FO 371/115571 PRO. Whitehall to British embassy Tel Aviv, 14 October 1955 to Tel Aviv, FO 371/115571 PRO

141. FO 371/115571, 11–18 October 1955, PRO

142. P. Bernet, *SDECE Service 7* (Paris: Presses de la Cité, 1980), p. 15068. See D. Porch, *The French Secret Services* (Oxford: Oxford University Press, 1997), p. 421

143. Broadcasts: BBC Summary of World Broadcasts IV, Daily Series no. 7: 'Unidentified Broadcasts Attacking Gamal Abdul Nasser in Arabic', 28 July 1956. See K. Kyle *Suez: Britain's End of Empire in the Middle East* (London: I.B. Tauris, p. 151). Two agents: Faligot & Krop, *La Piscine*, pp. 116–8. Diplomatic bag: Faligot & Krop, *La Piscine*, p. 149

144. Embargo: Pineau's letter to Geoffrey de Courcel, Sécretaire Générale de la Defense Nationale, 2 February 1956

145. SDECE chief interviewed by Crosbie, op. cit., p. 58

146. Targets: Plans to strike Syria were part of 'Operation Straggle', a joint British–American operation to stop Syria falling into Soviet hands. The French had been only tangentially involved in this operation. Preparations: These included eighty-two Mystère Mark IVs, 120 AMX tanks, forty Super Sherman tanks and eighteen 105mm guns.

147. Question: Shimon Peres, 'The Road to Sèvres: Franco-Israeli Strategic Cooperation' in Troen & Shemesh (eds.), *The Suez-Sinai Crisis: A Retrospective and Reappraisal* (London: Routledge, 1990). Meeting: J. Cointet, 'Guy Mollet, the French government and the SFIO' in Troen & Shemesh, *The Suez-Sinai Crisis 1956*, p. 133. See also Bar-On, *Gates of Gaza*, 1956, p. 207

148. Israel informed: Bar-On, 'Challenge and Quarrel: The Road to the Sinai Campaign' (Beersheba: Kiryat Sde Boker, 1991), pp. 183–5

149. Pineau to Dulles, 1 August 1956. See also DDF (Documents Diplomatiques Français), 1956, II 105, pp. 209–10

150. Selwyn Lloyd, op. cit., pp. 80, 174

151. Jebb: Sir Anthony Nutting and Selwyn Lloyd noted how Mollet and Pineau felt 'double-crossed' by the Americans. See Nutting, *No End of a Lesson: Story of Suez* (New York: Constable), p. 99; PREM 11/1100 f.22, 9 September 1956, PRO; DDF (Documents Diplomatiques Français) 1956, II 169, pp. 348–9

152. US commentators: *New York Herald Tribune*, 2 October 1956. Dillon: FRUS, XVI, 31 July 1956, pp. 74–7

153. See in general, Wall, op. cit., p. 27

154. Wall, op. cit., p. 20

155. Bourguiba: Wall, op. cit., pp. 103–4. The strategic importance of north Africa was a powerful and recurrent theme in French military publications, such as the *Révue Militaire d'Information* and *Révue de Defense Nationale*, in the mid-1950s. See for example General L. M. Chassin, 'Vers un encirclement de l'Occident?', RDN, May 1956

156. FO 371/124472 PRO

157. Letter to K. L. Stock at the Ministry of Power, 26 April 1956

158. Soustelle: 'The Wealth of the Sahara', *Foreign Affairs*, July 1959. Sahara: D. Yergin, *The Prize: The Epic Quest for Oil, Money & Power* (London: Simon & Schuster, 2009), p. 526. State Department: See State Department Memorandum of 26 June 1958, FRUS, vol. XIII, 1958, p. 640. See also Statement of John Dulles, 'American Foreign Policy: Current Documents' 15 April 1958, pp. 1091–2

159. M. Golani, *Israel in Search of a War: The Sinai Campaign 1955–6* (Portland, Oregon: Sussex Academic Press, 1998), p. 154

160. Thomas, Hugh, *The Suez Affair* (London: Penguin, 1970), p. 172

161. US intrusion: An accompanying document labelled simply 'Note' appears to assume the falsehood of the charge that American oil companies were implicated by materials in Ben Bella's possession at the time of his arrest. See Wall, op. cit., p. 47. Filling stations: Wall, op. cit., p. 61

162. Wall, op. cit., p. 49

163. World power: See R. J. Barnet, *The Alliance: America-Europe-Japan Makers of the Post-War World* (New York: Simon & Schuster, 1983), p. 217

164. Oil history: Yergin, op. cit., p. 170. Sahara: Jebb's Memorandum on France, 17 January 1958, FO 371/137237 PRO

165. Quoted in M. G. Klapp, *The Sovereign Entrepreneur: Oil Policies in Advanced and Less Developed Capitalist Countries* (Ithaca: Cornell University Press, 1987), p. 32

166. De Gaulle's rage: Battenburg, 'English versus French: Language Rivalry in Tunisia', *World Englishes* vol. 16, no. 2, 1997, pp. 281–90. Muehlenbeck, op. cit., p. 162

167. Michel Debré: See I. Wall, *L'Influence Américaine sur la Politique Française, 1945–1954*, and 'The United States, Algeria, and the Fall of the Fourth French Republic,' *Diplomatic History* vol. 18, no. 4, Fall 1994: pp. 489–511 and R. Murphy, *Diplomat Among Warriors* (New York: Doubleday, 1964), p. 382. US and North Africa: NSC 5911/1, 4 November 1959, FRUS, vol. XIII, North Africa 1958–60, p. 615

168. NSC 5911/1, 4 November 1959, FRUS, 1958–60, vol. III, p. 622

169. Alphand: Wall, op. cit., p. 129–30. Adverse effect: Wall, op. cit., p. 119

170. National Assembly: In the letter, Eisenhower asked France to 'show comprehension of the practical limits on the Tunisian government. Sentimental ties unite the Tunisian and Algerian people who seek an opportunity for self-government and self-determination. Is this not only consistent with French interests, but also a way to promote them?'

French influence, it continued, must be freely accepted by Muslim peoples and could not be imposed on north Africa. It added that France's policies towards the region were also the business of its Western partners. Coup: G. Ball, *The Past Has Another Pattern* (London and New York: Norton, 1982), p. 155. Meeting: UN Resolution 1167, 26 November 1957. 'De Gaulle's fixation with Algeria and rage at US abstention in [the] UNGA vote plays major role in our problems with him.' The French ambassador, Hervé Alphand, also 'linked French project [to] withdraw their Mediterranean fleet from NATO with de Gaulle's anguish at attitude we have adopted towards FLN'

171. M. Couve de Murville, Ministre des Affaires Étrangères, aux Représentants Diplomatiques de France à Londres, Washington, 17 Juillet 1958. Telegram reprinted in AMAE, 1958, Tome II, pp. 89–91

172. Memorandum from the Secretary of State's Special Assistant to Secretary of State Dulles, 6 February 1958, FRUS, vol. XIV, 1958–60, p. 2; NSC meeting, 7 August 1958, FRUS, vol. XIV, 1958–60, pp. 19–20

173. *Foccart Parle: Entretiens Avec Philippe Gaillard* (Paris: Jeune Afrique, 1995), p. 227

174. M. Robert & A. Renault, *Ministre de l'Afrique : Entretiens Avec Maurice Robert* (Paris: Seuil, 2004), p. 112

175. 'La Françafrique' appears to have first been used in 1955 by the leader of the Côte d'Ivoire but was later used by French journalists and authors. Colonial treaties: For example, Article 2 of the second annex of the defence agreement between France and Gabon stipulated that the Gabonese Republic 'engages itself to call exclusively on the French Republic for the maintenance and renewal of its materials'. This clause was also integral to most of the other agreements that France struck with its former African colonies. These treaties were secret until 2008, when the Sarkozy government decided to publish them. See the French Defence Ministry document, 'Défense et Sécurité Nationale: Le Livre Blanc', June 2008, pp. 154–5. French officials: Telegram from the Embassy in the Congo to the Department of State, 19 November 1960, FRUS, vol. XIV, Africa, 1958–60, p. 243

176. Guinea is different from the Portuguese colony of Guinea-Bissau

177. Quoted in G. Chaffard, *Les Carnets Secrets de la Decolonisation* (Paris: Calmann-Lévy, 1967), p. 189

178. Western observer: This was the description of the Belgian ambassador to Moscow, who observed Sekou Touré's trip to Moscow in November 1959. Memorandum to Brussels, 3 December 1959, 51QO20 AMAE

179. French ambassador in Tunis to Foreign Ministry, 9 October 1958, 51QO20 AMAE

180. Charles Lucet to Maurice Couve de Murville, 29 January 1959, 51QO/2, Guinée 1958–1959, AMAE

181. Alphand to Maurice Couve de Murville, 9 October 1958, 51QO/18 AMAE

182. Hungarian team: Pierre Siraud, French ambassador to Conakry, to Paris, 2 September 1959

183. Telegram from Chauvel to Foreign Ministry, 24 April 1959, 51QO/18 AMAE. Judge and Jury: Lucet to Paris, 19 October 1959, 51QO/18 AMAE

184. British government: French chargé d'affaires, Conakry to FM, 10 September 1959, 51QO20 AMAE. British ambassador: Memo of the French ambassador in Washington to Paris, 3 September 1959. Memo of the British ambassador in Washington to Whitehall, 24 August 1959, 51QO20 AMAE. Czech delivery: Francis Huré, French chargé d'affaires to Guinea, letter to the Min. of Foreign Affairs, 10 June 1959, 51QO/2, Guinée 1958–1959, AMAE

185. French ambassador: Maurice Dejean to Paris, 18 September 1959, 51QO20 AMAE.

Alphand to Paris, 20 October 1959, 51QO/18 AMAE. Pierre Siraud to the Minister of Foreign Affairs, 22 October 1959, 51QO20 AMAE

186. Robert, op. cit., p. 112

187. Karim: This statement was made under duress during a trial in 1970–71. The transcripts of the interrogation were published in *Revue Tricontinentale*, February 1972. See Faligot & Krop, op. cit., p. 193

188. Robert & Renault, op. cit., pp. 108–9

189. The French company was the Societé des Pétroles d'Afrique Équatoriale Française (SPAEF) and its chief joint ventures were the Compagnie Shell de Recherche et d'Exploitation au Gabon. SPEAF also had separate operational agreements with Mobil Oil Française and Mobil Exploration West Africa

190. Memo from French intelligence chief to the Prime Minister, Paris, 17 March 1959, CA 5.1, 40QO17 AMAE

191. Katha: Telegram from Marine Paris to Marine Dakar, 12 January 1960, CA 4.4, 40QO13 AMAE. Telegram from Cominterarm, Cameroon, 31 January 1961

192. Telegrams from Maurice Dejean, French embassy, Moscow, to Paris, 20 August and 10 September 1959, 40QO6 AMAE

193. *Time*, 11 January 1960

194. Equipment: Foreign Ministry telegram, 7 June 1961, 40QO17 AMAE

195. Charles Van de Lanoitte, 'Beti Main Basse', in R. Joseph (ed.), *Gaullist Africa: Cameroon under Ahmadu Ahidjo* (Enugu, Nigeria: Fourth Dimension, 1978), p. 96

196. Faligot & Krop, op. cit., pp. 188–9

197. The Swiss authorities opened formal legal proceedings against Bechtel in 1974

198. Memorandum of Conversation, 16 April 1959, FRUS, XIV, Africa, 1958–60, pp. 45–7

199. Report: Memo from Ambassador Bonnet in Washington to Paris, 2 October 1951, 10.H.173 SHD

200. R. Denard: Pierre Lunel, *Le Roi de Fortune*, 1st edition, Paris, 1991

201. See M. G. Kalb, *Congo Cables: The Cold War in Africa – from Eisenhower to Kennedy* (London: Macmillan, 1982)

202. Rusk: Dwight D. Eisenhower, *Waging Peace 1956–61* (London: Heinemann, 1961), p. 576; Rusk, 'Address before the American Historical Association at Washington DC, 30 December 1961; and 'Statement before the Subcommittee on African Affairs of the Senate Foreign Relations Committee', 18 January 1961. The CIA concurred with this view: See the telex of Lawrence Devlin to CIA director Allen Dulles in 'Alleged Assassination Plots Involving Foreign Leaders' 1975, 94th Cong, 1 Session, S.Rept, 94–465, p. 14

203. Rusk: Statement before the Sub-Committee on African Affairs' in EK Lindlet (ed.), *The Winds of Freedom: The Speeches of Dean Rusk* (Boston: Beacon Press, 1963), p. 222

204. *Foccart Parle*, pp. 310–11; Robert, op. cit., p. 163

205. Schraeder, 'From Berlin 1884 to 1989: Foreign Assistance and French, American and Japanese Competition in Francophone Africa', *Journal of Modern African Studies*, vol. 33, no. 4, 1995, p. 548

206. Kennedy: See P. E. Muehlenbeck, *Betting on the Africans: John F. Kennedy's Courting of African Nationalist Leaders*, p. 157

207. Muehlenbeck, op. cit., p. 158

208. De Gaulle, op. cit., pp. 266–7

209. Francis Terry McNamara, *France in Black Africa* (New York: US Government Printing, 1989), p. 177

210. Muehlenbeck, op. cit., p. 162

211. Kennedy: Muehlenbeck, op. cit., p. 171. De Gaulle quoted in F. Costigliola, *France*

and the United States: The Cold Alliance since World War II (New York: Twayne, 1992), pp. 139–40. See Muehlenbeck, op. cit., p. 162. Common Market: See J. Fenby, *The General*, p. 503

212. 'Possibilities and Limitations in Dealing with de Gaulle', State Dept, April 1963. See Muehlenbeck, op. cit., p. 171

213. Robert, op. cit., p. 174

214. Robert, op. cit., p. 201. Whiteman, 'The Man Who Ran Françafrique'; S. Decalo, *The Stable Minority: Civilian Rule in Africa, 1960–1990* (Gainesville: Florida Academic Press, 1998), pp. 130–31

215. Robert, op. cit., p. 194

216. Gabon's natural resources are discussed in the following chapter

217. Robert, op. cit., p. 204

218. Robert, op. cit., pp. 263–4

219. De Gaulle and 'US expense': Interview with C. L. Sulzberger, *New York Times*, 3 February 1964. In Laos, the French and Americans were backing different candidates, and de Gaulle was keen to keep out the Americans from a French-speaking region of south-east Asia. Newspaper stories began to appear noting de Gaulle's interest in winning Chinese support to keep the Americans at bay

220. Secret Meeting of the British Cabinet, 30 July 1969, CAB 128/44 PRO

221. Telegram 551, 28 July 1969, PREM 13/2833 PRO

222. 'France and Nigeria', 23 October 1969, FCO 65/267. FCO Telegram no. 1142, 10 December 1969. 'Use of French Rockets by Biafrans', FCO 65/269 PRO. Anti-British feeling: 'Anglo-French Talks', 21 October 1969, FCO 65/272 PRO

223. British tabloid: *The Sun*, 3 October 1968. Proxy war: 'Military aid and assistance for Nigeria', 29 July 1969, PREM 69/69; Telegram Number 1552, 28 July 1969 PREM 69/69 PRO

224. R. Steiner, *Carré Rouge* (Paris: Laffont, 1976)

225. De Gaulle: '*La France et le Biafra*', République Française, Ministère des Affaires Étrangères, Paris, 1969, p. 20. Houphouët-Boigny's influence: In October 1969, the French ambassador to London claimed that Houphouët-Boigny had put 'pressure to bear' on Paris to support Ojukwu 'as a result of a TV programme he saw on starvation in Biafra'. See 'Anglo/French talks on Africa', 28 November 1968, FCO 65/267 PRO

226. British official: 'France and Nigerian Oil', 4 December 1968, FCO 65/267 PRO. French companies: 12 November 1968, FCO 65/266 PRO. In 1967, French oil interests in Nigeria were registered in the name of SAFRAP, which was partly owned by the French government. It had six prospecting licences in the Benue-Plateau, the East Central, the Rivers and the Mid-Western states, covering a total of 24,178 square kilometres. It was producing oil only from the Obagi field and moving it to Bonny along the Shell pipeline. By 1967 it had one other field with proven oil reserves, at Owopele in Mid-Western State, but was not exploiting it

227. French officials admitted this in their dialogue with British counterparts, 'pointing out that French economic interests were about equal on either side of the River Niger'. Telegram no. 5, 29 January 1969, FCO 65/268 PRO. See also House of Commons Debates, vol. 769, c. 1462, 27 August 1968. K. E. Klieman, 'US Oil Companies, The Nigerian Civil War and the Origins of Opacity in the Nigerian Oil Industry', *Journal of American History*, vol. 99, 2012

228. Internal Foreign Office Memorandum, FCO 65/269, March 1969, PRO

229. Fashoda analogies: 'Nigeria and France', FCO 65/266, 31 October 1968, PRO. House of

Commons debate, vol. 775, c. 664, 12 December 1968; FCO 65/267, 28 November 1968. PR. P. Decraene, 'Les grandes puissances interviennent de plus en plus ouvertement dans la guerre civile du Nigeria', *Le Monde*, 1 November 1968

230. 'The Presidents' Man' by R. W. Johnson, LRB, 25 May 1995. French-speaking Quebec was conquered by the British in 1763 and later assimilated into an independent 'Anglo-Saxon' Canada

231. 'Anglo/French talks on Africa', 28 November 1968, FCO 65/267 PRO

232. One of the few analyses of the French position is D. Bach, 'Le General de Gaulle et la guerre civile au Nigeria', *Canadian Journal of African Studies*, vol. xiv, 1980; 18 August 1969, FCO 65/270 PRO

233. Robert, op. cit., p. 180

234. NATO depots: Information supplied to the author by Frederick Forsyth, who reported on the Biafran civil war. Telephone interview with the author, 4 September 2015. Prying eyes: FCO 65/266, 29 October 1968; FCO 65/266, 30 October 1968, PRO. 'Monsieur Foccart', FCO memorandum, 13 June 1969, FCO 65/269 PRO

235. Doran: Quoted in C. J. Korieh, *Religion, History and Politics in Nigeria: Essays in Honor of Ogbu U. Kalu* (Lagos: UPA, 2005), p. 164. Interview with the author, 6 February 2015

236. Air supplies: 'South Africa and France step up Biafra arms', *Sunday Telegraph*, 30 November 1969. A. J. Venter, *War Dog: Fighting Other People's Wars* (London: Casemate Books, 2008), p. 322. Forsyth, p. 146

237. 'French involvement with von Rosen', 23 October 1969, FCO 65/272 PRO

238. 'Strafe civilians': Foreign Office Telegram 573, 29 November 1969, FCO 65/272 PRO. 'Explosive Situation': FCO Telegram no. 1142, 10 December 1969, 'Use of French Rockets by Biafrans', FCO 65/269 PRO. Advice: 'Report on visit to Nigeria by RAF officers' 20–23 August 1969, 28 August 1969; 'Military aid and assistance for Nigeria', 17 September 1969, FCO 65/289 PRO

239. The covert airlift was reported in *The Times*, 3 January 1968 and *Financial Times*, 9 August 1967 and *Birmingham Post*, 15 August 1967. Shepherd's remark was made in the House of Lords on 29 January 1968, Hansard 22 July 1968 column 68. See in general Forsyth, op. cit., pp. 162–3. See in general Forsyth, op. cit., chapter 10. British fears of a wider 'Balkanisation' were voiced by Sir Leslie Glass in his memorandum to London on 21 October 1969, in which he referred to the way in which 'the intensification of tribal solidarity resulting from the creation of these new "nation states" would undoubtedly spill over the present borders of Nigeria', FCO 65/272 PRO

240. Defenceless targets: *Sunday Telegraph*, 11 February 1969

241. 'Discomfort us': 'Background Note', 2 April 1969, FCO 65/269 PRO. Telegram no. 5, 29 January 1969, FCO 65/268 PRO

242. Temperature: 'Sir J. Johnston to AM Palliser, 13 October 1969 PRO. Foccart: Foreign Office Telegram 578, 28 November 1969, FCO 65/272 PRO. 'Increase in de Gaulle's aid to Biafra: Anglo-French Row', *Daily Telegraph*, 11 February 1969

243. US commerce: Robert, op. cit., p. 263. OAU resolution: W. Attwood, *The Twilight Struggle: Tales of the Cold War* (New York: Harper & Row, 1987), p. 241

244. 'Partido Africano da Independência da Guiné e Cabo Verde' ('The African Party for the Independence of Guinea and Cape Verde')

245. The story of the SDECE-PIDE joint venture was published in the Portuguese newspaper *Expresso* on 24 January 1976

246. De Gaulle quoted in *Le Monde*, 24 November 1961

247. French bomb: Kennedy quoted in Constantine Pagedas, *Anglo-American Strategic Relations and the French Problem* (London: Routledge, 2000), p. 129. George-Henri

Soutou & Alain Beltran (eds.), *Pierre Guillaumat: La Passion des Grands Projets Industriels*, Institut d'Histoire de l'Industrie, 1995, p. 35

248. Article 4 of Gabon's independence treaty stipulated that Gabon '*facilité au profit des forces armées françaises le stockage des matières et produits stratègiques*'. The French Commissariat à l'Energie Atomique provided the venture capital through its subsidiary Compagnie Générale des Matières Nucléaires, which owned 18.8 per cent of the Compagnie des Mines d'Uranium de Franceville

249. See S. W. Smith & A. Glaser, *Comment la France a Perdu l'Afrique* (Paris: Calmann-Lévy, 2005), part 1, chapter 4

250. De Marenches: C. Ockrent & Count de Marenches, *The Evil Empire* (London: Sidgwick & Jackson, 1988), p. 64

251. J. Foccart, with P. Gaillard, *Foccart Parle: Entretiens avec Philippe Gaillard* (Paris: Jeune Afrique, 1995), vol. 1

252. Bakouma: author's interview with retired French geologist, April 2015. See also Thierry Parquet (ed.) 'La Mine et Les Mineurs de l'Uranium Français', p. 305: 'L'uranium est inclus dans le réseau cristallin de l'apatite, phosphate de calcium contenant du fluor et du chlore'

253. Carter later denied making the remark: See 'Inquiry into the Matter of Billy Carter and Libya', US Senate, 12 June 1980

254. Foreign Minister: British ambassador to Washinghton, FCO 93/1376, 6 November 1978, PRO. British diplomats: 'Libya seeks new oil fields to boost exports in 1980s', *Washington Post*, 29 July 1979; *Christian Science Monitor* 25 October 1978; FCO memo 93/1869, 18 June 1979, PRO

255. This version of the conversation is put forward by Arnaud de Borchgrave, 'Commentary: Regime Change à la Français', UPI, 14 March 2003

256. Debré: See F. Verschave, *Noir Silence: Qui arrêtera la Françafrique?* (Paris: Les Arènes, 2000), p. 155

257. Newspaper: *Depêche du Midi*, 27 August 1959. Analyst: D. Albo, 'L'intervention Française au Tchad', *Dernières Nouvelles d'Alsace*, 12 September 1969; C. Angeli, 'Des soldats pour le Tchad', *Le Nouvel Observateur*, 15 December 1969

258. 'Super Étendard for Peru', Secret UK Eyes Alpha Exclusive, 10 June 1982, FCO 33/5574 PRO

259. 'Falklands-Peru', Secret telegram from British embassy in Peru to London, 8 June 1982, FCO 33/5574 PRO

260. Sir J. Nott, *Here Today, Gone Tomorrow: Memoirs of an Errant Politician* (London: Politicos, 2002), p. 305

261. Fulsome description: See P. Short, *Mitterrand: A Study in Ambiguity* (London: Vintage, 2013), pp. 378–9. Mitterrand: press conference, Marseilles 9 June 1982. 'Falklands French Performance', FCO memo by Sir John Fretwell, 14 June 1982, FCO 33/5574 PRO

262. Madagascar's claims include the French territories of Bassas da India, Europa and Glorioso Islands

263. British officials: FCO Memo to Sir John Nott, 5 November 1982, FCO 7/4432 PRO

264. 'Entretien Avec Le Chancelier Camilion', Ambassador Destremau to Paris, 28 October 1981, 80QO 211 AMAE

265. Quai officials: 'Objet: Thomson CSF': 9 January 1980, 80QO 247 AMAE

266. Human rights document: 'Vente d'armes à l'Argentine', 19 June 1980, Foreign Ministry memo by Philippe Cuvillier, 80QO 247 AMAE. Licences: 'Vente de Matériels Militaires à l'Argentine', 4 February 1980, 80QO 247 AMAE. 'Note d'Entretien Pour le Directeur de Cabinet', 28 October 1981, 80QO 211 AMAE; Entretien avec le Ministre de l'Intérieur,

26 May 1981, Ambassador Destremau to Paris, 80QO 211 AMAE; Entretien avec le Ministre de l'Intérieur, 26 May 1981, Ambassador Destremau to Paris, 80QO 211 AMAE

267. 'Carlos Pastor – Visite du Chancelier Pastor à Paris', 4 July 1980, 80 QO 211 AMAE. In 2012, a French reporter, Pierre Ambrovici, showed the BBC confidential documents that he had accessed. These showed that in the mid-1970s France had become an intermediary for the supply of missiles on a nuclear rocket launcher called Pluto. See the BBC radio documentary, 'France and the Falklands', BBC Radio 4, 5 March 2012. Arms deliveries: 'Note d'Entretien Pour le Directeur de Cabinet', 28 October 1981, 80QO 211 AMAE

268. Whitehall official: FCO memo 21 May 1982, FCO 33/5574 PRO

269. Simon Webb, letter to Sir Anthony Acland, 23 June 1982, FCO 33/5574 PRO

270. Onslow to Rt. Hon. Peter Thomas, June 1982, FCO 33/5574 PRO

271. 'Falklands Crisis: Attitude of the PCF', M. J. Reynolds to FCO, 26 May 1982, FCO 33/5574 PRO

272. 'Cheysson's Leak': Memo from British embassy, Paris to FCO London, FCO 33/5574 PRO

273. Malvinas: Memo to President Giscard from M. Monod, President of the Centre of International Commerce, Paris, 30 December 1980, 80QO 211 AMAE. Fretwell: 'Falklands-French Attitude', from FCO London to Paris embassy, 14 June 1982, FCO 33/5574 PRO

274. De Margerie: 1930INVA/5224 AMAE

275. Old dispute: 'Falkland Islands', Fretwell to FCO, 9 April 1982, PRO. Latin America: 'Falklands: Mitterrand's Statement', memorandum from Sir John Fretwell, 9 June 1982, FCO 33/5574 PRO. Author's interview with former French intelligence official, London, 14 January 2016

276. Memorandum from Sir John Fretwell, 30 June 1982, FCO 33/5574 PRO

277. 'Thatcher's Blistering Attack on French over Exocets during Falklands', *Daily Telegraph*, 28 December 2012

278. 'Falklands: Mitterrand's Statement', memorandum from Sir John Fretwell, 9 June 1982, FCO 33/5574 PRO; Mitterrand press conference, reported in Telegram of 9 June 1982, FCO 33/5574 PRO

279. SIS: 'Allegations of French Help for Argentina Over Exocet AM39 Missiles', to 10 Downing Street, 26 July 1982, FCO 33/5574 PRO. 'Paris Shock on Exocet', *The Times*, 11 May 1982

280. The tapes were aired in a BBC radio documentary, 'France and the Falklands', BBC Radio 4, 5 March 2012

281. Nott: 'France and the Falklands', BBC Radio 4, 5 March 2012. British officials: 'Allegations of French Help for Argentina Over Exocet AM39 Missiles', 14 August 1982, FCO 33/5575 PRO

282. Onslow: Written Answer to Tam Dalyell, Hansard, 8 November 1982, PRO

283. Jacques Bence: 'Allegations of French Help for Argentina Over Exocet AM39 Missiles', Memo to 10 Downing Street, 26 July 1982, FCO 33/5574 PRO

284. 'Projets de l'Aérospatiale en Argentine', 8 December 1978, 80QO 250 AMAE. Amongst Aérospatiale's projects were the development of training aircraft, helicopters and satellites.

285. 'France and the Falklands', BBC Radio 4, 5 March 2012

286. Quai officials: Fretwell to Foreign Office, 2 June 1982, FCO 33/5574 PRO. Fretwell: 'Lt Commander Astiz', memo from John Holmes, Private Secretary, to Downing Street, 3 June 1982, PRO; Fretwell to Foreign Office, 2 June 1982, FCO 33/5574 PRO

287. 'Document', BBC Radio 4, 5 March 2012

288. Fretwell to Foreign Office, 2 June 1982, FCO 33/5574 PRO

289. FO diplomat: 'France and Arms for Argentina', 13 August 1982, FCO 33/5575 PRO. Hernu: Telegram Number 1168, 6 December 1982, FCO 7/4433 PRO

290. Plan: 'Exocet Missiles', 23 November 1982, FCO 7/4432 PRO; *Le Monde*, 17 December 1982

291. Five Exocets: *Le Monde*, 17 December 1982; Telegram from British embassy in Paris to London, 6 Dec 1982, FCO 7/4432 PRO. Disappointment: 'Argentina: Exocet Missiles Already in Country': 23 November 1982, FCO 7/4432 PRO. Corti: FCO Memo to Sir John Nott, 5 November 1982, FCO 7/4432 PRO

292. Thatcher on Mitterrand quoted in P. M. H. Bell, *France and Britain 1940–94: The Long Separation* (London: Longman, 1997), p. 247; Sir John Nott, 'France and the Falklands', BBC Radio 4, 5 March 2012

293. M. King, *Death of the Rainbow Warrior* (Wellington, New Zealand: Penguin, 1986), pp. 106–7

294. These allegations were made in *Libération*, 6 November 1981

295. De Gaulle, *Renewal*, op. cit., p. 239

296. New Caledonia parties: R. Aldrich & J. Connell, *France's Overseas Frontier* (Cambridge: Cambridge University Press, 1998), pp. 211–14

297. De Marenches, op. cit., p. 162

298. See R. Fisk, *Pity the Nation: Lebanon at War* (Oxford: Oxford University Press, 2001), p. 525

299. DGSE chief: De Marenches, op. cit., p. 161. BP: *Libération*, 6 November 1981

300. State Department official: Interview with the author, London, April 2015

301. Initially, Lane agreed with Secretary of State George Schulz that the US would not apply for a port visit within the first six months of the government's term. In January 1985, Lange agreed to allow the nuclear-armed destroyer USS *Buchanan* into Wellington harbour, but the following month withdrew his permission, allowing only a non-nuclear armed frigate, USS *Perry*, instead

302. De Marenches, op. cit., p. 162

303. Faligot & Krop, op. cit., p. 295

304. Other DGSE agents were probably also on the ground, and in September 2015, another former agent, Jean-Luc Kister, publicly apologised for his own role in the operation. In September 2006 one of the agents who placed the bomb was named as Gérard Royal by his brother, Antoine. Their sister, Ségolène Royal, was the Socialist candidate in the 2007 French Presidential elections

305. Interview with the author, London, February 2015

306. The militiamen were members of the RPF's armed wing, the Rwandan Patriotic Army (RPA). This version of events is based on the account put forward by Jacques Lanxade, who was at this time a presidential military adviser at Mitterrand's side. See *Quand Le Monde a Basculé* (Paris: Nil Editions, 2001), p. 164

307. Jean-Christophe: Prunier, op. cit., pp. 100–101. Agreement: On 18 July 1975, Pierre Delabre, the French *chargé d'affaires*, and Aloys Nsekalije, the Rwandan Foreign Minister, signed a 'Special Agreement for Military Assistance' involving the organisation and training of the Rwandan *gendarmes* (military policemen)

308. Warnings: See Dr A. Wallis, *Silent Accomplice* (London: I.B. Tauris, 2006), pp. 73–4

309. British ambassador: interview with the author, 21 September 2015. Exposure: in June 1992, Stephen Smith, the Africa editor of *Libération*, authored a front page exclusive on 'The Élysée's Secret War' in Rwanda

310. English-speaking region: Delaye's memorandum to Mitterrand, 15 February 1993; Meeting held at the Élysée 23 January 1991. Former ministers: statement of the former Minister of Cooperation, Bernard Debré, to the French Parliamentary Commission on Rwanda 1998. Quoted in section 1.4.3 of the Mucyo Report, a Rwandan government commission on the genocide that released its findings in August 2008

311. Testimony to the National Assembly's Inquiry on Rwanda, 2 June 1998
312. Prunier: 'Les enjeux diplomatiques de la tragédie Rwandaise', *La Lettre du Sud* no. 27, 23 May 1994. See Prunier, op. cit., p. 278. Pamphlet: quoted in Prunier, op. cit., pp. 278–9. French officer: Prunier, op. cit., p. 337. Pamphlet: Wallis, op. cit., p. 108
313. American non-military aid to Uganda between 1989 and 1992 totalled $183 million, which was twice what the United States granted to Rwanda during the same period
314. Training: Ugandan personnel were invited to the US and trained under the International Military Education and Training Programme (IMET), which had been set up to train soldiers and 'encourage effective and mutually beneficial relations and increased understanding'. Career diplomat: R. E. Gribbin, *In The Aftermath of Genocide: The US Role in Rwanda* (Bloomington: iUniverse, 2005), p. 59
315. Information provided to the author from a former US diplomat, London, September 2015
316. French intelligence: they may have detected this presence by using the DC8 Saringue eavesdropping planes that were based in neighbouring Central African Republic
317. Mitterrand and Vichy: In *Une Jeunesse Française*, published in 1994, Pierre Péan revealed that Mitterrand had worked for Vichy before joining the Resistance, and, sensationally, that he had been on friendly terms, well into the 1980s, with René Bousquet, the head of the Vichy police force which was responsible for the deportation of French Jews. Biographer: quoted in Short, op. cit., p. 13. Hafez al-Assad: Short, op. cit., p. 400
318. Modus vivendi: speech at Cancún, 20 October 1981. Cheysson's remarks were made in *Le Matin*, 21 October 1981
319. CIA campaign: Short, op. cit., p. 400. Star Wars: the French government was also afraid that SDI would bolster Greenpeace's anti-nuclear influence in the Pacific
320. Short, op. cit., p. 513
321. Védrine coined the term *hyperpuissance* in 1998
322. US presence: These remarks were made at the Bad Wiessee conference on 23 July 1991. Hubris: see for example the NATO communiqué that was issued during the NATO summit in London on 5–6 July meeting. 'Europe has entered a new, promising era. Central and Eastern Europe is liberating itself. The Soviet Union has embarked on the long journey towards a free society'
323. The allegations were based on communication between Saddam and the US ambassador to Iraq, April Glaspie, who, just before the invasion, reputedly stated that the US had 'no opinion' on the Iraqi–Kuwaiti dispute
324. Mitterrand: record of a conversation between Gorbachev and Mitterrand, 29 October 1990. The Wilson Center Digital Archive, document 118176. Independent policy: Mitterrand had made a speech at the UN General Assembly on 24 September demanding democratic reforms from the Kuwaiti leader after he was restored to power. This was a bid to show that France was still independent from the US. See L. Freedman & E. Karsh, *The Gulf Conflict* (Princeton: Princeton University Press, 1995), p. 117
325. Chevenèment also justified his resignation because of French links with the Iraqi oil industry. He gave an account of his resignation in his book *Une Certain Idée de la République M'Amène* (Paris: Albin Michel, 1992). Sanguin: Lawrence Kaplan, *Nato and the UN: A Peculiar Relationship* (Columbia: University of Missouri Press, 2010), p. 122
326. Méhaignerie: National Assembly debate of 27 August, pp. 3220–25. 'New world order': see above, footnote 321
327. Cohen: see P. Schraeder, *United States Foreign Policy Toward Africa: Incrementalism, Crisis and Change* (Cambridge: Cambridge University Press, 1994), p. 102
328. Big stakes: The Atlantic Charter 1941 had underscored the right of all nations to

free trade and to 'access, on equal terms … to the raw materials of the world which are needed for their economic prosperity'. US official: Herman J. Cohen, Assistant Secretary of State for African Affairs, speaking before a US–African Trade and Investment Conference, February 1995. Quoted in *Jeune Afrique*, 9 March 1993, p. 40

329. In 1989, France gave over $100 million ODA to most of its former African colonies (except Guinea). It also gave over $2,200 million to all francophone African countries in the same year

330. Zaire was the new name given in 1971 to the Republic of the Congo

331. Aggression: Quoted in Short, op. cit., p. 63. Roussin: interview, *Le Monde*, 6 September 1993. Lissouba had needed to finance a large budget deficit and requested an advance payment from Elf Aquitaine, the French state-owned oil company. When Elf refused, Lissouba turned to Occidental Petroleum, which forwarded him $150 million

332. The Congo had been renamed as 'Zaire' in 1971. In 1997 it was then renamed again as the Democratic Republic of the Congo

333. Quoted in Schraeder, op. cit., p. 103

334. These were mostly veterans of the Zairean *Mouvement National Congress*. See Prunier, op. cit., p. 319

335. The Zairean leader also appears to have been convinced that later events in Rwanda – a plane crash that killed Habyarimana – were 'part of a larger plot to destabilize the region', rather than just Rwanda. See the US National Security Archive Document 7 Kinshasa 02123, 15 April 1994, accessed at: http://nsarchive.gwu.edu/NSAEBB/NSAEBB117/

336. Robert, op. cit., pp. 293–4

337. Pipeline: Information to the author from the Northern Corridor Transit and Transport Coordination Authority, September 2015. Ambassador: author's interview with Sir Christopher Mallaby, former British ambassador to France, London, 21 September 2015

338. United Germany: On 28 November 1989, Chancellor Helmut Kohl had announced his own plan for a speedy reunification of East and West Germany. By April 1990, the prospect of a unified Germany appeared inevitable. Bad mood: Mitterrand quoted in *New York Times*, 6 December 1989; D. Moïsi, 'The Trouble with France', *Foreign Affairs*, vol. 77, no. 3 (1998), p. 94. UN seat: author's interview with Sir Christopher Mallaby, former British ambassador to France, London, 21 September 2015

339. Eyewitness account: Author's interview with Kathi Austin, 6 May 2016

340. Both quotes, and on America's military role in general, see 'US military role in Rwanda greater than disclosed', *Washington Post*, 19 August 1997

341. Right decisions: 'Rwandans Led Revolt in Congo', *Washington Post*, 9 July 1997. Author's interview with Kathi Austin, 6 May 2016

342. Testimony to the Committee on International Relations House of Representatives, 16 July 1997, p. 79

343. Mining sector: On the strength of American commercial interest in Zaire, see Robert Block's article 'US Firms Seek Deals in Central Africa', *Wall Street Journal*, 14 October 1997. Pentagon briefing: 'United States Security Strategy for Sub-Saharan Africa' (Washington DC: US Department of Defense, 1995), p. 3

344. Simpson: F. Reyntjens, *The Great African War: Congo and Regional Politics 1996–2006* (Cambridge: Cambridge University Press, 2010), p. 74

345. Communications: Reyntjens, op. cit., pp. 68–77. Campaigner: Author's telephone interview with Kathi Austin, 6 May 2016

346. Debré: Testimony to the Parliamentary Committee of 2 June 1998. Eyewitnesses: Reyntjens, op. cit., p. 73. Security services: Colum Lynch, 'US Agents were seen with

rebels in Zaire: Active participation is alleged in military overthrow of Mobutu', *Boston Globe*, 8 October 1997; Hubert Coudurier, 'What the French Secret Services Knew', *Valeurs Actuelles*, 30 August 1997

347. Within a year, the US administration had openly embraced Kabila's new regime and offered substantial economic support. 'On Visit to Congo, Albright Praises the New Leader', *New York Times*, 13 December 1997

348. *Le Monde*, 5 December 1996

349. UN: France had argued for an alleviation of UN sanctions against Iraq, and 23 October 1997 joined China and Russia in abstaining from a UN resolution, 1134, condemning Iraq for refusing to grant UN weapons inspectors access to a number of military sites. Foreign Minister Hubert Védrine criticised Washington because the sanctions would give Baghdad the impression that 'there would never be a way out of the tunnel'

350. Michel Roussin, the Minister for Cooperation, admitted that these meetings were held. A. Glaser & S. W. Smith, *L'Afrique sans Africains: le rêve blanc du continent noir* (Paris: Stock, 1994), p. 187; Jacques Chirac, speech in Gambia in July 1995 quoted in 'The End of an Affair?', *The Economist*, 12 August 1995

351. Reyntjens, op. cit. p. 117

352. Reyntjens, op. cit. p. 115; *Le Figaro*, 5 April 1997

353. *L'Événement du Jeudi*, 20 February 1997

354. See Sean Boyne's article 'The White Legion', *Jane's Intelligence Review*, June 1997

355. The financial support of the Pasqua network to Mobutu has been detailed by F. Verschave, *La Françafrique: Le Plus Scandale de la République* (Paris: Stock, 1997), pp. 255–65. Professor T. Chafer, 'Franco-African Relations: No Longer So Exceptional', *African Affairs*, 101, pp. 343–63, 2002

356. The French aid budget to Africa fell sharply between 1994 and 2000 from 0.64 per cent to 0.37 per cent of GDP. Smith & Glaser, *Ces Messieurs Afrique 2: Des Réseaux aux Lobbys*, Calmann-Levy, p. 25

357. Scandals: For example, Michel Roussin (former Cooperation Minister) and Charles Pasqua (former interior minister), Jean-Christophe Mitterrand and several directors of Elf have been investigated; Alfred Sirven (Elf's long-standing director of finance) was extradited; and Mitterrand, Michel and Roussin were briefly jailed before being bailed

358. CFA franc: The 'African' or CFA franc (Communauté Financière Africaine) was used by Senegal, the Comoros, Burkina Faso, Ivory Coast, Chad, Benin, the Central African Republic, Congo, Gabon, Niger, Togo, Cameroon and Mali. In 1948, France had guaranteed a fixed parity of one French franc to 50 African francs

359. EU ties: This initiative crystallised into a French-led peacekeeping programme RECAMP (Renforcement des Capacités Africaines de Maintien de la Paix). This relies more upon 'Africanisation' of regional security – the Africans taking a more proactive role than before – and, by involving France's Western allies, 'multinationalisation'. St Malo: Foreign and Commonwealth Office briefing paper, Saint-Malo summit, 3–4 December 1998. Chafer, op. cit.

360. Obama made the comments to the American magazine *The Atlantic* in March 2016

361. A. Seldon & P. Snowdon, *Cameron at 10: The Inside Story 2010–2015* (London: W. Collins, 2015), p. 103

362. Seldon & Snowdon, op. cit., p. 107, 111

363. February supplies: This information is based on leaked emails, made public on 22 June 2015 and published in *New York Times*, that were written to Secretary of State Hillary Clinton by her adviser Sidney Blumenthal. June supplies: 'Les hélicoptères français sont entrés en action en Libye', *Le Figaro*, 4 June 2016

364. Hugh Roberts's article 'Who Said Gaddafi Had to Go?', *London Review of Books*, 17 November 2011 pp. 8–18

365. Roberts, op. cit.

366. Bashar al-Assad 'betrayed Col Gaddafi to save his Syrian regime', *Daily Telegraph*, 30 September 2012

367. Seldon & Snowdon, op. cit., p. 109

368. 'Gaddafi wants EU cash to stop African migrants', BBC News, 31 August 2010

369. Above, note 361

370. Author's interview with Libyan oil analyst, London, 14 December 2015

371. Thomas Vampouille, 'Guerre en Libye: La France a dépensé 300 millions d'euros', *Le Figaro*, 21 October 2011

372. Archer: 'Tripoli Talks Advance U.S. Army Relationship with Libyan Land Forces', US Africa Command Press Release, 20 May 2010. US–Libyan relations emerged from several confidential memos that were released on the website Wikileaks in August 2011. See for example 'A/S Welch underscored the importance of increased defense cooperation as a signal of normalcy in the bilateral military relationship', 11 January 2008

373. Interview with the author, 14 April 2016

374. Sarkozy 'shared values': 'Nicolas Sarkozy: "J'aime l'énergie et la fluidité de l'Amérique"', *Le Monde*, 9 September 2006. On his first official visit to Washington, Sarkozy recalled his adolescent fondness for a pop song 'If the GIs hadn't come', which celebrated the liberation in 1945

375. 'Sarkozy turns back on 'Anglo-Saxon model', *France 24*, 13 April 2012. Regulation: 'Sarkozy claims credit on tighter regulation', *Financial Times*, 2 April 2009. Falklands: 'Sarkozy launches new era with gaffe', *The Independent*, 3 November 2010. Bring sides together: 'Falklands/Malvinas – Sarkozy willing to bring sides together to address the issue', *Merco Press*, 31 August 2015

376. S. W. Smith, 'Nodding and Winking', *London Review of Books*, 11 February 2008

377. General Salan quoted in Keiger, op. cit., p. 9

378. Foreign visits: Bogdan Koszel, 'The Union for the Mediterranean in the Policy of France and Germany', *Przegląd Zachodni*, no. 9, 2013. Sarkozy had first publicly proposed 'Club Med' at an election rally in Toulon on 7 February 2007: see in general Koszel, op. cit., p. 65.

379. Alliot-Marie: 'Violences en Tunisie', National Assembly debate, 11 January 2011. Mitterrand: 'Tunisie: PS et Verts condamnent la répression, le gouvernement français embarrassé', *Libération*, 11 January 2011

380. 'L'intervention en Libye a évité 'des milliers de morts' selon Sarkozy', *Le Monde Afrique*, 25 March 2011

381. 'NATO runs short on some munitions in Libya', *Washington Post*, 15 April 2011. Retired British general: author's correspondence, 21 June 2016

382. Sarkozy's press statement at the G8 summit, Deauville, 27 May 2011

383. Covert DGSE support: Claude Angeli, 'Une intervention limitée préparée par l'OTAN en Syrie' *Le Canard enchaîné*, 23 November 2011; X. Panon, 'Dans Les Coulisses de la Diplomatie Française: De Sarkozy à Hollande' (Paris: L'Archipel, 2015); 'Hollande admits arming Syrian rebels in breach of embargo – book', *RT News*, 6 May 2015

384. Fabius: 'Sur le terrain, ils font du bon boulot'. See 'Pression militaire et succès diplomatique pour les rebelles syriens', *Le Monde*, 13 December 2012

385. Fabius: 'Syria crisis: Geneva talks sound death knell for Assad regime', *The Guardian*, 1 July 2012

386. 'France risks being sidelined with tough Syria stance', *The Times* (South Africa), 28 October 2015

387. Speech to the 20th French Ambassadors' Conference, Paris, August 2012

388. Isolated: 'Syrian influence grows in the new Lebanese government', BBC News, 14 June 2011

389. Diplomat: Author's interview with former Western ambassador to Syria, 14 May 2016

390. Arms to Syria: 'Exclusive: Arab states arm rebels as UN talks of Syrian civil war', *The Independent*, 13 June 2012

391. Syria's links with Iran go back to the Iraqi invasion of Iran in 1980, when the Syrians supported Tehran on the axis. See for example 'The Enduring Iran–Syria–Hezbollah Axis', American Enterprise Institute, 17 December 2009

392. US State Department memo, 30 December 2009, Wikileaks reference 09RIYADH1684_a

393. Heated exchanges: 'France's Approach to a Nuclear deal with Iran', European Institute, April 2015. Iran nuclear deal: 'France Voices Doubt on Iran Nuclear Deal', *Wall Street Journal*, 18 December 2013. 2006: Author's conversations with an EU nuclear negotiator, London, October 2006 and March 2016. 'France voices support for Saudi campaign in Yemen', *France 24*, 12 April 2015

394. 'The Future of U.S.–Saudi Relations': F. Gregory Gause III, 'The Kingdom and the Power', *Foreign Affairs* July/August 2016

395. Ryan Crocker quoted in 'America's Fading Footprint in the Middle East', *Wall Street Journal*, 9 October 2012

396. Seymour Hersh, 'Military to Military', *New Yorker*, 7 January 2016

397. 'First GCC-France summit makes history', *Arab News*, 12 May 2015

398. Yemen: 'We support the Saudi Arabian military intervention in Yemen following President Hadi's request for support by all means and measures to protect Yemen and deter Houthi aggression', Foreign Office statement, 25 March 2015. 'UK licences £2.8bn of arms sales to Saudis since kingdom entered Yemen war', *The Guardian*, 19 April 2016. Police: *The Times*, 8 June 2016

399. Mali: See Jean-Paul Chevènement & Gerard Larcher, 'Rapport d'information fait au nom de la commission des affaires étrangères, de la défense et des forces armées par le groupe de travail', 'Sahel', p. 10, Paris: Sénat, 16 April 2013. See http://www.senat.fr/notice-rapport/2012/r12-513-notice.html. Quote: Chevènement & Larcher, op. cit. Sarkozy had 'officially' repudiated *la Françafrique* during trips to the African continent in July and September 2007, when he had called for 'a healthier relationship' and 'a new partnership between equal nations'. However, in practice French policy did not substantially change as the interventions in Mali in 2007 and 2013 revealed

400. By 2013, the French had reduced their presence in Djibouti to just 1,900 troops, less than a third of the number at independence. There were also far fewer family postings, and soldiers were rotated much more frequently than before. France currently retains bases in Chad (N'Djamena), Gabon (Libreville), Côte d'Ivoire (Abidjan) and Djibouti (Camp Monclar), as well as on the French territories of Mayotte and La Réunion.

401. Drian: Quoted in 'France launches new Sahel Counter-Terrorism Operation Barkhane', *International Business Times*, 14 July 2014. Author's interview with defence source, London, September 2015

402. In May 2011, the EU launched its 'Strategy for Security and Development in the Sahel'. This declared that 'the EU has an important role to play both in encouraging economic development for the people of the Sahel and helping them achieve a more secure environment'

403. 'The US and France are Teaming Up to Fight A Sprawling War on Terror in Africa', *Vice News*, 15 September 2014

IMAGE CREDITS

INDEX